ENDORSEMENTS IN ADVERTISING

ENDORSEMENTS IN ADVERTISING

A Social History

Kerry Segrave

McFarland & Company, Inc., Publishers
Jefferson, North Carolina, and London

Library of Congress Cataloguing-in-Publication Data

Segrave, Kerry, 1944–
    Endorsements in advertising : a social history / Kerry Segrave.
        p.   cm.
    Includes bibliographical references and index.

    ISBN 0-7864-2043-X (softcover: 50# alkaline paper) ∞

    1. Advertising — Moral and ethical aspects — United States —
History — 20th century.   2. Advertising — United States —
History — 20th century.   I. Title
    HF5831.S44   2005
    659.1'042 — dc22   2005001968

British Library cataloguing data are available

Cover photograph ©2005 Comstock

Manufactured in the United States of America

*McFarland & Company, Inc., Publishers
    Box 611, Jefferson, North Carolina 28640
    www.mcfarlandpub.com*

Contents

Preface

This book looks at endorsement advertising from the period just after World War I up until the present time. Endorsement ads—known as testimonial ads—feature a person, usually a celebrity, paired with a product; the person explicitly or implicitly endorses that product and urges its purchase. Though usually drawn from the ranks of the well known, sometimes endorsers are unknown testifiers—ordinary citizens or people in some way considered "expert" in relation to the product. For the purposes of this book, the words endorsement and testimonial are treated as synonyms.

Prior to World War I, endorsement ads had existed in a minor way, but their most highly visible usage, in patent medicine ads, left the testimonial promotion with a bad reputation as the quackery involved was exposed to the public. After a period of quiet, that ad format resurfaced following World War I and quickly became a significant part of the advertising industry.

As testimonial ads spread, the ethics of the format were debated. Most of those in the industry regarded endorsement ads as unethical if they were solicited and paid for. Still, the testimonial ad survived and prospered, while the ethics debate simply faded away.

Once they became established, endorsement ads went through a long period of stagnation with seemingly no gains or losses. Then, in the mid–1970s, testimonial ads took off again, with the money received by the testifiers growing enormously. By the early years of the twenty-first century, however, such ads were quite different from those of the 1920s and 1930s.

Back then Lux soap had, by its own estimate, more than 600 of Hollywood's actresses on its roster of endorsers and reportedly did not pay any of them. In the modern period the most favored testifier is the athlete, not the film star, and basketball star Michael Jordan alone made tens of millions of dollars annually from endorsements in the 1990s. Despite the huge sums of money now spent on endorsement ads, no one knows for sure if such ads are more effective than ads featuring no endorsements.

Research for this book was conducted using various hard-copy and online databases at Simon Fraser University, the University of British Columbia, and the Vancouver Public Library.

1

Testimonials Get Off to a Rocky Start: The Years to 1919

I have taken three bottles of Lydia Pinkham's Compound and feel like a new man.   — Lillian Russell, 1890s

I am told that my commendation of Pears' Soap has opened for it a large sale in the United States. I am willing to stand by every word in favor of it that I ever uttered.
                                    — Henry Ward Beecher, 1890s

Modern testimonial advertising began in the wake of World War I. That rise of endorsements paralleled the growth in the advertising industry in general as the United States settled back into a peacetime economy and the rise of mass production and mass consumption really got under way. Magazines and newspapers became more accessible, as more and more people could afford them. Also, the general literacy level improved as education spread; more people were able and willing to read more material. In order to catch people's attention, advertising tried a variety of strategies. One of those was the use of testimonials and endorsements in ads, with the testifiers and endorsers ranging from the ordinary citizen to the expert to the famous athlete to the film star or other celebrity. Such ads were not absent prior to World War I, and indeed went back at least to the 1600s. However, they were few and far between until at least the 1880s, at which time they began to appear more frequently, often in conjunction with advertisements for patent medicines. Those concoctions, which offered to cure virtually every medical ailment then in existence, usually contained a lot of alcohol and little else. A crusade against patent medicine was begun around 1890, and by the first decade of the 1900s advertisements for such preparations had largely disappeared from the newspapers and magazines— at least the respectable ones, the ones with the majority of the circulation. While the criticism and crusade were against the products—the worthlessness of patent medicines and their exaggerated claims—endorsements in ads in general suffered and lost some of their credibility and viability. Before World War I, ads that featured endorsements were associated with patent medicines more than any other item. After the war, a major difference was that endorsement ads were associated only with products that were accepted by society and regarded as legitimate. Because patent medicine ad claims were false, it was understood the testifiers were not truthful, in one way or another. When they became associated with legitimate products (including cigarettes, which, of course, were regarded quite differently by society then), that assumption of falsehood was absent, or at least had to be shown since it could not be assumed.

One of the earliest testimonial ads to appear showed up in a small volume printed in 1666 by the charlatan Valentine Greatrakes, a quack who claimed to effect cures by the laying on of hands. His book, *A Brief Account of Mr. Valentine Greatrakes, and Divers of the Strange Cures by Him Lately Performed*, contained "the Testimonials of several Eminent and Worthy Persons." One was from a woman named Mary Glover, signed and dated May 17, 1666, who declared Greatrakes's laying on of hands cured her of a deafness and blindness she had suffered from for five years. One phrase in her endorsement, "I have received perfect Cure of the stroke of Mr. Greatrakes' hand," appeared, word-for-word, many times in the book in other endorsements. A century later, the London *Chronicle* newspaper of November 17, 1770, published an advertisement containing the endorsement of one Mary Graham, who testified to the healing power of Dr. Rysseeg's Balsamic Tincture. After trying several other remedies without success, according to Graham's ad, Rysseeg's concoction cured her of a "Scorbutic humour" that she had for 12 years.[1] According to Frank Presbrey, in his 1929 book, *History and Development of Advertising*, one of the earliest testimonials in advertising appeared in an ad for a teething preparation in 1711.[2]

Writing in 1929, journalist Charles Merz found that many famous people endorsed products in the pages of *Harper's Weekly* in the spring of 1879. One was Harriet Beecher Stowe, endorsing Baker's Chocolate. Frank Leslie testified on behalf of Burnett's Cocaine that it was "far preferable to anything he had ever used for his hair." Whitcomb's Asthma remedy was offered with the assurance that Oliver Wendell Homes, Washington Irving and former president Martin Van Buren all benefited from using it. James W. Husted, the speaker of the State Assembly of New York, pitched on behalf of Alcock's Porous Plasters that his prompt application of three plasters eradicated an incipient case of pneumonia when he had "so bad a cough that his friends thought nothing but a trip south would save him."[3]

Reporter Loring W. Batten Jr., in 1931, looked back to the July 1896 issue of *Harper's* and found in it five advertisements based on testimonials by the great Sarah Bernhardt. Then he mentioned the text of the Gilbert and Sullivan operetta *The Gondoliers*, which was first produced in 1889. One of Gilbert's specialties was taking shots at contemporary events, and in that operetta a song was sung by the Duke and Duchess of Plaza-Toro in which they lampooned the paid testimonials used by dressmakers, tailors, patent medicine, soap, and so forth.[4]

One of the better-known testimonials became notorious when the manager of Lillian Russell carelessly okayed the use of her signature below the following: "I have taken three bottles of Lydia Pinkham's Compound and feel like a new man."[5]

Ray Giles was another reporter who looked back, in 1930, to ads from the early 1890s in the pages of *Harper's*, *Scribner's*, and *Century*. In those magazines he found what he described as an "abundance" of advertising that included the use of testimonials. A full-page ad from March 1891 had well-known financier Russell Sage declare: "For the last twenty years I have been using Alcock's Porous Plasters. They have repeatedly cured me of rheumatic pains, and pains in my side and back." Giles felt that such ads of the 1890s were built on the assumptions that the testifiers were known, famous people and that they were telling the truth. Another Alcock ad asserted: "Endorsements by men and women of the character and standing of those who recommend Alcock's Porous Plasters are unquestionable proof of their merit." Following that was a quotation from Mrs. Henry Ward Beecher, who said that "the above is the only testimonial I have ever given in favor of any plaster." A second quotation was attributed to the Reverend Mark Guy Pearse, who said, "I find them a very breastplate against coughs and colds."[6]

Among other discoveries made by Giles was that in June 1891 Oliver Wendell Holmes endorsed Waterman's Ideal Fountain Pen — "works admirably. I have given up every other pen in its favor, and of late have done all my writing with it." Reverend Thomas K. Beecher declared in a round-up ad for the pen (ten different endorsers were featured in the single ad) that "it is the very best of them all." In early 1890, Royal Baking Powder had one ad that consisted of a "fac-simile" reproduction of a one-page letter from ordinary citizen Marion Harland and nothing else. Another one reprinted a certificate of the United Cook and Pastry Cooks Association of the U.S. to the effect that "the Royal Baking Powder has been used by our Members, and we recommend the same for fine pastry, cakes, biscuits, etc., as superior to all other baking powders or articles used for quick raising." It was signed by four officers of the organization.

Another Royal ad featured a testimonial from Henry A. Mott, Ph.D., United States Government Chemist. Henry Ward Beecher endorsed Pears Soap by noting, "If Cleanliness is next to Godliness, Soap must be considered as a Means of Grace and a Clergyman who recommends moral things should be willing to recommend Soap." Beecher added, "I am told that my commendation of Pears' Soap has opened for it a large sale in the United States. I am willing to stand by every word in favor of it that I ever uttered. A man must be fastidious indeed who is not satisfied with it." For a different brand of soap, a Professor Cornwall of Princeton University testified that "Ivory Soap is very well made and cannot injure anything." Williams Shaving Soap, in a June 1890 page, declared: "Genuine Yankee Shaving Soap—used by 22 presidents of the U.S., by leading men in all departments of life ... used by Senator Ingalls, the fastidious President of the U.S. Senate." An advertisement from June 1888 for Linden Bloom Perfumes stated that "Mrs. Grover Cleveland uses and recommends Linden Bloom."[7]

Around the 1890s, Edward W. Bok, publisher of the *Ladies Home Journal*, was involved in a crusade against patent medicine advertisements and the paid testimonials often associated with such products. Among the disclosures he made during the course of his investigation was the fact that a Washington journalist had a regular price list for testimonials that he guaranteed to secure from senators and representatives of Congress.[8]

Investigative reporter Arthur J. Cramp spent some 20 years studying testimonials, especially ones for medical concoctions. One of those ads was produced for George H. Mayr, who advertised his Wonderful Remedy for Stomach Trouble. One of his copy sheets with instructions to the printer consisted of a 16-inch by 32-inch page containing over 40 alleged testimonials—unsigned—each describing how the writer had been saved from death by taking Mayr's preparation. Each sheet had a heading with a blank space that was to be filled in by the compositor before the newspaper ran it. The instruction sheet emphasized: "Insert name of your city in heading of each ad." It read "Old _____ Resident Given Up By Physicians" (old Cleveland resident, old Seattle resident, and so on). Cramp observed that the newspaper publishers could have been under no confu-

Opposite: A round-up type of endorsement ad, one that featured more than one endorser in the same copy. This one was for Tuxedo tobacco in 1914. The endorsers were Grantland Rice, sportswriter; D.N. Travis, president of the Michigan Board of Pardons and "lecturer, lawyer and dramatist"; E. Ysaye, "world-famous violist"; Allan H. Frazer, a "leading attorney of Detroit"; Penrhyn Stanlaws, "celebrated artist"; and George Galvin, M.D., "founder of Boston Emergency Hospital" (who commented that Tuxedo tobacco "gives a man that old joy-of-living feeling").

sion as to the copy's obvious fraudulence, and thus the newspaper, in accepting the copy, participated with Mayr in his campaign of falsehood. "Seldom has even a patent medicine vendor shown a more cynical disregard for elementary business honesty. Yet Mayr seems to have had little difficulty in getting his advertisements accepted," he concluded.[9]

For Cramp, the patent medicine ads—and their testimonials—reached a "quack" peak in the 1890s and the first decade of the 1900s. Peruna was a famed nostrum of that time, another alcohol-laden cure-all. Peruna's manufacturer claimed to have testimonials from 50 members of Congress, some of which he published. Also, he claimed that 25 American Army generals had sent him letters of endorsement. He published all 25, including the names and addresses of the individuals to whom they were credited. Prominent admirals of the U.S. Navy were also declared to have pitched for Peruna. Another nostrum, Paine's Celery Compound, compared favorably with Peruna in its alcoholic potency. In fact, it was so powerful in that regard that Paine had to discontinue the product because "it was impossible to prepare this product without an excessive amount of alcohol." Prohibition had arrived. Before that happened, though, Paine made use of some highly respected people to pitch his concoction — not the least of whom was Sarah Bernhardt, who was quoted as stating that she was convinced that Paine's Celery Compound was "the most powerful nerve strengthener that can be found." Other testifiers included a prominent Chicago clergyman, a mayor of Lowell, Massachusetts, a congressman from Virginia, a U.S. senator from North Carolina, and a Kansas attorney general. Paine's Celery Compound contained 20 percent alcohol and an insignificant amount of other drugs.[10]

During this period there were many examples of what Cramp described as self-canceling testimonials. Miss Ida S. of Wisconsin was treated for consumption by a Michigan quack, who published the girl's testimony and added that "she is now cured." She had died of consumption about a year before her testimonial was circulated. Another endorsement for the same remedy came from Otto B., also of Wisconsin. His death certificate showed Otto had died of tuberculosis two years earlier. Frank W. of Illinois gave a testimonial to the value of the same "cure" but died three months after giving it (of tuberculosis); his endorsement was still making the rounds 23 months after he was buried. A California firm that sold

Opposite: This 1914 ad for Tuxedo was one of the earlier ones to use professional athletes. These six baseball players — Napoleon Lajoie, Christy Mathewson, Joe Tinker, John McGraw, Jimmy Archer, and Jack McInnis — were all stars, from six different teams.

"cures" for diabetes also published many glowing testimonials. Edward Z. of Iowa consumed 30 bottles of the remedy and gave an endorsement, but his death certificate recorded his cause of death as diabetes. Daniel McH. of Virginia took the same company's remedy for kidney disease and had his testimonial published with the case declared by the company to be a "nice recovery." His death certificate recorded interstitial nephritis as the cause of death.[11]

In the files of the Bureau of Investigation of the American Medical Association, continued Cramp, were reported to be large numbers of testimonials for remedies for cancer, tuberculosis, diabetes, Bright's disease, and other conditions; "filed with them are the death certificates of the individuals who gave these testimonials!" The testimonial of W.A.M. of Nashua, Iowa, appeared in the Nashua *Reporter* endorsing Doan's Kidney Pills. Also appearing in the same issue of that newspaper was the death notice of Mr. M. Mrs. Nettie W. of Glenwood, Iowa, also testified to the virtues of Doan's Pills in an ad that appeared in the Glenwood *Opinion*. Her death notice also appeared in the same issue. H.G.F. of Kankakee, Illinois, had his endorsement run in June, although Mr. F. had died during the previous March. Cramp declared that the medical profession of the day (he was writing in 1929) was not "addicted to the testimonial habit" as it had been a generation earlier. During the period 1907 to 1911, the American Medical Association indexed and tabulated more than 10,000 American physicians whose names had appeared in one form or another in praise of some proprietary medicine. Many of those occurred, said Cramp, in the form of so-called original articles and were published "in those commercialized and nostrum-subsidized medical journals so prevalent until about 1915."[12]

By around then, 1915, most patent medicine advertising excesses had disappeared from the respectable media, largely due to the crusade against them. However, there were a few exceptions, one of which was a heavy advertising campaign that started near the end of World War I for a patent medicine called Nuxated Iron. Chemists with the American Medical Association reported the item contained practically no "nux" and only a negligible amount of iron. It was advertised intensively by the testimonial method. First came endorsements from physicians, some of whom were described in the advertisements as noted, well-known specialists, but who

Opposite: Thomas Edison endorsed this industrial product in 1916. He represented the "expert" category of testifier, one whose opinion carried more weight due to a real or perceived expertise in a specific area or in a general sense. This ad, of course, was aimed at industrial buyers and not the general public, although it appeared in a general magazine.

on investigation, said Cramp, "proved to be superannuated advertising quacks." Then there were testimonials by retired generals and judges and from former U.S. senators William E. Mason and Charles A. Towne. The Nuxated Iron people even went so far as to run an ad in 1921 containing a picture of Pope Benedict XV along with the heading, "The Vatican at Rome Recommends Nuxated Iron." Two years earlier, ads for the product announced, "Sarah Bernhardt Sends Nuxated Iron to the French Soldiers to Help Give Them Strength, Power and Endurance." A signed testimonial from baseball legend Ty Cobb attributed his comeback in the sport to the renewed vigor instilled in him by Nuxated Iron. A series of advertisements featuring boxers opened with Jess Willard declaring that Nuxated Iron helped him to whip Frank Moran. When Willard was knocked out by Jack Dempsey, the world learned, through the company's ads, that it was this preparation that put Dempsey "in such superb condition" and helped him whip Willard. Dempsey did a series of those ads, after each victory. For example, "How Nuxated Iron Helped Me to Whip Tom Gibbons."[13]

When reporter Alva Johnston attacked the testimonial "racket" of the time she was writing, 1931, she looked back to find examples with which to make comparisons. Race car driver Barney Oldfield had endorsed "Goodyear Detachable Tires on Universal Rims" around 1906, but she felt it would have had no place in the testimonial market

ROSCOE ARBUCKLE of The Keystone Comedies is particularly enthusiastic about the **PARIS GARTERS** that are made with the 200% stretch Ridgeweave elastic. He finds that this new elastic feels so very comfortable he forgets he's wearing garters.

Mr. Arbuckle wears No. 1565, Silk, at 50c per pair. No. 1520, Lisle, retails at 25c. Look for the name on the back of the shield when you buy.

A. Stein & Co.
Makers
Chicago   New York

PARIS
GARTERS
No metal
can touch you

Screen comic Fatty Arbuckle, 1916. At first, film stars were used only occasionally as endorsers, but by the time the talkies arrived Hollywood was big enough and important enough to give onscreen faces real marketing value. This change, along with a boom in all advertising in the 1920s, soon made the Hollywood actor the most sought after endorser.

of her time because it was an example of someone endorsing a product they actually used — that is, it was truthful. Lew Fields, Sam Bernard, David Warfield, and George Arliss all endorsed Murads in 1905, said Johnston, "but they smoked Murads, and therefore have no place in the modern testimonial racket." Johnston declared the origin of "the modern, sophisticated" testimonial was difficult to trace. She felt one candidate who might get credit was J.C. Hommanns Jr., who in 1919 obtained endorsements for the Corona typewriter from authors and war correspondents, "but these endorsements were not quite in the modern mode. They fail in four particulars—first, they were true; second, they were signed by actual users of the typewriter; third, they were written by those who signed them; fourth, no cash was paid for them." In order to denounce the testimonial advertising industry of 1931, Johnston painted the industry of 1905 to 1919 as much more honest and corruption-free than it was, which made it easier to condemn the endorsement methods of the late 1920s and very early 1930s.[14]

The idea that famous people, and ordinary citizens, could help sell products through endorsements was a long-standing one, although such ads were not much used outside of the patent medicine industry. Being associated with such a corrupt industry helped make people cynical about such presentations; they all came to be viewed as dishonest. Banished from respectable newspapers and magazines— they still existed, of course, but in the equivalent of the supermarket tabloids, media that had little or no credibility to begin with — endorsement ads went through a period of relatively little use through the latter half of the 1910s and into the very early 1920s. Then they began to appear more frequently. Since they were mostly associated with acceptable products this time around, many of the negative attributes of testimonial ads were forgotten. They started this round with something like a clean slate.

2

Testimonials Arrive, 1920s

So abundant is the flock of women cigarette endorsers that the reader has become disgusted to see advertisements bearing testimonials which only lack the price tag to make them complete.
— H.S. Gardner, 1929

I suppose men such as Ford, Edison and Marconi were landed for the Simmons [mattress] campaign because those gentlemen were told they would be doing humanity a good turn if they preached the gospel of more and better sleep.
— Anonymous ad executive, 1931

Hollywood personalities began to figure more prominently in the testimonial industry of the 1920s. A 1919 report in the trade publication *Variety* observed that in the previous few months there had come to light a number of instances in which film studios with big stars under contract "have been collecting a considerable rake-off on the value of the names of their stars through endorsements of various market products." One film studio had made it a custom to prevent its stars from signing any letters of endorsements unless the permission of the studio was first obtained. A studio representative in that case saw to it that "the star gets the full value of the advertising and in cases where the commodity is one that will be of use to the star there are arrangements made whereby the star will get something of a rake-off, the studio usually receiving a cash consideration for the use of the name." Prices varied according to the prominence of the star. If the star was a major one, the studio extracted $5,000 as its price for allowing the endorsement. One of the stars with a major studio reportedly obtained all her gowns from a certain dress manufacturer in exchange for allowing herself to be painted in one of their gowns each season of the year and to have those paintings displayed in the dress maker's showroom. "She has carte blanche to anything there is in the establishment," said the account, "and it is not unusual for her to obtain as much as $25,000 worth of dresses in a year." The report also mentioned that Charlie Chaplin got "considerable royalties" out of the use of his name for various purposes, such as Chaplin statues, Chaplin dolls, and so forth. However, the gist of the account was that this practice was not widespread and just then seemed to be taking hold.[1]

When *Variety* reported on the same subject almost ten years later, it presented a picture of endorsement advertising that had grown enormously among Hollywood film personalities and the film studios. It paralleled a similar growth rate in endorsement advertising in general. According to the article, Hollywood film studio publicity offices were then being submerged with countless requests for exploitation tie-ups and film star endorsements for national and locally advertised products. "The racket has become so common that a number of the studios and screen personalities are refusing to lend their support to this form of publicity," stated the account, "believing that the value of the novelty has worked out its usefulness long ago and a continuance can only result in undermining their popularity." Because of that attitude, it was reported that a number of national advertisers were "forced" to spend large sums of money and to expend much effort to procure endorsements from big screen names. One of the largest cigarette advertisers (unnamed in the story), wanting to compete with Lucky Strike — described here as a pioneer in endorsement exploitation — found it necessary to engage the service of a fan magazine publisher to secure the endorsements for them. That publisher was said to have been given a $50,000 advertising appropriation for the work, but upon approaching some of the big film names, he found it necessary in a number of cases to make certain publication concessions, in the way of covers and space in his magazine, before he could get the players to sign. Another large national advertiser — a maker of soap — earmarked over $1 million to secure endorsements and found it necessary to have representatives in Hollywood who did nothing but maintain personal contact with the screen players and see that they were furnished with enough soap to keep them supplied. The endorsement form of exploitation had become so universally known and admired by all kinds of manufacturers, concluded the account, "that the studios receive hundreds of letters from all parts of the world seeking permission to use the names of their players in connection with the advertising of product. Some of these requests are pathetic in their sincerity and come from manufacturers of most any conceivable commodity."[2]

Cough drop manufacturer Smith Brothers launched an ad campaign in December 1928, to run through the following April in 27 magazines. Those ads were of the testimonial type, and it was said to be an easy matter to get leading stage stars, without remuneration, to join with Smith

Brothers in their campaign against the theater cough. Actors who endorsed the product included Peggy Wood, Glenn Hunter, Joe Cook, and Lew Fields (of Weber and Fields fame). In his ad copy, Fields recalled he had then been on stage some 6,000 times, "yet, on some nights, I still get pretty nervous. Those are the nights when the overture is nearly drowned out by coughing, and I know there is an army of coughers in the audience. How coughing can kill a wise crack dead!" One conclusion drawn in this account — which indirectly mentioned the pervasiveness of testimonial ads — was that in this case "the overworked actor and actress testimonial ceases to be hackneyed because in this instance the theater plays a legiti-mate part in the argument of the copy." The reporter added, "Then again, sincerity, which hides its face in shame in a great deal of professional tes-timonial copy, here reveals itself without a blush because the stage stars are endorsing, through Smith Brothers cough drops, something very much to their interest — a war on the annoying and disturbing, hoarse theater cough."[3]

One of the busiest endorsers among the Hollywood colony in the 1920s was silent film star Constance Talmadge, who, in the interests of pro-moting her latest films, established what ad executive Walter Goodman called a record in the field when she endorsed some 400 products, rang-ing from an aspirin tablet to a grand piano, all in a single day. Goodman, writing in *The Nation* in 1956, may have exaggerated the number, but Tal-madge certainly was active.[4]

Arthur Cramp observed wryly, in 1929, that the *Liberty* magazine issue for October 19, 1927, might well have been called the "Constance Tal-madge Testimonial Number," as her endorsement of products appeared in no fewer than nine different ads. First, there was the film star being awakened by an alarm clock, the Ansonia Squareclox; then, the Benrus Watch concern featured "on the alluring wrist of Constance Talmadge the watch of your dreams"; a few pages onward appeared Talmadge display-ing the Juliet Wedding Ring manufactured by J.R. Bowden and Company; then under the headline of "No More Flat Tires," the actress informed readers that "Air Containers are a blessing." An ad for the obesity remedy Marmola showed a full-figure photo of Talmadge pitching on behalf of the nostrum; then she was depicted using her "sure-fire Thorens" [a cig-arette lighter]; next she gave her alleged approval to Dentyne Chewing Gum, Gold Seal Radio Tubes, and the First National "Super-Movies" for the 1927–1928 season.[5]

So popular was the practice of joining movie stars and national man-ufacturers in endorsement advertising that at least one organization was founded in the 1920s to bring about such unions. Famous Names, Inc., of

Chicago, sent out mimeographed letters in 1926, one of which was addressed to the sellers of a nationally advertised table water. The company declared it was in business to sell the rights to use the names, pictures, and endorsements of certain film stars. According to the letter "managers of the most prominent moving-picture stars and stage celebrities have assigned to this organization the selling rights of their stars for commercial advertising purposes." It went on to add that any special poses for the ads "will be made according to your specifications and if it is desired the endorsements signed by the star can be of your dictation." A follow-up letter on the same subject listed the names of about a dozen film stars of both sexes, with the prices demanded for endorsements for each of them. Asking rates ranged from $200 to $275.[6]

One of the product categories that made heavy use of endorsement ads in the 1920s, and would continue to do so into the future, was the tobacco industry. These ads also reintroduced significant dishonesty into the area by often using as endorsers people who did not smoke. When the American Tobacco Company marked the sixty-fifth anniversary of its Bull Durham smoking tobacco in 1925, it asked author, humorist, and stage and film star Will Rogers to help in the celebration by writing Bull Durham advertising copy. Frank W. Harwood, advertising manager of the firm, claimed Rogers had given a new twist to testimonial copy. That new twist, he said, "lies in the fact that we are running a testimonial campaign written entirely by the individual who makes the testimonial." The format of the copy was that it was set up as an opinion column, "The Bull's Eye," in which Rogers was free to write anything he wanted. Reportedly, he did not have to say much about Bull Durham. In one of those early pieces he wrote, "I know people are going to say: 'What do you think of Will Rogers writing and endorsing Bull Durham?' That's where you're wrong. I am not endorsing it. I never smoked any tobacco in my life, not even Bull Durham." Such ads ran in national magazines and in newspapers from coast to coast.[7]

In that campaign, American Tobacco tried to develop sales through what it described as a "human interest" strategy. Irvin Cobb used the same theme in his endorsement copy for Sweet Caporal cigarettes. In another campaign, Mae Murray was one of several film and stage stars used to shill for Tuxedo pipe tobacco. A campaign for Melachrino cigarettes also used the testimonial strategy and included a series of from 12 to 15 endorsements from European and Asiatic nobility. For years Melachrino advertising had given prominence to the slogan "The One Cigarette Sold the World Over." In the new campaign that theme was reinforced by introducing the public to prominent individuals, representatives of various nationalities, who professed a preference for the brand. A media account declared that "every detail of the campaign has been developed to create a international atmosphere, and an impression of luxury in keeping with the class appeal." One of the first of these endorsers was Jagat Jit Singh, Maharaja de Kapurthala; others were Prince Wilhelm of Sweden, Prince Luis de Bourbon (brother to King Alfonso), and Count Boris of Russia. These ads also ran in national magazines and newspapers coast to coast. American Tobacco's Frank W. Harwood (vice-president by this time) said that in no case was any money paid directly for any of these endorsements. In some cases a donation was reportedly made to a selected charity. Those endorsements were arranged through the services of a woman who came originally from Swedish royalty. She married into Russian nobility and for 20 years had been in touch with European nobility, "so she has been able to get these signatures largely on the basis of personal friendship."[8]

Remarking on the number of women then endorsing cigarettes, journalist H.S. Gardner (who owned an ad agency) commented, in 1929, that it must have taken some nerve years earlier for a famous singer (unnamed) to pioneer in the endorsement of a cigarette, when smoking by women was still frowned upon. However, once the ice was broken many more rushed in. Speaking of the late 1920s, Gardner declared, "So abundant is the flock of women cigarette endorsers that the reader has become disgusted to see advertisements bearing testimonials which only lack the price tag to make them complete." Then Gardner related that a few months earlier a woman had astonished the world by flying across the Atlantic, a feat that gave her a lot of attention and made her a prime suspect for testimonials. (Although Gardner did not identify the flier, it was obviously Amelia Earhart.) In due course she turned up in an ad, a casual reading of which, wrote the reporter, would be taken as an endorsement of a cigarette, which the woman presumably smoked on the flight. Later the pilot contributed $1,500 to an Antarctic expedition, stating through the press that she was merely passing on the money that she had received for endorsing a cigarette that her male companions—not she—smoked on that transcontinental flight.[9]

Morton J. Simon, a member of the Philadelphia bar, told the story of the efforts of a group of tongue-in-cheekers to secure court approval of an organization to be known as the "Tobacco Society for Voice Culture." When the New York *World* commented on this, it said: "The apparent purpose of the application was to ridicule cigarette advertising which uses testimonials from singers." The court refused the application and labeled it as "frivolous."[10]

According to Arthur Cramp, over the course of 12 months ending in

1929, some 18,000 physicians were alleged to have testified that the "toasting process" to which a certain brand of cigarettes were allegedly submitted was likely to free those cigarettes from throat-irritating properties. Setting aside that the figure may have been exaggerated, Cramp went on to complain that not one physician in a thousand was competent to express such as opinion, "but a questionnaire, accompanied by the persuasive power of a free gift of a carton of a hundred cigarettes, seems to have brought a lush response from an easy-going and tolerant profession — a record that does not redound to its credit."[11]

One aspect of the testimonial industry that was refined in the 1920s (and into the 1930s) was that of a national advertiser using many, many different celebrities in a long-running campaign. Another development was the use of society people — invariably women — in endorsement ads, the so-called better classes. Combining both of those elements was a campaign begun around 1924 for Pond's Cleansing and Vanishing creams. Principle developer of that campaign was Stanley Resor, then head of the J. Walter Thompson advertising agency. Behind the campaign was the idea that since Englishwomen had complexions fabled the world over, then Englishwomen should endorse Pond's face creams as the secret of their creamy luster. That would cause American women to fall in line and buy the products.[12]

Writing about the Pond's campaign in 1931, Alva Johnston enthused that it modernized the testimonial and that "directed with audacity, tact and imagination, backed up by a well-filled war chest, the Pond's cream campaign made endorsing not only respectable but glamorous." While the campaign started with Englishwomen, very early on it expanded to include American women (as well as females from other parts of the world) as endorsers. But in all cases Pond's went after only "the cream of society." Early in the Pond's campaign, society reporters were called in to divide American aristocracy into two classes—"the $1,000 people and the $500 people." Women who possessed "personality" and Social Register acquaintances were engaged as wranglers. Reportedly it was hard going and unrewarding work at first, but, wrote Johnston, "Soon the important discovery was made that preliminary obstacles could be overcome in a surprising number of cases by the careful greasing of social secretaries. It was also found necessary to buy useful information and to split commissions with relatives and friends of the prospective endorser." Moral suasion was also brought to bear, as these women (the prospective endorsers) had an appeal made to their consciences that they constituted a moral force in society, were looked up to by the community for leadership, and had certain public duties to let the "masses know about valuable products," and so forth.[13]

Pond's endorsers included Mrs. O.H.P. Belmont, Mrs. Cornelia Biddle, Julia Hoy ($1,000, $500, and $500 people, respectively), Mrs. Marshall Field Sr., the Duchesse de Richelieu, and Lady Mountbatten. Queen Marie of Romania was said to have given an endorsement after receiving $2,000, two silver boxes, and a miniature of herself by the artist de Laszlo. Some endorsers, like Alice Roosevelt Longworth, declined several times before finally agreeing to endorse. She then committed what Johnston declared was the worst crime that had ever been perpetrated against the testimonial: she announced through the Associated Press that she received $5,000 for the endorsement. Johnston said that statement delivered a blow to the infant endorsement industry because "at that time many people still believed that the endorser was a good creature who gave the endorsement because of a generous impulse to spread the good news about Pond's. Few understood that the sale of a name had become an ordinary commercial transaction like the sale of a fish. The testimonial racketeers have never forgiven the daughter of the former President." Not only was public confidence shaken, but Longworth cost the testimonial industry a good deal of money because the wranglers could no longer swear that $1,000 was the ceiling endorsement fee. While the Queen of Spain cost Pond's ten times as much as Queen Marie, a large part of that sum had to be spent "in greasing governesses, noblewomen and princesses before the Queen could be propositioned."[14]

Reportedly, the aristocratic Vanderbilt clan resisted becoming endorsers for a long time because of a fear they would incur the wrath of the elder Mrs. Cornelius Vanderbilt, matriarch of the tribe. Finally, though, they began to sign on until, by the end of the 1920s, wrote Johnston, "the name is a drug on the testimonial market." Other Pond's shills were Mrs. Conde Nast, Mrs. Adrian Iselin II, Mrs. William Borah, Mrs. Asquith, Marjorie Oelrichs, the Marquise de Polignac, Viscountess Curzon, the Duchess of Alba, Lady Lavery, and the Duchess of Vendome. The theatrical profession, which had previously held a monopoly on endorsements, declared the reporter, was snubbed by the face cream maker. Two titled women — Lady Diana Manners and Princess Matchabelli — were the only stage people admitted to the Pond's ranks. Even at that early time the idea that some endorsers could actually have a negative effect on product sales — the bad boy testifier — was evident, although it would be decades before it became a major concern. Early in the Pond's campaign, explained Johnston, it was recognized that a "grave error" had been made in permitting divorcees, especially those on the "wrong end" of a decree, to endorse Pond's. Thus, the creams "may be endorsed by none but maids, widows and chaste matrons.... Pond's advertising account was closed forever to any woman who has been in a jam."[15]

By all accounts, the Pond's campaign worked well for the firm and was still doing so some 25 years after it began. At the later date the testifiers were young American women on the brink of marriage. Their pictures and testimonies came under a heading that read something like: "She's engaged ... She's lovely ... She uses Pond's."[16]

Every once in a while there was a slip-up in that usually well-oiled Pond's campaign. After having joined the highly placed ranks of Pond's face cream endorsers (a group ad executive Walter Goodman described as containing "2 Queens, a battalion of Princesses and several regiments of society women"), Lady Diana Manners told newspaper reporters that her beauty and flawless complexion were attributable to "fresh air, exercise and plenty of soap and water."[17]

Offering insight into the workings of the testimonial industry was a woman who anonymously wrote a lengthy article for the trade publication *Advertising & Selling* that was published in 1931. She had entered the "testimonial racket" (as she called it) back in 1923 and was still working in that field when her article was published. Over that time she had worked on over 25 different testimonial campaigns, with the endorsers including women of titles, athletes, authors, political leaders, members of first families, artists, and people in the theatrical profession. The use of middlemen, she thought, started "away back" (no year was given) in the days when a Community Plate ad appeared that startled the eyes of many magazine readers, as it showed the dining table of one of New York's most exclusive matrons. It was said to be the first time society had entered the testimonial field. Everyone was puzzled since the society woman could not have been paid for her endorsement. In any case she did not need the money, and there seemed to be no reason for her to seek publicity. So how was the endorsement arranged? The insider (call her Jane Doe) related the story that a poorer member of the society set was told there was money for her if she could persuade her more prominent friend to endorse. "The wealthy lady, wishing to do her less fortunate sister a good turn, agreed," explained Doe. "And I believe that is what started the 'liaison officers' such as myself in the testimonial business." That was her term to describe the middleman, or wrangler, function.[18]

National advertisers, explained Doe, realized that people of note could be approached much more easily and cheaply if done through the right entrée, such as being approached by a personal friend, and were more likely to agree to endorse "if they understand that their friend who is asking for the testimonial is going to profit thereby." Doe said there were many liaison officers such as herself with some being young society girls and some being married society women. Both of those types were looking for extra money. Another type of liaison person was the "man-about-town" who had a lot of contacts. Some advertising agencies used testimonials; some did not. Those that did believe in the use of testimonials kept on hand a list of liaison officers along with a list of celebrities and "important people" to whom those liaison people had easy entrée. Often Doe was called to a meeting with an ad agency and handed a list of people who were wanted as endorsers for a campaign. Sometimes she suggested names not on the list.[19]

She said it was generally understood that the liaison officer received half of the amount paid to the endorser. Sometimes, though, an advertiser told her he could afford to spend a certain sum to cover the testimonials of a definite number of endorsements. Then it was up to Doe to make deals at such prices as to leave something for herself. There were also cases where the advertiser asked her advice about how large a fee to pay an endorser. Bargaining sometimes took place over the fee, and inducements over and above cash were often involved. Besides the aforementioned $5,000 in cash, Alice Longworth also reportedly received a portrait of herself done by a prominent painter, which was used as an illustration in the Pond's ad. She also was said to have received the hospital expenses incurred at the time her daughter Paulina was born. Doe then wondered if much faking was going on in the testimonial industry. She thought all such talk was over-emphasized by the industry and that "my experience has shown me that most people who endorse articles are sincerely enthusiastic about them." Then she added that she knew several celebrities who had a rule about not endorsing things they did not believe in — "and it was useless to offer money unless they actually do approve of the product." One example she gave of a celebrity who refused to endorse no matter how much money was offered was Katherine Cornell. Charles Lindbergh was also cited as a firm resister, although she acknowledged he finally succumbed and endorsed Bulova watches. Former President Calvin Coolidge did not appear in advertisements, but Mrs. Coolidge was used, unpaid, in a 1930 Kodak campaign. In general, she thought men were much more difficult to secure as endorsers than were women, and she added, "I suppose men such as Ford, Edison and Marconi were landed for the Simmons [mattress] campaign because those gentlemen were told they would be doing humanity a good turn if they preached the gospel of more and better sleep."[20]

Returning to the subject of faking in testimonials, Doe admitted that "yes, it most certainly does take place.... I have been a party myself to some fakes in testimonials." In one campaign featuring famous businessmen who were endorsing a certain food product, she found one on her list who detested that particular kind of food. "But he wanted the publicity —

not so much for himself but for his firm — and I wanted the $300." And so it was done, but she blamed herself for the ethical lapse rather than the ad agency, which had warned her (in the face of a lot of media attention given to faking in endorsements) to make sure all endorsements were sincere. In a campaign featuring the maids of famous actresses, she used (with the consent and approval of the actress) a model instead of the real maid (the model was passed off as the real maid). Yet another campaign included a woman described as being well-known in social and political circles. She endorsed a product because she needed the $1,500. She had never used the article until the time she was given it when she signed on, even though the ad suggested and implied she had used it for years.[21]

In discussing endorsements more generally, Doe confessed, "I have a special theory about the use of testimonials. I really don't think the public swallows much of the actual testimonial stuff anyway." She felt the main value of endorsements lay in the name and photograph of the person featured, a person in whom the public was interested. "People will always be more exciting than products. So I honestly didn't feel that I was robbing the advertiser or the public in the few cases where I faked." Any number of stage and film stars told Doe their ad endorsement signing was entirely out of their hands. Some contracts included a clause stating that the stars would not sign any testimonials except through the film studio's manager or publicity director. On the other hand, the studio could sign for the star. Doe rationalized the situation by exclaiming, "But after all, the dear public has never taken theatrical endorsements seriously. The main value of using stars is that they are attention-getters." She thought that even people who seemingly did not need the money might nevertheless do testimonials to get a little more money, because one could never have too much; "it means she can run over to Cartier's for that latest trinket from Paris.... Personally, I think many of our society women have their tongues in their cheeks when they announce that their testimonial fee is going to their pet charity — though I have known cases where it has been true." Another reason she offered to explain the willingness of many people to do endorsements, who might seem unlikely candidates, was simply because it flattered them. "This business has taught me what a vain world we live in," Doe added. In conclusion she declared, with respect to paid testimonials, that "I don't see why people shouldn't be paid, provided they're sincere in their endorsement. Naturally, if it's simply a bribe, that's different."[22]

All facets of the endorsement industry grew strongly in the 1920s, including ads featuring testifiers who were ordinary citizens, and sometimes companies. However, the concept of the unsolicited testimonial letter arriving in the morning mail was mainly fiction. They were actively

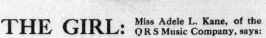

Ordinary citizens endorsed this Dictahone in 1921. That they presumably used the machine was thought to make their testimony more cogent.

sought. Willis Brindley was the manager of Hewitt-Lea-Funck (the firm sold farm silos), and he told how he obtained testimonials for his silos for use in company ads in farm periodicals. He explained, "Many farmers like to take their pen in hand and write the company a nice letter, but for three years past farmers have not felt exactly chatty in the mind." He had to admit that "We found in the file very few testimonials, and those not very hearty in tone." To overcome that problem, Brindley wrote a short letter to some 120 farmers who bought silos in 1922. He asked, in a few questions, how the silo had been for them and, if possible, to send along a photo of the silo for the company's catalogue. As of the date of his article, November 1923, he had received 16 replies from the 120 letters—a figure that he felt would eventually reach 40 to 50. A reply from L.H. Willet, with responses to company questions, went as follows: How do you like your H-L-F Silo so far? "There is no better." Did you have any frozen silage last winter? "No." How cold was it? "40 below." How much did you save by buying an H-L-F Silo? "150." Remarks: "I am satisfied with my H-L-F Silo. Would not part with it if I could not get another." Working with that material, Brindley turned out the following testimonial: "I like my H-L-F Silo fine. There is no better. I had no frozen silage last winter, with the thermometer 40 below zero. I saved $150 when I bought the silo. Would not part with it if I could not get another. Yours truly, L.H. Willett (Tomahawk, Wisconsin)." Anticipating that some critics might have felt it was a "little rough" on Willett and the others to write them and then make what they say into a letter of praise, Brindley said, "Not at all. There will be absolutely no complaint. Mr. Willett and other testimonial authors will be glad to see their testimony in print." He said he knew that would be so because he had been using testimonial letters for ten years and "in all that time, I have never had a complaint because a letter was used for advertising purposes."[23]

Photos were not so easily obtained by Brindley, and a second letter to the farmer was generally necessary. The farmer could take a photograph himself and send it in or have a commercial photographer (at Hewitt expense) come take it. Brindley noted, however, that the latter option could be a problem, because "county photographers are notoriously incompetent." Another problem the executive mentioned was that some years earlier they had discovered that prospective customers often wrote letters to the endorsers of testimonial ads, ostensibly for the sake of getting additional information, "but really to see whether the evidence offered is genuine." With that in mind, some advertisers avoided the publication of post office addresses. However, Hewitt felt giving the complete address added strength to the testimonial, and if the inquirer could get further direct information from a customer, that would increase the chances of a sale. One snag was that after answering one or two such inquiry letters, the endorsing farmer might get tired of the imposition and ignore any other letters. Thus, "the inquirer makes up his mind that the letter was a fake, and that the product must be a fake, and the deal is off." Hewitt got around that problem by writing the endorser to tell him they were going to use his letter and that many farmers would probably write to him for additional information and that Hewitt would like him to answer all such letters. As an incentive, they sent the endorser a correspondence pad, some stamped envelopes, and a piece of carbon paper. For each carbon copy of a letter the endorser sent to Hewitt, they sent him 25 cents. "This works very well," boasted Brindley. "The sum we offer is so small that it cannot be considered except as an honorarium." He added that such a letter, from one farmer to another, was "much more effective than anything we could write ourselves, and the farmer-correspondent can and does tell his inquirer that "the company is on the square ... the sort of thing that we cannot say very well for ourselves, and which would not necessarily be believed if we did."[24]

In a different case, a large manufacturing institution sent a letter to a Detroit company that had purchased certain machinery from it for its main factory building. That letter asked if they would write a testimonial letter, as the inquiring concern wanted to use it as part of their advertising material in trade journals. Detroit said no—it had a blanket policy against writing such letters. But the first company did not give up. It used photographs of the installation that it already had, and its ad merely stated that the company had made the installation and that everyone was pleased. That ad copy was submitted in proof form to the Detroit firm, which, in a reply letter, said it had no objection, explaining, "There is a vast difference between this simple statement of a fact and our actually writing a testimonial." In a different example, a firm received the contract for certain installations in a large transatlantic ocean liner and rushed those facts into an ad, along with a picture of the ship. A week after the ad appeared the steamship line sent a terse letter reprimanding the advertiser, as "no such liberties should have been taken without the complete sanction of the Lines." They did not want to be placed in the position of recommending the product of one concern over another. As a result, contracts for two other installations in boats of that line were canceled.[25]

Another company that used industrial testimonials was the General Fireproofing Company (GF). For them to be able to simply state in an ad that the Statler Hotels had specified GF fireproofing material was "certainly sufficient." The Republic Flow Meters Company also used what were called indirect testimonials in one of its ads. It featured the symbols of national advertiser Morton Salt Company — the familiar tilted container spilling salt and the Morton trade character, a little girl under an umbrella. The ad copy declared, "Power plant cost accounting is being adopted by every branch of industry. The Morton Salt Company, among many others, uses Republic Flow Meter equipment to give cost facts." Business reporter A.L. Townsend offered companies advice on how to avoid being refused an endorsement by other firms. He said it was "more effective to make up the advertisement in question and submit it in proof form exactly as it will appear. When the concern knows what is to be used, there is less likelihood of canceling permission, but to make an inquiry first leaves the thing in doubt."[26]

Believing that many testimonial campaigns were marred by the inclusion of a considerable amount of copy, which attracted attention away from the endorsing company, Imperial Oil Limited, Toronto, trimmed as much text as possible from its ads. With that end in mind, the facsimile letters from endorsers were conspicuously displayed in each ad while the text copy added by Imperial was limited to no more than 20 words, and sometimes as few as four. One ad read, "Large Vancouver Company Endorses" (followed by the Imperial trade mark). It was a campaign for Imperial's Polarine Motor Oils. Another ad read: "Alberta's largest automobile fleet lubricated with Polarine."[27]

Returning to citizen testimonials, a 1924 article by A.L. Townsend related that a new trend involved an increased sophistication in extracting parts from unsolicited testimonial letters (culls) received by a concern, with the fine print of the ad explaining that interested readers could send in for the complete document — that is, the full endorsement letter. Townsend concluded that "the testimonial letter is as powerful as ever, for advertising purposes, but there is a more conscientious and skilful method of culling the interesting from the dull, the picturesque from the drab, and the convincing from those which are a little too flagrantly boastful."[28]

A business article from 1926 discussed the trend away from using ordinary people as endorsers (still somewhat discredited from their use in patent medicine ads of old) to using famous and/or society people as testifiers. One reason was thought to be the high cost of ads. According to this account, "the socially elect, golf champions, movie and stage stars, explorers, authors of best sellers, scientists and .400 hitters are the pegs on which the most readable of copy is hung." One campaign then going against that trend was from the Quaker Oats Company, a campaign using endorsement copy from ordinary people to advertise its breakfast foods. Quaker asserted that "in no case has the advertising leaned on the personality or

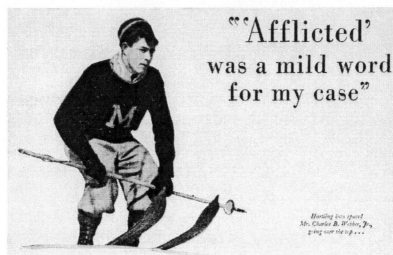

" 'Afflicted' was a mild word for my case"

Hurtling into space!
Mr. Charles B. Webber, Jr., going over the top . . .

In the early years of endorsement ads, ordinary people did the endorsing more often than Hollywood actors or sport stars. Fleischmann's Yeast was one company that made frequent use of ordinary citizen endorsement, as shown here in this ad from 1928. Here, a young man claims that Fleischmann's cleared his complexion; a woman remembers being nervous, underweight and constipated before using Fleischmann's; and a man says that Fleischmann's cured his indigestion.

reputation of anyone known to the general public." It was evident, therefore, went the account, "that this campaign stands out sharply from other
testimonial campaigns wherein manufacturers depend on the high position or popularity of some man or woman in the public eye." By using
famous people as testifiers, most advertisers expressed a belief that when
a person of prominence endorsed a product countless others, more or less
eager to follow the leader, would buy and use it. Quaker Oats held, however, at least for this campaign, that in matters relating to food the
plumber, policeman, and printer would be influenced the most by men of
their own ilk—average people. A Quaker executive commented, with
respect to this campaign, "Unquestionably in our sales promotion we did
not reach the enormous market made up of people who work with their
hands as well as their heads. We want to sell that market." He added that
"our newspaper advertising of 'Everyday Folks and Their Breakfasts' is one
approach to it. In it we are using the pictures and endorsements of men
from various trades who have found puffed wheat and puffed rice palatable and satisfying."[29]

One point of debate about endorsement ads at this time involved
what to include. The Everbrite Stove Company of Kansas City, Missouri,
wrote to the editors of the advertising trade journal *Printers' Ink* to ask
about the effectiveness of testimonials that gave the name and address of
the endorser versus those that gave the name only. Said the editors, "There
is little question that the use of addresses as well as names adds to the value
of advertising testimonials, except in the instances of such persons as
nationally known actors, baseball players, society women, and so forth."
Many years earlier, they said, the patent medicine makers discovered that
a letter signed "Mrs. John Smith, 100 Main St, Smithville" was a lot more
valuable than a letter merely signed "Mrs. John Smith" with no address.
That was because the average person was said to be a bit suspicious of testimonials that were not pretty definite. "The address takes up very little
space but does add the ring of authority to the testimonial." Those editors added that one method that avoided the use of addresses and "yet
makes the testimonial sound sincere is to use the familiar device, 'Name
on request.' Of course, it is seldom that anyone writes in to the company
to ask the name, but the mere fact that the company offers to reveal the
name to those interested makes the prospect believe that the testimonial
is bona fide." In conclusion, however, the editors stated that it was considered better practice to give both the name and the address of the person doing the endorsing.[30]

With the growth of testimonial advertising in the 1920s came,
inevitably, growth in the number of outright scams involved in that field.

Many were explained by journalist C.B. Larrabee. Suppose you made fudge boilers but you could not make any headway against Smith's fudge boiler — the market leader everybody liked. If you were steeped in the "old ethics," explained Larrabee, you searched around for a number of users of your product and got their testimonials. But that was laborious, took time, and produced problematic results. Alternatively, you sent a man out to Hillsdale College with a bunch of your fudge boilers. He might have found all the women at Hillsdale used Smith units and swore by them. But you gave away your product and asked the women to write a letter to your firm telling about the product and whether or not they used it. Some did write. Thus, through ad copy, the world was told, "The Double Star Fudge Boiler is the College Girl's Favorite." Also, carefully mentioned was that you had letters to back up that claim. In another example, Larrabee mentioned an advertiser who sent a quantity of his product to a number of professional men in various parts of the country. Along with the gift was a questionnaire made up "of cleverly worded questions regarding the merits of the product." Some filled them out and mailed them back, as they had been requested to do. One question asked if the respondent considered the product in question any more harmful than similar products on the market. The men said no. But that was changed by the company, and in some of their ads thereafter the company declared their product was endorsed by professional men, even though there was a big difference between a hearty endorsement and a statement that "your product isn't any worse than others."[31]

Another option for a company seeking endorsements was "to buy a couple of thousand dollars' worth of testimonials." Even if some one targeted as a potential endorsee had never used a product, explained Larrabee, that should not be seen as a bar to a testimonial. "If she has an elastic conscience she need never see the product," but if her dignity would not allow that, it was easy enough to present her with the product; "She will then write you such a testimonial — or let you write if for her...." One advertising agency executive argued that testimonials had not become meaningless as some thought (due to their proliferation), and that "they have but one intent and that is to convey the impression that the signer is a voluntary user and endorser of the product." The executive added, however, that testimonials which had been bought, directly or indirectly, from persons whose use of the product (if such use existed at all) was solely to give some validity to the endorsement, were "fraudulent in their intentions, deceptive to the public, and undoubtedly must tend to destroy whatever faith consumers may still retain for the dependability of advertising statements." Larrabee agreed with that sentiment, adding that "even the most adventitious logician can't argue you or me into believing that such testimonials are ethical. They are fraudulent and misleading." Worse, they handicapped "decent" advertisers who did not stoop to use the unethical endorsement and were thus placed at a competitive disadvantage. "The testimonial fever has swept advertising. It has become worse and worse during the last year or so."[32]

Another type of endorsement ad that may have first emerged in the 1920s, at least to any extent, was the endorsement from an "expert"— or as reporter W. Livingstone Larned described them in 1924, the "Men Who Know" type of testimonial. A new series of ads for Colt revolvers carried that slogan as a standing head over photos of testifiers, although those pictured did not write their testimonials. Ads for Western Ammunition featured photos of one of its workers in the factory and out in the field with dog and gun. The advertising copy read: "The men who make Western Ammunition are sportsmen. They not only know how to make ammunition, but how to shoot it, and have learned from personal experience just what you expect, and should get, in the shells and cartridges you buy." A maker of golf clubs and balls had the same idea and was said to have successfully used a similar theme in its ads. Its copy described how its factory men, during their leisure hours, played golf with the very equipment they themselves produced. Another company, one which targeted new mothers with its advertising material, used a nurse in its copy, "of mature years and judgment," who was supposed to have worked in a maternity ward of a local hospital and to have had experience with thousands of babies. As a consequence, said Larned, "so many young mothers began writing this supposed 'expert' for advice along specialized lines, that the company was compelled to find just such a woman to join their organization."[33]

Larned pointed out that this type of campaign did not contain a widely known famous person because fame had nothing to do with it, as experience and know-how were the important points. The classic example of the expert endorsement from this era was the locomotive engineer endorsing a well-known watch. In Larned's opinion, the approbation of that engineer meant "far more than the most extravagant praise from a world-wide celebrity, although it is not asked that the engineers shown be photographs of real railroad men." He explained further that "the mere fact that a great many drivers of engines are partial to a certain make of watch, supplies the desired advertising ammunition. An engineer can't take any chances when it comes to the question of time." Calling his time an age of specialization, Larned concluded that public respect and confidence thus was then going to the "Person Who Knows" as compared to the person who was merely famous.[34]

A few years after that, Larrabee returned with an article about how some advertisers were using expert testimony, or scientific reports, in a fraudulent way. One example was of a national food advertiser who published in an ad a "remarkable" endorsement for his product. That endorsement was taken from a scientific paper of "unimpeachable authenticity." In no uncertain terms, noted Larrabee, it said a certain type of cooked food was ideal for breakfast. The scientific body that sponsored the paper read the ad with some surprise since the man who prepared the paper knew he had not endorsed the product. In that report the man had endorsed whole wheat cereal, but the advertiser's product was not whole wheat. Nevertheless, the paragraph quoted in the ad seemed to be an endorsement of any kind of cooked cereal. That impression was given because the advertiser used a strategy of long-standing even then — they took something out of context.[35]

According to Larrabee, some advertisers pointed out in their copy that scientists everywhere were almost unanimous in their recommendations that a certain medicine be used to correct certain medical conditions. An advertiser then noted his product contained some of that medicine and therefore it must be a cure for the condition. Not pointed out by the ad was the tiny amount of that ingredient actually contained in the product. Another national advertiser announced his product was the final answer to insomnia. Just put a little of it in hot milk and the user would quickly fall asleep. Not mentioned was that if someone drank hot milk without the product he would receive the same effect. Larrabee argued that these modern fakers differed from the old patent medicine falsehoods because they were not "plain liars" for if you hauled one of them into court he could show documents to prove that doctors said the very things the advertiser claimed they said. "He could point out to you, furthermore, that no place in his copy is there a statement that his product is a sure cure for these things about which doctors were so upset."[36]

Reporter Henry Lee Staples was one of the few investigators who bothered to find out how many testimonial ads were actually appearing in magazines. When he looked at three issues of the *Saturday Evening Post* for February 1929, he counted nine testimonials in total (three from one advertising agency and six from all the other agencies in America). He found actor Peggy Wood shilling for Smith Brothers, Gloria Vanderbilt for Holeproof Hosiery, polar explorer Commander Dick Byrd for Sergeant Dog Remedies, foreign medical personnel for Fleischmann's Yeast (the American Medical Association did not approve of U.S. physicians giving testimonials, believing self-diagnosis to be a great danger to the public), and five from ordinary citizens. From the February 1929 issue of the *Ladies*

Home Journal he found 11 testimonials (eight from one agency, three from all the others) out of a total of 228 advertisements therein. Although Staples did not mention the name of the agency responsible for most of the endorsements, it was almost certainly the J. Walter Thompson agency, one of the very few agencies of the time that was a proponent of such ads.[37]

Also little explored was the question of the efficacy of endorsement ads. A.E. Little was the advertising manager of the Thew Shovel Company (a maker of heavy equipment for road building work, such as power shovels, cranes, and backhoes). With a certain amount of media attention then devoted to fake endorsements, Little argued that "counterfeiting proves the value of the thing counterfeited. Men don't imitate bad money. We do not condemn all money because we know that an occasional banknote might be spurious.... Believability is based on the source of the testimonial rather than the thing said." For Little the real question was not "are testimonials believed" (which he took to be a given), but "why are they believed?" One reason he offered was that people were lazy and were content to let others think for them on subjects aside from their immediate pursuits. Little declared the belief in testimonials went back to the biblical Eve: "All Mother Eve needed to convince her the apple should be eaten was a voice outside herself to accelerate her decision to do that which she would have done anyhow sooner or later." In conclusion, Little added that "timeliness is the strength of a testimonial, and its proper time is after something has built up a leaning toward the article advertised ... but the preparation is essential."[38]

By the end of the 1920s, the endorsement ad had strongly re-established itself as an important part of the advertising world. Types of such ads that would remain common up to the current time — using celebrities, experts, and ordinary citizens — were all well established again by the 1920s. Not that endorsement ads were the dominant format used, far from it, but they attracted an attention and notoriety disproportionate to their prevalence. (See Appendix A for statistics on their prevalence.) It all culminated in a huge media debate in 1929 over the ethics involved in the testimonial area. Although the debate started a little earlier than that, and lasted a little beyond that date, for the most part it was centered in 1929. Generally, it revealed little support for the endorsement ad, at least rhetorically, within the advertising industry and without.

3

The Ethics of
Testimonials, 1929

Advertising is to-day the most truthful matter which appears in print ... I never question a statement in the *Saturday Evening Post.*
— Claude C. Hopkins, 1928

I am informed that one can buy almost any kind of testimonial for a price. The scourge has spread and it takes in social leaders, shipwreck heroes, aviators, baseball favorites, par golfers, etc.
— A.W. Erickson, 1929

The advertising world has been bitten badly by the prostituted testimonial....
— H.S. Gardner, 1929

One of the earlier articles to address the issue of ethics at length appeared in late 1926. Business reporter D.M. Hubbard worried about a trend to endorsements being bought from the famous. He felt that just a few years earlier the use of testimonials had been a very minor part of advertising. But then someone stirred up the situation, and the use of "testimonial copy, obscure and in none too high repute from its patent medicine associations of a generation ago, gathered new force with the evidence from the new-era endorsement not counting at all as the testifier was the whole show." For him, what he sarcastically called the dawn of the golden age in testimonials had begun around four or five years earlier, when a smoking tobacco manufacturer obtained the names, photographs, and written endorsements of a group of nationally known athletes for use in advertising their product. Since then, he continued, "the trail of the testimonial writer has led straight upward through the ranks of the stars of ring, diamond and gridiron, the ingenuous folk of the movies, popular novelists, and the social register to throne rooms and chancelleries." It was just two years previously, wrote Hubbard, that the newspapers first published a brief account that those testimonials might not be all they seemed. An unidentified woman — whose husband was reportedly then being talked about as one of the next nominees for U.S. president — wrote a testimonial for an advertiser and received $5,000 for it, although that amount was purportedly donated to charity.[1]

Many more people got insight into the testimonial field in the summer of 1926 when Gertrude Ederle received fame, and countless endorsement offers, after swimming the English Channel. "I was an honest amateur and I intend to be an honest professional at any cost. I'm not going to endorse things that I do not know anything about," commented the swimmer. "I'm not going to say for a few thousand dollars here and a few thousand dollars there that I trained on some malted product when I didn't do any such thing or that I like Punko cigarettes when I never smoked." Then there was the case of star football player Red Grange, who was quoted in the newspapers to the effect that he expected to receive several hundred thousand dollars for endorsing a host of products. Other stories about purchased testimonials also came to the public's attention. For Hubbard, it was all very annoying that celebrities, for a fee, would endorse outboard motors they would never know how to start, food items they would never eat, and other products "they wouldn't use on a bet."[2]

The American Medical Association's monthly magazine *Hygeia* published an editorial called "The Testimonial Game," which was summarized and sent out by the Associated Press (AP). It was an editorial based on a letter sent to an advertiser by Famous Names, Inc., offering to supply the names, pictures, and endorsements of famous celebrities for advertising purposes. Enclosed with the letter were the names of 13 film actors and the "moderate" fee each required. "With the star's endorsement," ran the AP dispatch, "the advertiser may have a specialty posed picture of the celebrity and the exclusive right to that name against all competitors." According to Famous Names's literature, pictures of movie stars "have unlimited possibilities for attracting greater attention to your advertising." Another news account told of a New York firm that had Queen Marie of Romania ready to furnish her endorsements of products to advertisers, presumably for a consideration. Wondering what those news accounts meant, Hubbard answered his own question when he wrote: "First of all, they plant the idea in the minds of the buying public that the use of testimonials in advertising is a trick; sharp practice if it is not a fraud. Then, they lead the reader to question whether there is such a thing as a genuine bona fide testimonial. And by doing this, they tend to destroy faith in all advertising." John F. Ditzell, president of Famous Names, defended the sale of celebrity testimonials as entirely ethical and legitimate by arguing that competition among advertisers and competition between the advertising and editorial sections of publications for reader attention had reached the point where the manufacturer had to get new pulling power into his advertising to make it pay.[3]

Ditzell went on to explain he believed there was no better way of increasing pulling power than to use the picture and endorsement of some famous person on behalf of the product. "The public today creates its own idols and once it has created them apparently it cannot see enough of them. It wants to know what they do, what they say, eat and wear," said Ditzell. "The picture, alone, of a famous movie star or athlete will stop readers of a publication as nothing else." Emphasized by Ditzell was that the stars he had under contract would not endorse any patent medicine or quack merchandise. Before his firm obtained an endorsement, he claimed a sample of the product was sent to the star under consideration, or his manager. The product was tried by the star, he insisted. And while it was true that Famous Names let the advertiser write his own endorsement for the star's signature, "he also emphasized that the signature is not forthcoming unless the star actually uses and approves the product. Notwithstanding this, it is in the star's photograph, not his written endorsement, on which the greater part of the advertising value rests." When Will Hays, president of the Motion Picture Producers and Distributors of America (MPPDA— the Hollywood cartel lobby group comprised of the major Hollywood film studios) was asked to reply to the claim by Famous Names that it could furnish within 48 hours the endorsement of any film star for any nationally advertised product, he cited a vigorous denial from some of those studios— First National, Famous Players, Metro-Goldwyn-Mayer, and Warner Brothers— that any of their stars or featured players had contracted for the exploitation of their names. Also, 35 leading players had been surveyed by a motion picture magazine, Hays pointed out, and 33 of them flatly denied having had any dealings with Famous Names.[4]

With respect to purchased testimonials, an unidentified advertising executive wondered who was deceived by the sold names of celebrities. Not the public, he thought. "The deceptive testimonials do not deceive. They merely interest.... If the name of a tobacco or vanishing cream sticks in the public's mind, the advertisement accomplishes its purpose. If not, not. In either case there has been no deception." Taking a different position was a member of the National Commission of the International Advertising Association who said the faked endorsement was unfair both to the manufacturer who competed against the advertising using it and to the public at large. "Perhaps those of us who are intimately concerned with advertising are not deceived, but others are. A good many of the products advertised with the help of professional testimonial writers, whose main concern is the money they get, affect health." An officer with the American

Association of Advertising Agencies said the faked testimonial was a false basis for advertising for the reason that the majority of the public was credulous. It was clear to him that people were being deceived, that they were led to buy certain merchandise because they felt it had sufficient merits to prompt some famous person to sit down voluntarily and, without thought of compensation, to write his endorsement. "Among many advertising men the testimonial has become a joke," added the executive. "We know it is as meaningless as the blanket claim 'Best in the World.' It is the consumer, led to believe in advertising after a long process of education, who is deceived." And the ethics debate was underway.[5]

By early in 1928 a debate was in process in the pages of *Forum and Century* magazine as to whether advertising as a whole was ethical. Claude C. Hopkins, an advertising man with 37 years of experience, recalled the old days of patent medicine advertising when he observed he had lived through an era in advertising that "we blush to remember now." But it had been reformed from the inside he insisted, as had been business in general, through a campaign often called "truth in advertising." With respect to the era in which he was writing, he said: "Advertising is to-day the most truthful matter which appears in print. We always have some doubts about a news item. It is almost never quite correct. But we never have questions about an ad which appears in high-class magazines. Most large advertisers employ censors." Mentioning the "thousands" of toothpaste ads he had written himself, Hopkins said that all had been censored by two authorities, one a college professor, and one an ex-assistant to a Dr. Wiley in the U.S. Bureau of Chemistry. Then, he went on, there was the Federal Trade Commission (FTC): "They have spent weeks in checking up some lines of my advertising." Also, there was the Better Business Bureau and the Associated Advertising Clubs with its Vigilance Committee to endorse truth in advertising. "I buy in absolute confidence when I see an ad in reputable publications. I always check up on a salesman. He has latitude," declared Hopkins. "But I never question a statement in the *Saturday Evening Post*." Regarding testimonial ads, Hopkins stated that "I do not believe in them. I have never used one in all my experience. I want no layman to tell my story for me. I ask nobody to confirm what I say. That to me would be humiliation."[6]

Early in 1929, Paul Hollister delivered an editorial in the trade publication *Advertising & Selling* in which he recommended that publishers should not run testimonial ads unless every endorsement was unpaid and that every such endorsement was given voluntarily. He wanted to see that recommendation take hold and spread to all magazines, newspapers, and so on. All publications should refuse paid endorsements. That led to a flood of letters in response. C.D. Newell of the Newell-Emmett Company, New York, argued testimonial advertising would always pay and as long as it did advertisers would be tempted to use it, either legitimately or not, according to their own ethical standards. Testimonial patent medicine advertising was still running, he observed, "wherever it is allowed by the publisher and running successfully." He told of a man he knew who made a worthy product, wrote his own testimonials, paid for the signature of celebrities, "and in perfect good faith claims that the benefit he brings to an individual every time he makes a sale justifies the underlying insincerity of the method. He will never believe that he is doing anything against public welfare and the 'good of advertising' is of minor importance compared to the rapid development of his own business." Merle Sidener, president of Sidener, Van Ripper & Keeling, Inc., of Indianapolis, Indiana, felt in the previous few years competition had become so intense that advertising men had turned to the use of a modern adaptation of the old huckster methods of patent medicine and that current ad men "have elaborated and expanded the old schemes for misleading the public."[7]

H.C. Osborn, president of American Multigraph Company of Cleveland, Ohio, declared that "I have become thoroughly disgusted with certain concerns who are concentrating on paid testimonials; and I consider it very bad advertising practice, particularly where it is so generally known that the testimonials are paid for." John Ring Jr., president of the St. Louis, Missouri–based John Ring Jr. Advertising Agency, had asked people he met socially what they thought of paid testimonials. In every instance, he said, they regarded them as nothing more than "bribed testimony." None of them considered them as representing anything that could be regarded as truth in advertising. W.G. Armstrong, of the Youngstown Pressed Steel Company of Warren, Ohio, complained that the Lucky Strike cigarette advertising (Luckies was then a big user of endorsements) had done more to hurt advertising and advertising men than any one factor during the past ten years. Most worrisome to him was Luckies's "destructive attitude" toward the candy industry (reach for a Lucky instead of a "fattening sweet" was a favorite theme), which, "together with their fictitious testimonials, will eventually prove to the American Tobacco Company that advertising is high-powered stuff and ... if improperly handled it will blow out in all directions and destroy those who have tinkered with it." He applauded Charles Lindbergh and "many others" who had quietly refused to be bought and thus had earned "our utmost respect."[8]

L.F. Calahan, secretary of the Periodical Publishing Company, of Grand Rapids, Michigan, related that the English publishers had asked cigarette makers using the same strategy in England as Lucky Strike used in

America to cease using endorsements because of their "distastefulness" to readers. John Benson, of Benson, Gamble, Johnson & Read, Chicago, declared that a testimonial was an old stand-by for creating confidence and probably always would be: "when it is voluntary it is entitled to every respect; when it is not voluntary or is paid for, directly or indirectly, it becomes insincere on the face of it, regardless of the conviction of the writer." Stuart Peabody, advertising manager for the Borden Company, complained that his firm had used legitimate testimonials for many years, but because testimonials were abused by a few Borden was forced to consider giving them up. Borden urged magazines to implement Hollister's recommendations. F.H. Pepper, sales manager of the Herpicide Company, Detroit, felt that voluntary, unpaid endorsements represented the advertising form that had the greatest sales potential, but that the public

Showman Flo Ziegfeld for Lucky Strike cigarettes, 1928. A popular pitch by this brand was that cigarettes should be smoked as a weight control method. So outrageous were the claims that the federal government stepped in to halt them, but only after other large capitalists trusts such as the candy industry kicked up a fuss.

was viewing them with skepticism and doubt and questioning the sincerity of the testimonials that were appearing in newspapers and magazines. As a result, testimonial advertising was becoming ineffective and destroying the faith, confidence, and belief of the public in all advertised products in general. Pepper believed each testimonial ad should carry an advisory, which should read as follows: "This is a voluntary testimonial reflecting my actual experience, for which I receive no compensation." W.A. Hart, director of advertising for E.I du Pont de Nemours & Company, Wilmington, Delaware, pointed out that at their annual meeting in New York in November 1927, the Association of National Advertisers had one session devoted entirely to "Sincerity in Advertising." He said they had tried to get their members to censor their advertising not only for "truth" but also for "insincerity"— typified by exaggeration and bought testimonials.[9]

Another advertising industry trade publication whose pages were full of the debate was *Printers' Ink*. In all such debates in all such publications, people within the advertising industry, and without, lined up to condemn the endorsement ad. A.W. Erickson, president of the Erickson Company, recalled that 25 years earlier (around 1904) there had been a lot of falsehood in advertising, especially for patent medicines, but not limited to that area. A New Englander told him he had once answered an ad which read: "Send 10 cents and get 12 useful articles." He forwarded the dime and received 12 pins. "Hundreds of offers like this ran regularly in newspapers and periodicals," he added. Then a few honest men attacked the evil, he explained, but it took years. First to respond and eliminate such material were the national magazines, followed by the "better class" of newspaper, although he did admit some places still ran patent medicine claims. Erickson continued by saying: "Of recent years, however, bunk and fake advertising seem to be increasing. It is not so blatant and crude as before, but it smells equally bad and is a rank imposition upon the readers of all publications that carry it." What Erickson particularly wanted to condemn in his article "is the fake testimonial advertising that is so rampant today. I am informed that one can buy almost any kind of testimonial for a price. The scourge has spread and it takes in social leaders, shipwreck heroes, aviators, baseball favorites, par golfers, etc." As others had done, Erickson praised Lindbergh, "and a few others of his ilk," for refusing to do endorsements and to take "tainted money." Because several endorsers had let slip that they were paid and because several such cases had received wide publicity, Erickson concluded that the public was coming to recognize "bunk." As far as he was concerned, the advertisers of 1929 who cared for their reputations hesitated to use legitimate testimonials (unpaid ones) because of the cloud of suspicion that had been thrown over all testimonials.[10]

Calling for a crusade against the fake endorsement, Erickson declared it was an issue the American Association of Advertising Agencies, the Better Business Bureau, the publishers' associations, the International Advertising Association, and even the FTC might well consider a matter suitable for action: "No honest man can excuse dishonest advertising and if associations such as those mentioned get on the job the testimonial evil will soon be a thing of the past," he explained. "After all, no permanently successful advertising campaign can be built up on a reader reaction that is founded on fake, not fact! The Tainted Testimonial must go!" In a separate aside, the editors of *Printers' Ink* noted they had been fighting against the fake testimonial for many years. Also, they said they agreed with the views expressed by Erickson and had printed many such similarly themed articles in their pages over the years.[11]

Raymond Rubicam, president of advertising agency Young & Rubicam, Inc., added his name to the debate on tainted endorsements, but he preferred to describe his article not so much as a protest but as a lamentation. "That the testimonial as employed today by some advertisers is a destructive influence seems beyond question," he began. That something should be done, and done quickly, to regulate it was self-evident to him. Wondering how a tainted testimonial should be defined, he felt the position of those who believed an endorsement was tainted if it was asked for and did not come as a free-will offering in the mail as too extreme. He thought there could be no valid objection to a manufacturer asking bona fide users of his product to state why they preferred it and then to publish those reasons in testimonial form. As to critics who felt any endorsement was objectionable if money had been paid, Rubicam wondered exactly what constituted a paid testimonial. Was the "truthful" testimonial to also be damned because money was received, regardless of circumstances? An example he wondered about was the case of a society woman who endorsed a product and was not paid, but the individual who secured her endorsement was paid by the agency or by the advertiser. Rubicam felt in that case there was no paid testimonial. For Rubicam, it was apparent that rules alone would not be adequate to regulate the area since a little thought made it evident that testimonials could be illegitimate whether paid for or not, whether solicited or not, whether secured through a intermediary or not. Reform, therefore, had to go deeper than a set of rules and regulations. "There must be some kind of working code, of course, and it seems to me that it is up to the advertising agents of the country to take the lead in bringing this about." Rubicam concluded, "In fact, to stop the present flood of objectionable ones [testimonials], I would, if necessary, see this old and legitimate tool of advertising given up entirely rather than have the present unbridled abuses continue." Still, he didn't think it would come to that because "It is beyond possibility, though, that the leaders of advertising cannot devise and enforce a way to remove the taint and yet leave the testimonial." Clearly Rubicam was worried that all the negative publicity being generated by endorsements might lead the government to step in and regulate them, and perhaps even advertising in a more general sense, more than it did already. His article, after playing both sides of the street on the subject, was a call to the ad industry to regulate itself—

or give the appearance of having done so— to forestall any possible government intervention.[12]

At the laying of the cornerstone of the Ayer Building on February 4, 1928, Wilfred W. Fry, of N.W. Ayer & Son, declared the greatest peril in the path of advertising was that those who knew its power, "but have no regard for the principles upon which that power rests, will abuse advertising by the use of misleading statements, insincere testimonials and exaggerated claims. The very cornerstone of advertising is threatened by those who thus willfully debauch it. I commend the attitude of those publishers who have refused great contracts because of insincerity of statement, and take this occasion to urge upon those who use advertising, those who prescribe advertising, and those whose livelihood depends upon advertising, to fight its prostitution." A year later, when a reporter looked at the situation, he said that while several publishers were individually considering a method of tightening up on censorship practices as they applied to paid testimonials, each one hesitated about being the first to take decisive action. An advertising director of a nationally known magazine complained that things were actually getting worse and that "today I am okaying copy that eight years ago would not have gotten beyond our make-up table — scarcely would have been submitted to us." He felt the onus of control was on the advertising agent and the advertiser. The advertising director of another publication said that until the present they had not established a definite policy that would eliminate all testimonial advertising from their magazine but from time to time "we have had arguments with agencies concerning flagrantly paid copy of this nature, and in some instances we have refused to accept the copy. We are most emphatically in favor of any course of action which will bring about the elimination of advertising testimonials which are bought and paid for." According to this account, although there was much talk against the practice of paid endorsements, no real action had been implemented. "In the meantime, celebrities and near celebrities of all kinds and degrees are finding a more or less ready market for their names in the advertising market."[13]

Even the respected general interest magazine the *Nation* got involved in the issue with a 1929 article of its own. Mentioning the recent furor over testimonials, such as the one in which boxer Gene Tunney endorsed, as a supposed user, a certain laxative, it said: "So much discussion has been aroused by the orgy of testimonial advertising that even the advertisers are becoming aware of a moral issue involved." Although the *Nation* article admitted it did not know what the answer was to control endorsement ads, it was cynical of the campaign begun by the business magazine *Sales Management* to create an Audit Bureau of Advertising "to combat fakery and misrepresentation" in the advertising world. It was skeptical because it thought the business community might eliminate some of the grosser advertising abuses, but for the "important" reforms one had to look to the community of consumers. One positive sign found was that the government was described as having taken a step in the direction of debunking testimonial advertising by rebuking General Robert Lee Bullard (retired) for lending his name for commercial exploitation when he declared in a cigarette ad that "any army man must keep fit" and the best way to do that was to smoke the brand Bullard was endorsing. Another example involved Captain Fried of the steamship *America* who allowed his picture to be printed in a cigarette advertisement. After that endorsement, the general manager of the United States Lines issued an order barring such action in the future. Concluded the *Nation*: "Meanwhile the constructive way to combat the exploitation of the public through its pet heroes and heroines is the creation of consumers' agencies which will analyze advertised articles for the benefit of their members." And that "one page of government analyses from the Bureau of Standards would cancel a hundred pages of fake testimonials from the public's darlings."[14]

Business reporter Roy Dickinson did man-in-the-street interviews about testimonial ads with ordinary passers-by. All knew exactly the type of ad he was talking about, none needed any explanation. Remarks were presented from about a dozen people, none of whom liked or believed in the ads, although some thought they were good advertising. None believed those ads and none said that such an ad had made them go out and buy a certain product. Some admitted the endorsement ads caught their attention and that they did read them. Said Peter L. Gregory, a Brooklyn chauffeur, "I think that all that stuff is good advertising but I don't believe it." A store floorwalker commented that "I have always been suspicious about the whole thing.... It looks phony." Camden, New Jersey, drug store clerk Ellwood Smith stated: "Bunk. I don't believe anything I read in those kinds of ads." Agreeing with such sentiments was nurse Lies Arenthorst, who said that "never could I quite believe." Insurance salesman Andrew A. Allen commented that "when you see [tennis star Bill] Tilden or a man who has just leaped into fame, or some big athlete endorsing a cigarette, it looks to me like it's overdone. It doesn't exactly destroy my confidence but it isn't convincing."[15]

Journalist Charles Merz mentioned one of the more excessive and bizarre testimonial ads from the period. On the afternoon of January 23, 1929, Chief Officer Manning, and others, of the steamship *America* lowered a lifeboat into a stormy sea and made their way to the side of the foundering freighter *Florida* and saved 32 men from that vessel. Eight days later, on January 31, the world learned that Manning and the others had not been alone in that brave feat, but driven on by the spirit of Lucky Strike cigarettes. As Manning put it in his endorsement ad, seafaring men had to keep physically fit and always prepared for an emergency. He said he had managed to keep fit by avoiding sweets and reaching for a Lucky. It was a glowing testimonial for Luckies and opened up a storm of public debate about the ethics and good taste of that ad. So valuable were Luckies, deposed Manning, and so cherished by good seamen, that out in a full gale on the North Atlantic with the sea running wild and 32 survivors in a lifeboat, "We really couldn't wait to get back to our ship and Luckies.... As an actual fact, in returning to the America I noticed one of our men rowing with one hand and lighting a Lucky with the other."[16]

Merz argued the testimonial had been flourishing for a good half century but that what was different in the previous few years was an "enormous increase" in the volume of such testimonials, "plus a suddenly far more graphic method of presenting the messages they carry"— that is, large ads, more photographs, more intimate details of the endorser, and so on. He mentioned many celebrity or society endorsers of the time he was writing, including Mrs. Frederick Cameron Church (nee Muriel Vanderbilt, for Simmons mattresses); Miss Natica de Acosta (Woodbury's facial soap); Constance Talmadge (the articles from the aforementioned *Liberty* magazine issue); Marilyn Miller (Kolynos toothpaste); Ruth St. Dennis (Tangee, a product for chapped lips); the Count de Beaumont (Clicquot liquor); Mrs. Douglas MacArthur (Maxwell House Coffee); the Baroness de Grazia (Mello-Glo face powder); Mrs. Fifi Widener Holden (Lincoln automobiles); Lady Heath (Cutex manicure products); Mrs. Jerome Napoleon Bonaparte (Borzoi books); Naomi Johnson of the *Vanities* (Blue-Jay corn plasters); and most of the royal families of Europe (Melachrino cigarettes).[17]

In Merz's opinion, the situation had been inevitable since people lived then in a "headline age" with news and opinion pouring in from all over the place and "nothing has more permanence and luster than great names made familiar by constant repetition," and it was logical that national manufacturers should seek to identify their wares with "these vast reputations." For Merz it was, therefore, no surprise that endorsement advertising prospered then and that it had increased enormously in volume and had rapidly enlisted one celebrity after another. He felt certain risks were involved in such ads. If testimonial ads were to achieve a maximum effectiveness, the experiences they related had to seem credible and the praise lavished on a product had to appear to have come from the endorser spontaneously and unsolicited. One that he wondered about in that regard came from race driver H. Siemer, "the crack driver" who, in his ad endorsement for Lucky Strike cigarettes, claimed he smoked two packs a day "to keep his nerves in trim." So public had the issue become, said Merz, that some advertisers were then pointing out that they did not use testimonials. Kelvinator (an appliance maker), for example, went on record to say it declined to publish the names of the celebrities who had bought its electric ice-boxes, declaring that "the distinguished owners of Kelvinators do not desire notoriety — no Kelvinator testimonial has ever been bought — in money, publicity or any other way." Testimonial ads were then so pervasive, certainly in the media and the public mind if not in fact, that they attracted what Merz called the ultimate accolade — ridicule. A mock ad in the *New Yorker* paid its respects to a mythical Countess de la Fouchette, who had just endorsed (for $800) a cigarette she never smoked, a bathtub (for $30) she never used, and a bed (for $90) that she gave her dog to sleep on. "Ridicule, especially in the advertising section, is bad business," concluded Merz.[18]

At the end of February 1929, a questionnaire was sent out to 4,650 names chosen by Edward L. Greene, general manager of the National Better Business Bureau, New York. It asked the single question, "Is the use of the purchased testimonial harmful to advertising in general?" Greene took that action in response to numerous inquiries regarding the use of testimonials, after much public discussion. Those names included 693 advertising agencies, with the remainder being national advertisers in various lines of business. As of March 16, 766 usable replies had been received, with 138 agencies and 581 national advertisers against paid endorsements. Only 11 agencies favored that form of advertising, and all of those except four added one or more qualifications to their approval. Of the 36 national advertisers voting in favor of paid testimonials, only 16 of them gave the method their unqualified approval.[19]

A few weeks later Greene gave updated results for his survey, based on 923 replies. Opposed to the use of purchased testimonials were 694 national advertisers and 149 advertising agencies. In favor of using them were 41 national advertisers and 13 advertising agencies; 26 responses were classed as indefinite. After reading the replies to the Better Business Bureau survey, Greene declared he got the impression that the opposition to the use of purchased testimonials was actually "an outburst of criticism against advertising insincerity. It seems to be an awakening on the part of the industry to not only condemn a practice which is detrimental to its best interest, but also appears as a beacon of warning against the use of so-called poetic license, pseudo scientific claims, unfair competitive copy and exaggeration." Noting the fact that in the past fake testimonials had been condemned and eventually kicked out of advertising, Greene asserted there was a "strik-ing change" in the present era of testimonials: the naïve person of old who signed a fake patent medicine endorsement and received payment in the form of a bottle of the quack remedy was quite different from the person of public prestige who signed an insincere testimonial for a product that really merited public confidence. In the latter case, he argued, "the upper structure of business has become diseased by deception." With regard to those advertisers who defended "insincere" testimonials, saying no harm was done as they made interesting reading, Green continued, "We believe that such reasoning fails to acknowledge that the foundation of advertis-ing is truth."[20]

H.S. Gardner, president of Gardner Advertising and former president of the American Association of Advertising Agencies, complained that "the advertising world has been bitten badly by the prostituted testimonial and the hue and cry which has been set up in protest is providing the publicity needed for the cure." He believed the surest way to stop the commercial-izing of matinee idols, heroes, debutantes, society leaders, and royalty was to do more of what they were doing then — that is, "increase the agitation against the practice." Acknowledging that if a campaign against endorse-ments was successful then "honest" testimonials would disappear along with the paid ones, Gardner pointed out that "one can always fall back on a sim-ple statement of a product's merits and have an effective advertisement."[21]

C.T. Southwick, head of the advertising agency the Southwick Com-pany, took a slightly different attitude when he claimed he had more faith in testimonials than in any other definable type of copy. Stating he had never paid for any testimonials he had used in advertising, he pointed out the many "miracles" testimonial ad campaigns had performed for clients after all other kinds of copy had failed. For example, George Eastman and a half dozen other great inventors, by willingly giving their opinion of AutoStrop razors, "literally turned the tide and brought success to that razor." Other products, he added, such as Dictaphone, and Savage pistols, had enjoyed similar success from endorsement campaigns. "The point is that most testimonials would cost nothing, beyond a courtesy gift of the goods, if nothing were offered," declared Southwick, as he laid the blame with the middlemen. "The graft starts with the employment of an inter-mediary," he explained, saying he had turned down one such person who offered the endorsement of the film studios, and another who offered the signatures of stage and film stars. Southwick argued the current campaign against tainted testimonials was too broad: "The advertiser, the agent and the famous testifier should be warned against the intermediary who will represent that the testifier demanded payment."[22]

One of the very few people who spoke in favor of the paid endorsement in 1929 was Stanley Resor, president of the J. Walter Thompson advertising agency of New York. By far, that agency used paid endorsements more than any other ad agency at that time. Whoever was second was not even remotely close. The article Resor published in *Advertising & Selling* was an address he delivered to a weekly meeting of the executives of his firm. First, he discussed why people liked to read about other people. One reason people wanted to know about other people was the "spirit of emulation," he believed. "We want to copy those whom we deem superior in taste or knowledge or experience. The desire to emulate is stronger in women than in men," he explained. "Lombroso, the celebrated psychologist, explains it in terms of women's ability to excite her imagination with external objects. It enables her to become princess or movie queen by using the cold cream or toilet soap they recommended." Additionally, he argued that people were eternally searching for authority. Democracy, even in name, was new, with royalty, aristocracy and feudalism having dominated the world for scores of centuries and, in doing so, having instilled in the masses a sense of inferiority "and an instinctive veneration for 'their betters.' This respect for authority is so little discriminating that we seriously listen to a motor maker's opinions of history, an inventor's dicta on religion and a theatrical producer's theories on education."[23]

Resor went on to say the newspapers and magazines presented the news, and prospered, because the news was presented in terms of people, with the editor who simply selected from material submitted to him having become obsolete. A modern editor was said to decide what subjects he wanted for articles and stories "and has them written to order." Because an editor wanted to see his magazine's issues studded with big names, he sought articles by famous authorities, commenting on the situation in their chosen fields. However, Resor continued, such people would either produce "ponderous" works, or decline to write at all. So the editor assigned writers who could produce acceptable material, items to be signed by the big names. "In addition to the articles signed by pugilists and golf, tennis and baseball players who did not write them ... even the real interviews are altered and often improved by the reporters," he explained. "It is clear, then, that the public wants its news, education, and entertainment conveyed to it through the medium of personalities who are regarded as authorities in their respective fields. If these authorities do not volunteer their services, they are sought out and engaged," remarked Resor. "If they lack self-expression, the deficiency is supplied." With that Resor ended his set-up, before justifying paid testimonials. He had first painted a picture of all news as presented in magazines and newspapers as essentially nothing but dishonesty, falsehoods and corruption. Given that background, advertising in general, and testimonials in particular, could not possibly come off any worse. By comparison they had to be at least average.[24]

With the background he had sketched, Resor went on to state that since the featuring of prominent people had become an integral part of almost every editorial program, it was logical for advertising to do the same since advertising was in direct competition with editorial features for the reader's attention. If it compared unfavorably with the reading matter in any aspect, it was not doing justice to the advertiser's interest: "When practically every publication of large circulation relies on personalities to secure and hold readers, it is obvious that the public will relish personalities when properly employed in advertising." Resor did concede that testimonial ads were not equally applicable to all products, but he did not identify which were which. He did agree that people who gave endorsements should definitely be users of the products endorsed and that their testimony should be expressions of their real opinions of the products. As to whether testimonials should be spontaneous and unsolicited in order to be considered legitimate, he exclaimed, "The answer is that very little that is worthwhile in this world is secured without solicitation. Sales volume, charity funds, wives, even justice, one obtained by asking for them, not waiting for them to happen." Regarding whether endorsements had to be secured without payment to the endorser to be seen as legitimate, he said that many ad campaigns had used famous people who were unpaid, because those people placed a high value on the publicity accruing to them, the endorsers, from those ads. On the other hand: "Other very successful campaigns have used a few names at a considerable cost. It happened that they were not interested in publicity." If only testimonials were used from people who used and liked the product, he said, payment had no effect on their opinions. However, the mere fact that a person was an enthusiastic user of a product, even of many years standing, did not in any way lessen the obligation of a business to compensate him for his cooperation. J. Walter Thompson had been using testimonials for six years, and in that time, Resor said, the number of cases in which it was later discovered that an endorsement was not wholly sincere "has been negligible." In conclusion, Resor wrote: "sincere testimonial advertisements are a tonic to the reader's interest, not a deterrent. He will read them because they are what he likes to read, and as a result he will have an increased interest in all advertising."[25]

Frederick C. Kendall, editor of the publication *Advertising & Selling*, said the controversy over the use of the purchased testimonial had long passed the confines of the advertising profession, making itself felt in all areas of business. He believed endorsement advertising, whether bought or unpaid, possessed the rare quality of being able to achieve more success than other methods of advertising. It was only natural, he argued, that a prospective buyer, of whatever station in life, should be impressed by the enthusiasm of someone else who used the product advertised. Patent medicine manufacturers discovered that principle many years ago, he reminded readers, and reaped a golden harvest until they were finally discouraged from further preying upon a gullible public. Now, after a period of comparative dormancy for endorsement ads during which advertising had attained new and higher standards, said Kendall, the testimonial idea "has been exhumed, dusted off, and dressed up in new and modern frills and type treatments." The testimonial was a boon to advertisers, he declared, because "it offers unlimited possibilities of injecting romance and action and human interest into an otherwise prosaic advertisement for a distinctly unromantic product." That quickly created an offshoot industry, that of middleman, the object of which was to obtain endorsements. One thing that worried Kendall was that "whether or not the endorser had ever used the product in question was too often considered a matter of minor importance." Advertising executive Earnest Elmo Calkins, commenting on the predilection of celebrities to endorse items, remarked sadly, "we are accustomed to find that our heroes have feet of clay. He mentioned that so far only Charles Lindbergh had spurned "the seductions of the testimonial hound."[26]

All the furor over testimonials brought a couple of literary heavyweights into the fray, each authoring a scathing, and sarcastic satirical piece. Noted humorist James Thurber penned a one-page piece for the *Magazine of Business* in which he ridiculed the testimonial industry. As a candidate for the fictional All-American Endorsing Team, Thurber suggested no one could leave off the first team a tenor to whom he gave the mythical name of Jascha Jaschavitz. "He won the pentathlon event easily, by endorsing three different cigarets, two shaving creams, a bathtub, a book publishing company, and three pianos."[27]

Famed author Sinclair Lewis wrote his mocking, cynical attack on testimonials for *Advertising & Selling*. Referring to all the society folk endorsing products such as Simmons Beautyrest mattresses, Lewis rejoiced that "Thank heaven those stuffy old days of which Mrs. Edith Wharton wrote in *The Age of Innocence* are now gone! At last we plebes are admitted, per full-page advertisements, to the society of the select!" More seriously, he said he resented them all and that "I have left out the more obvious vulgar advertisements — the boisterous assertions that Douglas

Fairbanks, Chief Officer Manning, George Gershwin, and a few score opera singers owe their success to smoking Lucky Strike cigarettes." Even with those left out, he continued, "I want to protest, as a layman, against those types of advertising: the testimonial advertisements which differ from old-fashioned medical advertisements only in being printed on better paper, the snob advertisements which suggest that I must buy something because Mrs. Umptidink of Paris or Terre Haute has bought it and advertisements which intrude on my personal life as brashly as a life insurance agent." Lewis believed that millions of people must have resented those types of ads as much as he did and that "it is not a hunch but a certainty that when you get twenty soaps all advertising against one another on the snobbish-ad-testimonial basis, they will all cancel out, and the successful advertiser will be the one who tells factually what he has to offer at what price, and why, with no extraneous pictures...."[28]

Perhaps worried about the impact of the Lewis article, the editor of the magazine first declared that the piece had not been censored at all, but printed as Lewis wrote it. "Mr. Lewis' frankness will please some — and probably offend others. As a decidedly articulate representative of the inarticulate average man, we think his views are worth reading," explained the editor in what almost amounted to an apology. "To those who disagree interestingly enough, we shall be glad to give space in reply. Advertising can only progress if its practitioners are broadminded enough to listen to intelligent criticism."[29]

G. Lynn Sumner, president of the G. Lynn Sumner Company ad agency, reminded people then in the business that they should never forget that advertising rose "from the gutter of quackery. The first large users of periodical space were the proprietary fakers." Out of that dark period slowly emerged modern advertising. As recently as 1905, he related, *Collier's* magazine launched its "memorable campaign" against the patent medicine frauds. And as late as 1915 the battle for "Truth in Advertising" was at its height. Only in the brief 20-year period since 1910 had advertising been treated with respect, said Sumner. "It has won a goodly measure of public confidence, it has carried on educational campaigns of incalculable benefit, it has helped to raise the standard of living, it has helped make possible mass production and low prices, it has helped to bring undreamed of comforts and conveniences and luxuries into the homes of many, it has helped to keep factories busy, give employment to millions, increase wages, pay huge dividends, it has made an enormous contribution to the prosperity we all enjoy," explained Sumner, with no shortage of exaggeration. He worried that after building up this good reputation, by playing fast and loose with endorsements it had been "trifling with its most priceless possessions."

He remarked that no newspaper or magazine could keep faith with its public and deliberately trifle with the facts.[30]

After mentioning the Better Business Bureau survey and the overwhelming sentiment against testimonials, Sumner discussed another survey, by the Erickson Company. That survey, conducted in five cities, asked business and professional men their opinion of familiar types of paid testimonial advertising: 17 percent said they believed them, 83 percent did not. Among male undergraduates, 6.3 percent believed endorsement ads while 93.6 percent did not. On the other hand, among male factory workers, 45.8 percent were believers, 54.2 percent were not. Among retail clerks, 55.5 percent believed endorsement ads, 44.5 percent did not believe. "The credulity of women in all classes was slightly higher, but the total investigation showed that only one-third of all men and women interviewed accepted the paid testimonial advertising at its face value," concluded the survey. Sumner pointed out the growing amount of ridicule directed at testimonials. From Sinclair Lewis to Corey Ford's "Meetings of the Endorsers' Club" in the *New Yorker* to *Life* magazine, which gave a glimpse of the future, wherein the aristocracy had the ancestral portraits assembled from the advertising pages, to Will Rogers, who observed that American sportsmen could not win golf's Ryder Cup when they arrived in England "all worn out with endorsing." Another reason sometimes given for the increased use of testimonials was the high cost of advertising in general. Full-page ad rates for some of the more popular magazines in 1929 were as follows: *Saturday Evening Post*, $3,000; *Woman's Home Companion*, $8,800; *Pictorial Review*, $8,500; *McCall's*, $8,200; *Cosmopolitan*, $4,200; and *True Story*, $4,000.[31]

The Association of National Advertisers (ANA) went on record in 1929 as being strongly opposed to the use of paid testimonials in advertising. Most of one session of an ANA semi-annual meeting was given over to the discussion of endorsement ads. George Fowler, vice-president of the Simmons Company (that mattress maker was a big user of paid testimonials), told the meeting that they were living in the age of autobiography and it was that same influence that caused newspapers to devote so much space to personalities. "People are interested in other people — what they are doing and what they think. It is easy to see, then, why personality advertising is one of the strongest and best forms of advertising," he exclaimed. As to standards for such ads, he said the advertiser who used testimonials "should place an absolute ban upon anything that is unfair, untruthful or in bad taste. I believe in testimonial advertising only when it is true, in good form, interesting and productive." With standards like those, argued Fowler, celebrities could be used properly and profitably, and a failure to use them, at least for some product lines, "would be to ignore one of the more fruitful methods of creating and increasing consumer acceptance." Questioned as to what was to be done to prohibit the "unfair and untruthful" endorsement ad, Fowler replied that corrective measures, if any, would have to be applied by advertisers themselves." Despite his pleas in favor of testimonials, the ANA went on to adopt a resolution opposing them, albeit a somewhat weakly worded one. It read: "Whereas, we believe that advertising in order to be lastingly effective and profitable must not only be truthful and sincere, but must also appear to be, and Whereas this being our belief it naturally follows that we view with disapproval the use of the so-called paid testimonial; therefore be it Resolved, that our members continue carefully to scrutinize their own advertising from this standpoint and that they express this opinion of the association on insincere testimonials, gratuitous or paid for, at every opportunity."[32]

Taking a similar stand just a few weeks after the ANA issued its resolution was the American Association of Advertising Agencies. At its July 15 quarterly meeting, the executive board of that organization issued the following statement after an inquiry into testimonial advertising: "We deplore the insincere testimonial as a breach of good faith." By insincere, they meant any endorsement (voluntary or solicited) that did not reflect the true opinion of the testifier, or that concerned a product the endorser did not use or enjoy. Making a practice of

This 1931 ad for Lux soap was over the top in its claims of the soap's ability to block the aging process. The ad claims that "605 of the 613 important actresses" in Hollywood used Lux — including Evelyn Laye and Lupe Velez, pictured in the ad.

paying for testimonials was something they considered to be an "unfortunate development" in advertising, although they noted that a paid endorsement could be sincere and thus not unethical, "but it commercializes what has long been held in personal, social and business relations to be an act of good-will. It strikes at the very heart of belief in testimony, which should be without bias or suspicion of bias," continued the statement. To make the statement even more vague, the American Association of Advertising Agencies release added that "we believe that the sought testimonial if it is competent and sincere is above criticism."[33]

Advertising executive Earnest Elmo Calkins, in chronicling the "descent" of testimonials to the point where so many were paid for, observed that advertising agencies had soon learned that if enough money was offered, the supply of endorsers could be increased indefinitely and they could buy all the well-known names they desired. Calkins found it "disillusioning to learn how many public and even distinguished people would lie for a few thousand or even a few hundred dollars. He remarked again that Charles Lindbergh remained about the only public figure "who was approached and remained incorruptible."[34]

Robert Tinsman, president of the Federal Advertising Agency, New York, had been in the advertising business for 29 years. Above all else, he said the one thing he wanted to see eliminated from advertising was "the bought-and-paid-for testimonial.... Advertising as a legitimate force in modern business is discredited by that sort of thing."[35]

By early in 1931 the editor of the *Outlook and Independent* magazine wrote that the practice of buying endorsements for nationally advertised products was under fire in many quarters and that "indeed, the testimonial industry seems to be on the wane...." Actually, that was not true, as the endorsement industry remained just as strong in the 1930s as it had been in the 1920s. What was on the wane by 1931 was all the media attention and public debate on the issue. Even though the vast majority of the ad agencies and national advertisers claimed to be opposed to the practice, no attempt was even made to rein it in. Likely they had just jumped on the perceived bandwagon of a strong public sentiment against paid endorsements, and the so-called insincere testimonials in general. By loudly proclaiming its own opposition, the advertising industry hoped they would be seen by the public, and any potential government regulators, as actually taking steps against an unethical practice, or getting ready to do so. That is, the industry hoped empty rhetoric would be seen as positive action. And, also, that such talk would forestall any government intervention that might have been under contemplation.[36]

4

The FTC Looks Askance: Hollywood Loves Lux Soap, 1930s

The [testimonial] racket is too useful to be abandoned merely because the mean old Federal Trade Commission gets up on its ear.
—*New Republic*, 1931

Not only have our American physicians been selling their names to advertisers, but foreigners have been brought in almost wholesale [to endorse]. —*American Journal of Public Health*, 1931

The European physicians got an average of $500 for their beards, names, and services, and the sales of Fleischmann's Yeast continued to soar. —*Fortune*, 1947

As early as the beginning of 1930, it was noted that the focus on testimonial ads and their ethics was on the wane. An account in *Printers' Ink* observed that the furious debates on the issue of a year earlier "have died down now to a mere whisper." Also noted was something much more ominous, something that industry had worried might happen. That was the involvement of the federal government, in the form of the Federal Trade Commission (FTC), in the endorsement business. Very early in 1930 the FTC issued a statement that said, in part, that a cigarette maker had signed a stipulation with the federal agency agreeing to discontinue certain practices. In the stipulation the tobacco manufacturer (unnamed by the FTC) agreed to cease and desist forever from the alleged unfair methods of competition as set forth in the statement. One of those alleged unfair methods consisted of "featuring what purported to be the testimonials of famous people who smoke respondent's products and found they protect from irritation."[1]

According to the FTC statement, certain of those testimonials were obtained by the respondent company for a valuable consideration from the alleged authors thereof. Additionally, the advertising matter "also contained a testimonial or endorsement purporting to be that of certain actresses in a musical show who were credited with the statement to the effect that through the use of respondent's cigarettes 'that's how we stay slender'; when in truth and in fact the said actresses were not cigarette smokers and did not stay slender through the use of respondent's products." Other uses of endorsements cited as unfair by the FTC included a testimonial given over the radio by a well-known musical comedy star. That actor, said the statement, described a variety of benefits which he claimed he derived from smoking the firm's cigarettes. But, in reality, said the agency, that actor authorized the testimonial, received a consideration for the statement attributed to him "but which statement he did not prepare, see prior to its use, or sign." The respondent firm also agreed to cease and desist from the use in all forms of advertising of any and all testimonials unless the same represented, and were, the genuine, authorized and unbiased opinions of the authors of the endorsements. Further, the FTC said the respondent company had agreed that if a monetary or other consideration were given for an endorsement the respondent company would publish, along with the said advertisements, in an equally conspicuous manner, the fact that the said testimonials had been paid for.[2]

When *Business Week* reviewed the above FTC case, summarized as one in which the respondent firm was foregoing the use of endorsements written by authors who had not used the product and from the use of paid testimonials of any kind unless the fact that they were paid for was also published, it pronounced that action as "major. The decision is more sweeping than the daily press indicated." As to the identity of the cigarette maker, *Business Week* pointed out the obvious, in ironic fashion: "Though the Commission did not name the respondent, the makers of Lucky Strikes have wasted a good many millions of dollars if everyone doesn't recognize them." This article pointed out an unofficial reason why the FTC may have gone after Lucky Strike, of all the many companies engaged in extensive, and similar, endorsement ad campaigns. That reason could be found in a part of the consent agreement whereby Lucky Strike promised it would not broadcast or publish statements that smoking Luckies would bring slender figures. It was an especially important stipulation to the candy industry and their allies, who had long been annoyed by Luckies' slogans, such as "reach for a Lucky instead of a sweet," and "whose indignation over what they labeled the 'anti-sweets campaign' of the advertiser in question carried them almost to the length of supporting radical demands for an advertising censor at Washington." Such a move by the FTC, hoped the account, would go a long way toward restoring to its original value the voluntary personal endorsement, "Which is the best form of advertising that the world has known since Eve endorsed the apple." It was also felt the FTC action would cause a testimonial pullback offensive by many firms that was, in many cases, a defensive "because our competitors are doing it" campaign in the first place.[3]

Later in 1930, a code of trade practice designed to modify certain methods in sporting goods advertising, and to bring to an end the widely used endorsement ad, was adopted by representatives of 90 percent of the sporting goods manufacturers of the United States, at a conference held by the FTC. Resolutions adopted were directed at misrepresentation of the use of sporting goods products by outstanding athletes and sportsmen. Manufacturers would be compelled to disclose the obligation (that is, the endorsement fee, for example) existing between the athlete and manufacturer in the use of an endorsement, or the name of the player on the maker's products. Prohibited were false advertising or falsely representing that a prominent athlete designed certain athletic goods. Also barred were the names of prominent athletes on athletic goods when the athlete did not design, endorse, or use such goods himself, if from the use of the name the purchasers were led to believe the goods were designed, endorsed, or used by the athlete.[4]

Official action against testimonials also took place abroad, in 1931, when German courts condemned the paid endorsement in German advertising, although they did not bar them completely. It came about through a suit brought by the German Association of Toilet Soap and Perfumery Manufacturers against the Colgate-Palmolive-Peet company. Palmolive was using endorsements given by "experts" in its German advertising, a technique said to be new to the Germans. The German Association investigated, tried to reason with Palmolive, failed, and then brought suit for violation of the Unfair Competition law. In the first court decision, handed down about a year earlier, the Association won; Palmolive then appealed. In a final judgment handed down in July 1931, by the highest court in Germany, the Association won again. At the expense of Palmolive, that judgment had to be published in 19 German newspapers and periodicals. The court ruled the statements given out in the form of experts' endorsement opinions were supposed by the public to be impersonal statements made voluntarily by disinterested experts on the basis of conscientious investigation, and for that reason such statements carried weight with the public. Consequently, added the court, "the use of such testimonials for advertising purposes is especially effective.... At this point Defendant's gross deception of the reader of the advertisement begins."[5]

Palmolive's deception had to do with how those testimonials were really obtained, said the court. It held those endorsements were not the result of conscientious and disinterested investigation and written by the endorser himself, but that the testimonial was presented already written to the experts, who then merely signed them because "they get a free advertisement for their own business, which is of immense value to them." If the public knew the real story, said the court, "the public will conclude that these business people have sold their signatures for a free advertisement which bears no relation to anything they themselves have done, since all they have done is to affix their signatures to a form already prepared." The court prohibited Palmolive from including in its ads statements of a general nature, such as "No other soap works like Palmolive," and from publishing in its own statements prepared ad copy composed by itself in such a manner that they appeared to be the statements of disinterested experts.[6]

Back in the United States, the FTC had again become involved. Near the end of 1931, the Northam Warren (NW) Corporation, maker of Cutex manicure products, filed an appeal with the Circuit Court of Appeals following an order issued by the FTC that would not prohibit the use of paid endorsements in advertising but which did order NW to cease and desist using paid testimonials unless its advertising disclosed the fact that payment was made. If the order was upheld, worried the NW counsel, there would seem to be no limits whatsoever to the censorship the agency could exercise over advertising. Specifically, the case dealt with endorsements from the following: Ethel Barrymore, who received $1,000 for her endorsement; Anna Pavlowa (who was paid £100 in London); Atlanta (Mrs. Michael) Arlen ($500); and Mrs. Howard Chandler Christy, who received $500 while Miss Lassie Homeyman, a personal friend of Christy, received $150 for services rendered in helping to obtain the testimonial from Christy.[7]

A complaint against the NW corporation had been first issued by the FTC on April 8, 1931. Northam began to use testimonial advertising late in 1928 and voluntarily discontinued that form of advertising in May 1930. According to the complaint, the firm had obtained endorsements from people prominent in the public eye; they were published as genuine, voluntary, and unbiased opinions of the alleged authors when, in fact, they were not genuine, voluntary, or unbiased opinions, and they were obtained through the payment of large sums of money or other valuable considerations. A hearing was held by the FTC at which Christy was a witness. She admitted receiving a payment of $500 for her endorsement but insisted that she had been using Cutex preparations over a period of four or five years, that she used Cutex preparations regularly, that her endorsement was made voluntarily, and that in fact she sought out the opportunity to endorse Cutex products. At that hearing the agency admitted they had no proof to bring forward that the endorsements were not honest or were not sincere. In the end, the FTC conceded that only one question was involved in its case against NW: that is, whether it was an unfair method of competition to publish admittedly true statements as advertising without stating in the advertisement that the person giving the testimonial received money or other consideration for the use of his or her name. Northam's counsel argued the FTC exceeded its power in making its order and that constitutionally guaranteed rights were involved — the right of an advertiser to contract and the property rights of an individual in the use of his name for advertising purposes. However, he did concede there would be some justification for the claim that unfair methods of competition were used if it appeared that the statements made by the endorsers in their testimonials were fake, or that such persons in fact did not use and approve the product.[8]

When the *New Republic* commented on the case, it predicted that if the FTC ruling was not overturned many advertisements featuring endorsements would probably follow a precedent recently set by Lucky Strike, in which it was clearly stated in one of their endorsement ads that nothing had been paid for the testimony. Still, concluded the piece, "The racket is too useful to be abandoned merely because the mean old Federal Trade Commission gets up on its ear."[9]

When Ethel Barrymore endorsed Cutex products, she signed the following release for her $1,000 from Northam: "I hereby give the Northam Warren Corporation and/or the J. Walter Thompson Co. (advertising agency) permission to use in its advertising, my photograph and/or my name and/or a statement to be submitted to me and which, when approved by me, I agree to sign. I agree not to endorse any other manicuring product, and to test adequately the complete Cutex outfit with which the Northam Warren Corporation will supply me. Ethel Barrymore (signed)." Note the company worded the agreement to protect itself against any charge that its endorsers did not use the product, by mailing an item to the testifier and getting their acknowledgment that they used it. That was a common strategy used by advertisers to blunt frequent criticisms of unethical testimonials from endorsers who never used the products themselves. After getting Barrymore's signature, NW produced the following statement that was used in her endorsement ad: "'Everything must flatter us to our finger tips,' says Ethel Barrymore. The best loved actress on the American stage adds, 'and of all the ways of grooming the finger tips I find new Cutex Liquid Polish the most flattering.'"[10]

As it awaited a decision on NW's appeal, the FTC took further action.

Near the end of 1931 the agency cited the Fleischmann Company in an order concerning its use of paid testimonials. Allegations were the same as those leveled at Cutex. Around the same time, the Trade Commission announced that another stipulation very similar to the one between itself and Lucky Strike cigarettes had been signed by an advertiser in a different field from tobacco. When Lucky Strike ran an endorsement ad that featured an actor by the last name of Lowe, the ad copy proudly stated, "You may be interested in knowing that not one cent was paid to Mr. Lowe to make the above statement. Mr. Lowe has been a smoker of Lucky Strike cigarettes for six years. We hope the publicity herewith given will be as beneficial to him and to Fox, his producers, as his endorsement of Luckies is to you and us." The *Printers' Ink* article felt the most important thing was the assurance that the testimonial came from a genuine user and that it was a true statement of fact; "Adherence to this principle, together with proper release, should answer the requirements of the law."[11]

With the Cutex decision still pending in the spring of 1932, the FTC issued similar orders against the Ponds Extract Company and Standard Brands, Inc. The latter order covered the use of paid endorsements for both Fleischmann's Yeast and Chase and Sanborn coffee. Then, in June of that year, the U.S. Circuit Court of Appeals for the Second District declared in favor of the Northam company and against the FTC order. The endorsements, held the decision, "are said to be neither exaggerations nor untruthful. There is no claim of monopoly. It would seem, therefore, that there was no violation of the Sherman Anti-Trust or Clayton Acts." Also, the court felt it was doubtful if the public was gullible enough to believe that such endorsements were given without compensation. If they were paid for, provided they were truthful, then no one was deceived. In no sense could they be regarded as unfair competition or as involving a tendency to restrain competition unduly, declared the court. "Because a prominent person ventures an opinion without being requested to do so, is no guaranty either of veracity or good judgment," said the decision. If the testimonials involved represented honest beliefs, there was no representation concerning the product, and no unfair competition was created, said the court, "we have no right to presume that endorsers of commercial products falsify their statements because they have received compensation."[12]

In its assessment of the Cutex decision, *Business Week* declared it dealt a "vital blow" to the FTC's attempts to place restrictions on testimonial advertising. According to this article, "the Trade Commission dug a legal grave for its case when it announced that it did not suggest that Northam Warren's testimonials tended to create a monopoly or an undue restraint of trade." Instead, the Trade Commission mistakenly argued that the failure to state the price paid for their endorsements amounted to deception and misrepresentation which by itself enabled the company to deprive "honest" manufacturers of a market, summarized the account.[13]

Several months after the Cutex decision was released, the FTC dismissed its complaints against Ponds and Standard Brands, Inc., and its subsidiaries for their use of endorsements because those complaints hinged on the same principle as in the Cutex case. One element present here that was not present in the Cutex case centered on the claim that in some of the ads people were dressed to be what they were not. In one instance, it was alleged that a young man in an ad photographed as a hockey player was not a hockey player. No evidence had ever been taken by the Commission on that subject, and the fact the complaint was dropped by the FTC led some observers to conclude that no such evidence was available.[14]

Thus, FTC involvement in the testimonial business came to an end, at least for well over a decade. So half-hearted and unenthusiastic was the FTC prosecution of its complaints that it seemed almost as if the agency wanted to lose. There were more than a few examples involving endorsements where the testifier was known not to use the product, for example, yet the FTC chose not to target any of those. When Christy gave evidence at the Cutex hearing, her answers to questions made it appear she had been coached in advance. Yet the FTC did not probe deeply. Perhaps the FTC moved at all only because the public controversy on the issue was loud and insistent and the agency may have felt compelled to act, dragged in, as it were, as a reluctant prosecutor. By unwisely choosing which case to prosecute and then prosecuting it poorly, the FTC guaranteed a defeat and perhaps provided itself with a reason for withdrawing from the ring, giving the appearance of having tried to regulate the endorsement area.

Debate over the ethics of testimonial ads had indeed tailed off to a whisper by the early 1930s, with that whisper centered on people in the medical profession. An editorial in the *American Journal of Public Health* complained that newspapers were full of "the most preposterous statements" and that for some time supposedly reputable physicians and health officers had lent their names to statements, many of which went beyond knowledge or facts. "Not only have our American physicians been selling their names to advertisers, but foreigners have been brought in almost wholesale," went the editorial. In practically every case the ads stated that those men were "noted," "famous," or "experts." It continued, "Now and then they get hold of people who are actually well known and who should know better than to lend themselves to such deception of the public." This publication had long taken a stand against such practices and at its annual meeting back in October 1930 had passed a resolution that any member of the American Public Health Association who thereafter "permitted the use of his name, or otherwise to have allowed himself to be quoted or used for illustration in the advertising of a commercial product, in such a manner as to reflect discredit upon the Association" shall have his membership in the Association terminated. Then the editor added that "we earnestly beg that those who have the honor of being members or Fellows of this Association refuse the use of their names in advertisements of any and every sort." One of the great functions of that Association was said to be to instruct the public in matters of health. When a member sold his name for the exploitation of commercial products, "he strikes a blow at the dignity of the profession to which he owes allegiance, and breaks down the confidence of the public in it."[15]

Meta Pennock, editor of the *Trained Nurse and Hospital Review*, complained about the unexpected pictures of cap and uniform (that is, people in ads dressed to look like nurses) that "fill the advertisements" in current magazines. With regard to those images in ads, Pennock remarked that "her definite recommendation is seldom stated in words, but her presence hovers in the background to carry the desired impression." She worried about the ethics of such ads, seeing them as bad for the public because they often promoted self-diagnosis and misdiagnosis, causing people to not go to a doctor, or delay going, when they might have a serious disease. As a matter of fact, she added, the woman depicted in such ads was seldom a nurse — just a model dressed in the uniform — but the public rarely understood that. For Pennock, another worry was that the emotion the public felt for the nurse — that combination of respect for her knowledge of health and sanitation and admiration for her spirit of service — was transferred to the product. And while that might have been good for the product advertised, it was also "cheapening to the exploited profession."[16]

Solon R. Barber, writing in *Hygeia*, an official publication of the American Medical Association directed at the layperson, complained that "One of the most reprehensible and misleading forms of medicine advertising is the use of testimonials," even if unsolicited and unpaid for and in other ways bona fide. He said that government officials enforcing the federal Food and Drugs Act had found that, in many instances, writers of testimonials were in their graves at the time their letters of endorsement appeared. Many had died of the very diseases that their testimonial letters said had been cured by the product endorsed. Evidence of the misuse of testimonials came to light at a trial before the federal court at Baltimore when the government was upheld in the seizure of a liniment billed as having value in the treatment of numerous maladies, including tuberculosis and pneumonia. The manufacturer of the nostrum had used the testimonial of a woman who claimed to have been cured of tuberculosis through the use of the remedy; however, the woman died of the disease. After she became too ill to answer letters that came to her from prospective purchasers, as a result of her name and address appearing in her endorsement ad, her son replied to them over her name. Some years earlier, in a memorandum to the U.S. postmaster general, the attorney general of the United States commented: "Speaking generally, it may be said that in all my experiences in this office never has a medical concern, no matter how fraudulent its methods or worthless its treatment, been unable to produce an almost unlimited number of these so-called testimonial letters." And all of this was happening at a time when the majority of egregiously fake patent medicine ads, and endorsements, had been purged from most of the respectable media, confined to each era's equivalent of the supermarket tabloids. Whatever the situation was in the early 1930s with respect to patent medicine ads, it had been much, much worse just a generation or so earlier.[17]

Barber argued that medical testimonials, as commonly understood, were almost always worthless. However, the reading of what purported to be a personal statement, reporting beneficial results from taking a particular patent medicine, he said, "has a powerful effect in persuading many sick people to buy the article." Although he conceded many of the endorsements were given in good faith, he felt a good number were based on faulty reasoning, wherein the endorser never really had the disease or the illness cleared up on its own, and thus was self-limiting. In any case, Barber added, the federal Food and Drug Administration had on file numerous death certificates of endorsers for would-be remedies for the ailment which eventually killed them. It would readily be appreciated, therefore, he concluded, that little confidence could be placed in most testimonials. Sometimes, even the names, addresses, and titles of the testimonial givers were faked. A favorite trick at that time, Barber wrote, was to use the names and pictures of medical specialists from foreign lands, knowing the chances of the patient's checking up on the reputation of the experts mentioned were extremely small. "What the testimonial giver says is of little importance," he said, "because the average layman who furnishes the testimonial is completely unable to diagnose his trouble." Barber admitted that a testimonial from a skilled physician would be valuable to an advertiser and carry a lot of weight. According to Barber, the purpose of his article was to warn the ill against the purchase of medical preparations that were "flagrantly" advertised or which were sold largely through the recommendation of testimonial givers, celebrities or ordinary citizens. Noted was the fact that a prospective buyer had little formal protection. Under the Food and Drugs Act (limited to interstate commerce), medical preparations were prohibited from being falsely or fraudulently labeled, nor could such claims be made on or in the trade package. That is, if a medical product's ad carried a lie in its magazine ad nothing happened. If that ad were reproduced on the product's package or appeared in the package as an insert, then a law would have been violated and the FDA could step in.[18]

Certain product types and/or companies embraced testimonials to a much greater degree than did others; they gave endorsement ads a larger prominence in their advertising campaigns. One of those products was tobacco. In June 1933, the R.J. Reynolds Tobacco Company started a new advertising campaign in a long list of publications, built around ordinary citizens who led "active" lives. Kicking off that campaign was an ad featuring famous tennis player Bill Tilden, "who has been a Camel smoker for years, after trying many brands he found that Camels do not tire his taste or get on his nerves." Headlining that ad was the following: "It takes healthy nerves to play like Tilden!" Following ads featured ordinary citizens, most of which were said to spend a lot of time engaged in various sports, as Camel shifted a little, at least in this campaign, away from athletes and celebrities and toward "real" people.[19]

In February 1937, rumors flew around at the Capitol in Washington, D.C., that ten U.S. senators had been persuaded, for $1,000 each; to give endorsements for a tobacco company detailing how little its cigarettes affected the throat membranes of great orators like themselves. Following the spread of that rumor, one senator came forward to confirm the story as fact, as far as he was concerned. Senator Robert H. Reynolds of North Carolina admitted he had given an endorsement that he had noticed no ill effects to his throat from that cigarette brand (not identified except that it was not the one made by the R.J. Reynolds Tobacco Company) and had received $1,000. Reynolds added that he was a smoker but that he smoked other brands as well.[20]

Much information about cigarette testimonials became public in 1944 (all the examples related to the 1930s, though) at FTC hearings in New York. For example, prices paid by the R.J. Reynolds firm for testimonials ranged from $5 to $500 according to witnesses as the hearing. The prominence of the endorser, rather than the length of time the endorsement was to be used, was the deciding factor in the matter of payment. At that hearing the advertising claims in general of cigarettes were under investigation. One part of the hearing dealt exclusively with the signed testimonials for Camel cigarettes and Prince Albert smoking tobacco. Helen Stansbury,

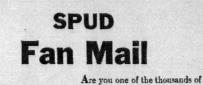

SPUD
Fan Mail

Are you one of the thousands of fans who have written us about Spud? If so, we want to take this opportunity of thanking you. It is pleasant and encouraging to receive letters like those printed below.

W. F. AXTON, *President*
The Axton-Fisher Tobacco Co., Inc.

NOTE: *Spud fan letters are spontaneous. No solicited or paid testimonials.*

Dear Mr. Axton:

The first time . . .
"Well, it was a Spud she gave me and for the first time in my life I can say I enjoy smoking. I even bought a carton to take to the Adirondacks with me."
(Mrs. E.) Edna L. Baggatt, Brooklyn, N.Y.

The last five years . . .
"In looking through a magazine the other day, I came across an advertisement of yours about Spud cigarettes. Every word of that advertisement was true. I think there isn't another cigarette on the market that can compare with Spuds.
"I've smoked them for the last five years and the last smoke was as delightful and wonderful as the first."
George Moller, McKeesport, Pa.

"Smoked out" feeling gone . . .
"I had that 'smoked out' feeling with other brands . . . so I determined to have a try at Spuds.
"The cool, clean, refreshing taste remains . . . and the 'smoked out' feeling is all gone."
Clair E. Stilwell, Akron, Ohio

Heavy smoker . . .
"I have been smoking them (Spuds) constantly now for nearly a year and find they are everything you recommend them to be.
"I changed from another brand because I am a fairly heavy smoker and as I work nights, as a linotype operator, I found my mouth and throat harsh and dry and with a disagreeable taste in my mouth after a night's work.
"After smoking your cigarettes for a while, I found that that condition does not exist."
Louis Frader, Camden, New Jersey

Smoked for hours . . .
"Yes, Spuds are really cool, enjoyable cigarettes . . . that can be smoked for hours at a time without ever lessening that clean, delightful taste one learns to like when he knows he is smoking the best.
"More than ever the men of our organization (aviation) are switching to Spuds permanently, for genuine smoking enjoyment." *W. L. Flager, C. E. Horseman Kansas City, Missouri.*

Passes "good word" along . . .
"You didn't ask me for the 'good word'; nevertheless, I am only too glad to give it.
"My pleasant experience has converted another Spud smoker. And, gentlemen . . . when you convert them, they stay converted."
F. G. Flack, Glendale, L. I., N. Y.

Intend to smoke . . .
"For the last two weeks I have been smoking Spuds and find them to be an exceptionally fine cigarette.
"I have had a cold for two weeks . . . but Spuds, being a cool smoke, had a soothing effect . . . I intend to smoke Spuds right along."
Clarence H. Haskins, Montpelier, Vt.

Down-right enjoyment . . .
"I know it is quite unusual for a manufacturer to receive an unsolicited letter praising his product.
"However, I have derived such pleasure and down-right enjoyment while smoking SPUDS that I feel I should let you know. For real honest to goodness smoke satisfaction SPUDS are ideal. Several of my friends who have consistently, to use slang, 'grubbed' SPUDS from me are now smoking them regularly."
Bernard Rosenblatt, Brooklyn, N. Y.

Appreciating more and more . . .
"I became interested and purchased a pack (of Spuds) for myself. Before I had them half smoked I began to like them. Not only did they have a pleasant taste, but better than that they certainly permitted me to smoke in comfort and enjoy it. And so I kept on purchasing them, and appreciating them more and more."
Arthur J. Mann, Hamden, Conn.

Outstanding clean taste . . .
"It has been my experience that the menthol taste is not noticeable after having smoked several packages of Spuds, although the effect of a cool smoke is still the same.
"The outstanding thing about Spuds, in my opinion, is the clean taste left in the mouth after smoking innumerable cigarettes, especially in the morning after a night's sleep. This, more than anything, has sold me on Spuds and it is only because of my appreciation for your having removed the unpleasant effects of cigarette smoking, that I write you this letter."
R. B. Lyman, Akron, Ohio

20 FOR 15c
(25c IN CANADA)

THE AXTON-FISHER TOBACCO COMPANY, INC., LOUISVILLE, KENTUCKY

an employee of United Air Lines, told she was paid $100 to give a testimonial for Camels, although she had not smoked more than three or four times in her life. At the time she gave the endorsement she was not a cigarette smoker. The advertising agency involved, William Esty Company, knew she was not a cigarette smoker because she told them. She said to the ad agency, "Well, my goodness, I don't know just why I should endorse Camels." Replied the agency; "Think of the publicity to your company." Believing that was one of the duties of her job, she discussed the matter with a couple of United executives, and "I was not coerced but I was told it would be a very good idea and why not do it." United Air Lines was said to have had an understanding "that the name United Air Lines would always appear in any advertising that showed my name or my face." Although she had never been a smoker, part of her endorsement in the ad, which appeared in May 1938, read: "So naturally, I chose a cigarette that is decidedly mild — Camels." Asked why she had signed that endorsement, apart from her employer wanting her to do so, Stansbury replied there was no other reason except the $100: "I would not have done it on my own responsibility because it would have incurred too much displeasure in my family." Another part of her testimonial read: "When I feel fatigued, I quickly light a Camel and get a 'lift' in energy." She agreed with her examiner at the hearing that from the ad and its statements was the inference that Stansbury was a Camel smoker and that she did smoke Camels.[21]

Another who appeared at the hearing was famed photographer Margaret Bourke-White, who was paid $250 for her endorsement of Camels. When asked why she did the testimonial, she replied that "frankly I was in business and was very glad to earn the money." At the time she was, admittedly, a "constant" smoker, although she smoked any of the standard brands and was not exclusively a Camel smoker. Another endorser was automobile mechanic Allen Patterson, who was discovered by a woman who represented the Camel ad agency and was searching his neighborhood looking for an "American-type" mechanic. After selecting Patterson, she got him to sit for two separate photo sessions for Prince Albert Smoking

Opposite: Testimonial letters from ordinary Spud cigarette smokers, 1933. Rarely did such letters simply arrive in a firm's mail, spontaneous and unsolicited, and then get used in ads. Usually they were indirectly or directly solicited. For example, a contest would be run on "Why I Love Spud cigarettes." Small prizes would be awarded, and the company would then pick out material from the submissions and run it as ad copy, after permission was granted by the letter writer. At least one letter in this ad rings true for cigarette smokers in general: "I became interested and purchased a pack (of Spuds) for myself. Before I had them half-smoked I began to like them.... And so I kept on purchasing them, and appreciating them more and more."

Tobacco, at $5 per sitting. He was not then a user of Prince Albert, saying that "I have given it a try, but just could not smoke a pipe." Then he was asked to do a testimonial for Camels, for which he received $25. He smoked Lucky Strikes then and had no preference for Camels. In part his endorsement said, "the Mrs. smokes Camels too because they hit the spot with her like they do with me." Mrs. Patterson had never smoked in her life. Another part of his testimonial had him say he reached for a Camel after a meal because it aided his digestion. At the FTC hearing Patterson admitted he did not believe, at the hearing or when he gave his testimonial, that Camels aided digestion.[22]

Still another witness at the hearing was Mary A. Wegener, who worked in the Student Placement Bureau at Columbia University. A Miss Fisher of the William Esty ad agency called on her (around 1930) for the purpose of obtaining students to give testimonials for Camel cigarettes. Fisher was looking for "American-type" students, and Wegener recalled she referred some. Each student was to receive $35 for an endorsement. Joseph Bolan was a farmer in New York State who did smoke cigarettes. He recalled that a man came to see him and, after hearing he smoked Camels and liked them, "made me an offer that he would give me so much money, $25 — if my memory is right — and I was to get, I believe, a carton of cigarettes for six weeks running [six in total] see, for the privilege of using my picture in a magazine as an advertising stunt." Walter Lanier Barber (better known as Red Barber, the famous radio sports announcer who was in his sixteenth year of broadcasting at the end of the 1930s) received $100 for his Camel endorsement. The agreement was that the ad was to appear once only and only in newspapers, at a time to tie in with the World Series of 1939, in which Barber was featured broadcaster. Barber was a regular Camel smoker. James L. Clark was director of preparation and installation at the American Museum of Natural History in New York City. Over the years he had conducted some 20 explorations to Africa, Asia, and so on. He got $500 for his testimonial. Clark did smoke Camels, but he also smoked other brands, such as Lucky Strike and Chesterfield. Part of his endorsement stated: "I have carried Camels on expeditions to three continents." At the hearing he said that he had also taken cartons of other brands with him on those expeditions.[23]

No advertising agency was more involved in testimonials than was the J. Walter Thompson firm. It led campaigns for Pond's face creams, Lux Toilet Soap, Parker Pen, and Fleischmann's Yeast, among others, all big users of endorsement ads. Around 1929 Thompson vice-president Bill Esty decided the way to sell more and more cakes of Lux Toilet Soap, a latecomer to a crowded field, was to acquire for it the praise of the female stars and starlets of Hollywood (see Appendix B). The campaign turned out to be a colossal success and was still running in the late 1940s. It sold tons of Lux and gave the Hollywood stars the benefit of free publicity for themselves, and for their current or upcoming films, since that was almost always mentioned in the ad, along with the name of the Hollywood studio involved. In a 1933 advertisement for Lux soap it was stated that "of the 694 important Hollywood actresses, including all stars, actually 686 use this simple, inexpensive complexion care!" According to one account, Lux paid no money at all for any of its many endorsements from Hollywood stars, with the actors apparently content, or forced to be content by their studios, with the publicity value of the ad, and a certain amount of free soap supplied by Lux. In its somewhat earlier campaign Pond's reportedly paid its endorsers fees ranging from $10 to $300. J. Walter Thompson's New York office contained a section known as the Personality Department presided over by Lucile Platt, a woman of connections who "is quietly ready at any moment to persuade some new name of the proper significance to go down the line for the product of one or another Thompson client," said a reporter.[24]

No fewer than 11 actresses in one Lux ad, 1933. Delores del Rio and Irene Dunne are featured at top. At bottom, left to right: Helen Mack, Dorothy Jordan, Ginger Rogers, Helen Broderick, Frances Dee, Arline Judge, Dorothy Wilson, Pert Kelton, and June Brewster.

While Thompson's love of testimonials led to many successful ad campaigns, none was more effective than the whole series of medical endorsements dreamed up by Thompson vice-president Bill Day for Fleischmann's Yeast in the late 1920s. For years it had been sold, in cake form, to serve the needs of women who baked their own bread. As that market declined in the 1920s (they were buying more store-made bread), sales of the product began to languish. So Thompson went to work on yeast in an example of product research activity, and out of the laboratory it brought the news that Fleischmann's Yeast was the best source of vitamins A, B, and G then publicly available. Thus, it was said to follow that the product was excellent to alleviate conditions such as acne, constipation, sallow complexions, and that tired, run-down feeling. A whole new strategy for restoring sales of the product to their old levels then revealed itself to Day and the Thompson concern. It seemed to observers to be a difficult task because, as a business reporter explained, "Now the basic idea of making any fraction of the U.S. public, however small, eat as much as one cake of yeast ever, except as the penalty on a lost election bet, might seem to have been an impossibility. Baker's yeast, in the mouth, has the texture of a deteriorated ink blotter, and a taste that defies description except as a mild blend of wet horsehair and acetylene."[25]

Despite the obstacles and difficulties the campaign "Yeast for Health" pushed sales up and up until in the 1930s they accounted for 75 percent of all the profits made by Standard Brands, which owned Fleischmann's. "Once again the principal device was the testimonial," noted an account, which also observed the American Medical Association had "stern views" on professional endorsement of commercial products: "any U.S. doctor who risked such an expression would find himself immediately up on charges before his county medical society." Aware of that situation, Day comforted himself with the fact there was no AMA in Europe, and he was apparently set on having medical endorsements of some kind for the yeast. Thus, from 1929 to 1936 the reading public in America was exposed to what seemed to be an endless series of European physicians (a total of 168 were signed up) endorsing Yeast for Health. Said one account: "the European physicians got an average of $500 for their beards, names, and services, and the sales of Fleischmann's Yeast continued to soar." One of those Thompson ads for Fleischmann's was a round-up style item that displayed nine doctors, mentioned 15 "noted" clinics, plus a "great U.S. medical college," and alluded to the idea that the product offered hope in treating no less than eight different human ailments— rheumatism, headaches, old age, and the common cold had been added to the originals, such as acne and constipation. Full-page ads (sometimes two-page spreads) appeared

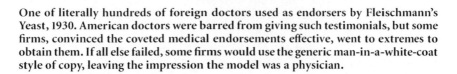

One of literally hundreds of foreign doctors used as endorsers by Fleischmann's Yeast, 1930. American doctors were barred from giving such testimonials, but some firms, convinced the coveted medical endorsements effective, went to extremes to obtain them. If all else failed, some firms would use the generic man-in-a-white-coat style of copy, leaving the impression the model was a physician.

in 26 national magazines, with space also bought in almost 300 newspapers. Crooner/band leader Rudy Vallee shilled for the product on some 54 radio stations as well. Nevertheless, by late in the 1930s sales of the product lagged again against a competition increase in vitamins put up as tablets in more concentrated, systematized and palatable forms. However, it was a great show while it lasted, wrote one reporter, "and it was also an extraordinary demonstration of the power of the testimonial ad, particularly when linked to the occult beauties of scientific discovery." By the late 1940s, Fleischmann's Yeast advertising could be most usually found in farm journals, where it carried the exhortation, "Feed it to your hogs."[26]

Others endorsed Fleischmann's Yeast, besides European doctors. One was Jean Norris, a New York City magistrate of seven years standing when she gave her testimonial in 1931, for a fee of $1,000. In her testimonial she said she had insomnia from poor digestion and that Fleischmann's Yeast cured her. When details of her endorsement became public (during a referee's inquiry into another matter), she was asked by the referee if she thought it was ethical to accept the $1,000 to endorse the product. "As I see it now, I think it was unethical," replied Magistrate Norris.[27]

Automobile companies also tied in significantly with celebrities in the 1930s. John McDonough recalled that in those early years of radio, most automakers regarded their brands as sources of prestige and sought "fitting" artists as endorsers. As radio became increasingly popular, the car companies stepped in. Jan Kurtz, national director of the American Advertising Museum, remarked, "The '30s, particularly, became the first real heyday of celebrity marketing. Broadcasting and sound movies came to maturity ... and gave the celebrity a power and influence in our culture it never had before." In 1935 Dodge sponsored *Major Bowes Original Amateur Hour* on radio. Packard first sponsored opera singer Lawrence Tibbett. Later in that decade they went for a broader appeal with Fred Astaire and comic Charles Butterworth. "In auto advertising, the idea in sponsoring a program was to find an artist whose prestige reflected the product," said Pat Weaver, a future head of the NBC network. Weaver produced that Packard program, for the Young & Rubicam ad agency. "With Astaire we saw a chance to broaden the appeal [of Packard] without lowering its quality image," added Weaver. Comic Jack Benny had Chevrolet as a sponsor in the early 1930s. His commercial urged listeners to drive to the 1933 Century of Progress Exhibition in Chicago in a new Chevrolet "priced as low as $445," while "Carole Lombard tells why she picked DeSoto" was the teaser headline of a 1938 ad for that automaker.[28]

Hollywood remained a prime location to sign up endorsers. By 1931 the Hollywood cartel — the MPPDA, the Motion Picture Producers and

Distributors of America—felt themselves so swamped by requests for its stars to endorse products that MPPDA head Will Hays placed a ban on player advertising tie-ups. Advertising agency personnel, however, simply put more effort into seeking out stars who happened to be without studio contracts—freelancers—insisting there were many names in the freelance field just as good as those with studio contracts.[29]

Not that the ban had much effect, for it was admitted early in 1932 that the banning of commercial endorsements by the Hays office had not stopped the practice. "Practically all studios have stars lined up for coming display or radio advertising tieup," said one account. Lucky Strike, Lux and Coca-Cola had reportedly met little resistance in getting big names from the studios as endorsers because of the widespread publicity those ads offered to the film studios. Having let down the bars a little, studios found it harder to refuse anyone. A representative of the Studebaker automobile firm was visiting the studios at that time for star tie-ins on a $2 million ad campaign "in which only picture names will be used in connection with the cars."[30]

At the same time it was reported that the use of misleading testimonials by screen stars in the national advertising of products that the celebrities frequently knew little about would be discouraged by the Associated Motion Picture Advertisers, Inc. That organization drew up resolutions condemning the practice and forwarded them to Will Hays and the MPPDA. According to Edward Finney, president of the Associated Motion Picture Advertisers, the intention was to eliminate misrepresentation and spurious endorsements by the stars, "while still maintaining a liaison between the national advertisers and the motion picture companies."[31]

A few years later, in 1935, *Variety* reported the endorsement business was booming in Hollywood: "Studios have gone wild on commercial tie-ups and have completely kicked wide open the Hays edict ... banning the printed plugs of their stars." All the film studios were reported to be racing to grab the best national accounts while national advertisers were rushing Hollywood with their representatives, fighting to get the best names. Agents then besieging Hollywood were said to represent General Motors (Buick and Chevrolet), Auburn, Packard and Dodge motor cars; Armour Company, Jantzen Knitting Company, Walkover Shoes, Pure Oil, Helena Rubenstein Cosmetics, and many other "potent" national advertisers. J. Walter Thompson's executive Danny Danker devoted all of his time to signing up Hollywood stars for the company accounts. So extensively were the celebrities involved that one reporter declared: "With the exception of [Greta] Garbo and Marlene Dietrich, almost every star in Hollywood has some sort of a commercial angle, and it is understood Dietrich now is open for propositions." Warner Brothers had at that point tied up the stars from its last ten movies with Buick cars. General Motors was trying to sign up big names to endorse Chevrolet "but finds it hard to have the big time stars work with them on a low priced car," went the account. No company had more success in signing Hollywood names than did Lux soap, made by Lever Brothers. Through Danker and the Thompson agency, Lux was then said to have "every actress in pictures, with four or five exceptions, on Lux releases."[32]

A beer ad in the *New Yorker* magazine annoyed the Hays office at the end of the 1930s. Hollywood's cartel had always frowned on the idea of its stars being used as "stooges" for alcohol promotion. In this instance four actors and newspaper columnist/emcee Ed Sullivan were featured in the ad, with Sullivan being the star of the item (he was not a Hollywood studio star and thus not subject to the wrath of Hays and the MPPDA). Sullivan said, in the ad, "My beer is the dry beer." His motion was seconded by Arthur Treacher, Marjorie Weaver, Betty Jaynes, and Bela Lugosi. The four actors had been members of Sullivan's troupe when he conducted his stage tour a few months earlier. Punishment of the four actors by Hays was limited to letting them off with a warning and telling them to see that it did not happen again.[33]

One of the few people who pointed out at this time that there might be negative aspects involved in the use of celebrity endorsers was business journalist Lawrence M. Hughes, writing in *Sales Management* in 1939. From the sponsors' standpoint, he argued, they wanted any stars they used as endorsers to stay in character, with the personal opinions of stars having the potential to "antagonize" part of the buying audience that was important to the advertiser. An example he gave of where it worked properly for the sponsor was Jack Benny, who, as endorser, had helped General Foods build a large sales volume for its Jell-O product, while always staying within his stage character. Hughes remarked that it was hard enough to get stars to click regularly as entertainers, without getting messed up in controversy. Acknowledging that controversy brought publicity, he warned that sometimes it was the wrong kind of publicity: "And always tending to obscure the purpose of the star system — to sell merchandise." He wondered that if the growing popularity of a star could increase sales of a product, could it not follow that the waning popularity of that star could diminish sales?[34]

Although the star system was then 25 years old, Hughes declared it was hard for the national advertisers to know who to pick or how to avoid the person who said the wrong thing. Because it was difficult and time consuming, advertising agents and public relations specialists were brought in to handle the process. National advertisers, thought Hughes, found it easier to tie their organization and product to a person already popular than to create popularity. So business rushed forward to get the influence of the stars behind the products. A lot of businesses had the same idea, and competition for big names became intense. And when the public began to discover that they had been paid, and even then often did not use the product, continued Hughes, the testimonial trend slowed down. However, he added, testimonials remained important in some areas, notably in tobacco promotion. Old Gold cigarettes had finally abandoned the use of testimonials, but only after a costly name-buying war with Lucky Strike. Camel and Chesterfield picked up the slack.[35]

Problems with using stars remained, said Hughes, even if the celebrity remained free of scandal; he could lose popularity, get sick, or die. And always, at the contract's expiration, he could switch to another sponsor. The public, he felt, remembered very few of the associations between star and advertiser; Jack Benny and Jell-O; Edgar Bergen (and his dummy Charlie McCarthy) with Chase and Sanborn coffee; Fred Allen and Ipana toothpaste; Major Bowes with Chrysler; and Rudy Vallee with Fleischmann's. Some stars were said to have worn out their appeal as endorsers by signing up for too many products; Eddie Cantor had been with Old Gold cigarettes, Sunkist oranges, Chase and Sanborn coffee, Pebeco toothpaste, Texaco gasoline, and Camel cigarettes. George Burns and Gracie Allen had gone from White Owl cigars to Campbell soup to Grape-Nuts cereal to Chesterfield cigarettes. Some stars, he believed, were so popular that they dominated the product in any ad and thus were not a good idea as endorsers. Readers would remember only the superstar. An example he used of a celebrity who became a person to avoid as an endorser, due to controversy, was Charles Lindbergh. (In earlier years he had often been cited by media accounts as one of the very few celebrities who had refused to do endorsements, after being approached. Usually he was the only one named, giving him even more weight as a positive example. In the end, though, he succumbed and endorsed.) After ten years the TWA airline had stopped using its slogan "the Lindbergh Line." The famed aviator was no longer in America and he was then reputed to be pro–Nazi.[36]

Wondering whether a person should tie their business to a star, Hughes replied to his question by observing that business executives needed to realize that the star system, "oftener than not, is full of more headaches than sales." Every few days in newspapers, every month in magazines, Camel cigarettes featured several stars in their ads. Each one was good reading in its own right, he said, but when you were through with each one of them it was only Camel that stuck in your memory. Hughes concluded that "The answer to the title of this story ["Should you hitch your business to a star?"] is largely to put the title in reverse. Don't hitch your business to a star. Hitch a star to your business—and then only as a part of your business and its promotional program."[37]

Society women continued to have prominence in endorsement ads in the 1930s but then fell out of favor. Some light was shed on the fees involved as the result of a court case, not related to testimonials. The Berkey and Gay Company, a Grand Rapids, Michigan, furniture maker, revealed in court documents that in 1930 Eleanor Roosevelt (wife of Franklin D. Roosevelt) accepted $1,000 from the J. Walter Thompson ad agency to endorse Berkey and Gay furniture. The same documents listed other women as receiving money for endorsements, including Mrs. Graham

Fair Vanderbilt of New York, $2,000; Mrs. A.J. Drexel Biddle, of Philadelphia, $750; and Mrs. J. Borden Harriman, of New York, $1,000. Invoices on Thompson agency letterhead listed an expense account of $51.89 for a trip to Northampton, Massachusetts, to obtain the endorsement of Mrs. Calvin Coolidge, but did not indicate that she gave an endorsement or received any money. Officials of the Thompson agency declined to discuss specific amounts paid but said that in many cases the women endorsers turned the money over to charities. Eleanor Roosevelt said she remembered the ad, could not recall the amount of money received, and had followed her usual custom of giving it to charity.[38]

A society woman testified for Pond's in 1938. For a time Pond's and other firms were fairly heavily into the use of society people (almost always women) as endorsers. Pond's especially favored the method. The underlying idea was that people were likely to imitate the habits of their "social superiors."

North Bay, Ontario, was the site of a momentous event on May 28, 1934 — the Dionne quintuplets were born on that day. Never before and never since has a multiple birth been covered so intensively by the media. The progress of the quints was tracked in minute detail and carried around the world, literally for years. Dr. Allan R. Dafoe, their obscure physician (who also quickly became a media personality), started the Dionne babies on Quaker Oats as their first solid food. When Quaker got wind of that, recalled Arthur Marquette years later, Quaker quickly signed up the quints as endorsers. Marquette, a Quaker account man with the firm's ad agency at the time of the birth, said cereal ads were very commonplace then and often so alike that the readership ratings for that class of advertising were consistently low. But a tie-in with the quints changed all that. "Quaker Oats advertising became the best read in the media, as high as 95 percent of the readers reporting they had read the ads featuring the Dionne quints," explained Marquette. Public interest in the Dionnes did not lag, but after two years of success pressure was put on Marquette, and his agency, to come up with something new. He came up with an idea linking together Amelia Earhart, the Dionnes and Quaker. Purdue University was then raising funds to finance Earhart's proposed flight around the world. Quaker Oats agreed to contribute $5,000 to the venture, in exchange for which she agreed to be featured in a series of ads as the "Quaker Oats World

The Dionne quints, and the family physician, shill for a candy bar, 1941. Hugely famous through the late 1930s and into the 1940s, the quints were enormously successful as endorsers. Decades later sets of quints would fare poorly, compared to the Dionnes. Apparently the novelty had faded.

Reporter." Several of those ads were to be devoted to her reports on the progress of the Dionne quints. None of it happened, though. Amelia Earhart disappeared on that flight, in June 1937.[39]

A detailed account published in April 1937 showed how extensive were the Dionne quints' endorsement contracts [see Appendix C]. With accounts receivable amounting then to $287,383.34 due, the total earnings of the quints to that date from endorsements were $861,148.39. Of that amount, $573,765.05 had been received from 24 contracts signed since their birth. And of the latter amount, $543,174.33 had been paid to their guardians since June 1935, when the babies had been made wards of the state. Many of their contracts had contingency clauses—certain percentages to the Dionnes based on sales of the products.[40]

Even more endorsement deals would come to the Dionnes after April 1937. Compare that with what happened to the Kienast quints that were born in February 1970 in Liberty Corners, New Jersey. Reporter James Forkan observed, three years after the birth, that major advertisers were not beating a path to the Kienast quints' door with endorsement offers. Partly he attributed that to changing times and attitudes and partly due to the parents' choice to try to give the babies a more normal upbringing. From 1970 to 1973 the Kienast family received an estimated total of $65,000, mostly from television appearances, "exclusive" *Good Housekeeping* articles, and a 1971 contract to do Ecolo-G phosphate-free detergent television commercials and print ads. South Dakota's Fischer quints, born in 1963, made about $80,000 a year their first couple of years from various business contracts, especially a long-term pact with Borden, Inc. Borden signed its advertising and promotion contract with the Fischer quints in late 1964, but let the pact lapse after its 1967 expiration. With options, that contract could have been renewed until 1984, when the children would have been 21. Forkan concluded, in 1973, "Industry sources indicated that whatever the reasons, few major dairy, food or diaper companies seem interested today in gaining publicity from tying in with such multiple-birth families." Officials at Pet Foods, for example, told him that multiple births "don't really fit in with out marketing approach." Perhaps another reason for the enormous interest in the Dionnes in the 1930s was that it provided a psychological relief of sorts for the hard times of the Depression years. As well, large families were still generally given much media attention and praise at the time.[41]

Writing in 1984, journalist Maurine Christopher remarked that Eleanor Roosevelt was the only First Lady to appear as an endorser on radio and television, but that she did not appear directly in ads until long after the end of her terms as First Lady (as wife of Franklin D. Roosevelt she was in the White House as First Lady from inauguration in 1933 until her husband's death in office in 1945). Her commercial radio career apparently started in 1932, when she managed to find time to conduct a weekly sponsored radio show on NBC while running her household and campaigning for FDR's election. She donated her salary to charity. That radio show was short-lived, as she gave it up before the Roosevelts moved into the White House. Eleanor returned to NBC with another sponsored, commercial radio program around the middle of 1934. Her program commanded ad rates as high as those for Ed Wynn and Kate Smith, two radio superstars of the time. She was sponsored by Simmons mattresses and later by Pond's cold cream. As in earlier times, she donated her salary to charity.[42]

Athletes were used as endorsers more systematically in the 1930s than ever before, although they clearly still took a back seat to film stars as the most sought after celebrities for testimonials. Cereal makers, and tobacco companies, were among the biggest users of athletes. General Mills (maker of Wheaties cereal) company president D.D. Davis sent a letter to the Kellogg cereal concern in 1938, and to the J. Walter Thompson agency that was then handling a Kellogg radio baseball tie-in advertising campaign. He observed that his rival could create a Kellogg's All-American baseball team but the firm could not tell the public that certain of those players enjoyed bowls of Kellogg's corn flakes every morning for breakfast because many of the leading baseball players already endorsed Wheaties and "we intend to see to it that these boys live up to their agreements with us not to endorse any other cereal." Kellogg's campaign involved a radio poll to pick an All-American baseball team. Davis said he had no objection to the idea of picking the team and that any player under contract to General Mills would not be prohibited from accepting any Kellogg award, should they win one. However, Kellogg needed to understand, emphasized Davis, that it had to refrain from implying directly or indirectly that those players endorsed any breakfast cereal except Wheaties. The awards to players winning spots on the Kellogg team were Buick cars, and it was planned to have them carry some sort of Kellogg identification, "but not conspicuously." Davis offered to furnish the Kellogg firm a list of the players who had signed on with Wheaties, but the latter said it did not intend to ask for such a list because it did not plan to involve any of the chosen players in testimonials for its corn flakes. General Mills declined to give the business periodical *Printers' Ink* a complete list of the baseball players then on the Wheaties' endorsement roll. Just a few months earlier a single ad for Wheaties, round-up style, contained testimonials from the following 12 major league baseball players: Joe Cronin, "Gabby" Hartnett, Charles Gehringer, Luke Sewell, Mel Ott, Louis Fette, Paul Warner, Carl Hubbell,

Bob Feller, "Lefty" Gomez, Joe Medwick, and Joe DiMaggio. That was, of course, not a complete list of baseball players who endorsed Wheaties.[43]

In order to secure testimonials from ordinary citizens, one method used was for companies to set up contests. John Caples, with the ad agency Batten, Barton, Durstine & Osborn, said one of the most common types of contest was the one that required entrants to submit letters: "What is more, a great deal of copy material can be quickly and easily obtained by offering prizes for letters about the advertised product." For example, the makers of Crisco shortening were then offering prizes for letters on "Crisco's quick digestibility." Prizes were $10 for each accepted letter, to be used, naturally, in future ads for the product. Lifebuoy Soap asked people to send in letters about true "B.O." experiences, with prizes of $25 for each accepted letter.[44]

Caples then described in detail a real contest but disguised the company involved by giving it the fictional name Maltex Beverage Company. Maltex had reached the point where it wanted letters from customers that might be used in testimonial ads. One method considered was the conventional manner: to send its representatives out to call on grocers and get the names of customers who purchased Maltex. The next step was to have the representatives call on the Maltex buyers and ask them to write letters on why they liked Maltex, then obtain signed releases to use those letters. That method was discarded by Maltex as being too time consuming and too much trouble. Also, there was no way of knowing if any letters actually written would be good enough to use. So a contest was created instead. Maltex limited the total prize money to a few hundred dollars and divided it into a number of small prizes instead of having just three or four bigger prizes. That method was said to draw more replies. Letters were limited to 150 words or less, and the contest was open for just 12 days, to speed up replies. An ad announcing the contest was run one time only in a large Sunday newspaper, at a cost of $225. Some 1,250 responses were received by the time the contest closed, considered a satisfactory response. Once received, the letters were read through and typed, or retyped, and edited. Grammar and spelling corrections were made. Quite a number of the letters mentioned other beverages, and since it was felt the best letters for advertising purposes would be those that omitted any references to other drinks, those references were left out of the contest letters when they were typed up for the final judging. About 100 letters were selected for that final judging. Winners were selected and checks mailed to them along with a release blank containing their winning letter and a space for the writer's signature.[45]

That letter sent to winners read as follows: "Congratulations! Your letter on 'Why I like Maltex' was chosen from among the twelve hundred entries as one of the prizewinners. Your check is enclosed. We would like to have permission to use your letter in our advertising, together with your name and address. Would you give us permission to do this by signing the statement at the bottom of the enclosed page, and returning the letter to us for our files?" Reportedly all the winners except one woman, who won a $1 prize, signed the releases and returned them. She returned her check with this note: "I certainly will not consent to having my letter used in an advertisement for only a dollar." Maltex's advertising manager sent the check back to her along with a letter stating the awarding of the prizes was in no way dependent on consent to use the letter in advertisements.[46]

Few articles on the philosophy or ethics of the endorsement ad appeared in the 1930s; the few that did were mostly positive and in favor of that format. Edward H. Gardner, executive secretary of the Advisory Committee on Advertising of the Proprietary Association, declared the testimonial had a secure place in the world of the advertisers because it was the voice of experience: "It dealt with results, not theories, and it speaks to the consumer in the language of his own kind." In Gardner's opinion, the strength of the testimonial lay in the fact that man was an imitative animal: "He does what others do; he is unhappy if he departs too far from the habit pattern of his kind. In everything that you and I do or say, the language we speak, the clothes we wear, the food we eat, the postures of our bodies and habits of our mind, in all these there is nothing that is not imitated consciously or unconsciously from other people." That idea that no one believed testimonials was so far from the truth, he argued, that it could almost be said that no one believed anything but testimonials, that no one could be persuaded to action other than through the use of example. A testimonial took the load of presenting evidence off the manufacturer's own shoulders, and more credible in the long run, he continued, was the story of the user rather than that of the maker because "he has no axe to grind, no profit to make or lose; he is my kind, he speaks my language. After all, who sold Adam the apple?"[47]

Business reporter Mark O'Dea offered a more subdued positive assessment. He felt dishonest, misguided endorsements led to public disillusionment but that people liked advertising itself—"it is a newsy, fascinating part of American life"—but it had to be believable advertising. Hence, the public felt deceived when the "paid testimonial racket" was exposed. But, he added, the power of sincere, honest testimonials would never decrease since testimony was evidence. So it was a basic principle in selling and advertising that allowed a user to speak for a product, freeing the manufacturers from "over-bragging." O'Dea concluded that "testimonials have a worthwhile job to do and their efficiency can be restored — if they do not overshadow the product they endorse, if they are believable, if they are not silly."[48]

Anna Richardson, associate editor of the *Woman's Home Companion* magazine, gave a talk in 1937 at an advertising class sponsored by the Advertising Women of New York, Inc., in which she stated consumers had confidence in ad endorsements given by middle-class women, but were skeptical of those obtained from society women or film stars.[49]

The 1930s was a busy decade for the endorsement business, as it remained a popular strategy for advertisers. What set it apart from the 1920s was that in the 1930s there was virtually no debate or discussion over the ethics of such advertisements. It was all business and no philosophy. Also, from the beginnings of the testimonial business through the end of the 1930s there had been no evidence presented that endorsement ads worked better than conventional ads; they certainly cost more, but the subject of effectiveness virtually did not arise. It was almost a given that such ads worked; an understanding that no one challenged or thought to question. Once in a while an observer pointed out that perhaps a celebrity might overshadow a product due to his superstardom or one might become involved in a controversy and have a negative effect on the product. But such criticism questioned not the endorsement format, but only the choice of endorser. As the 1930s ended, though, everyone seemed to lose interest in endorsement advertising, from the public to the media to the advertising agencies to the advertisers themselves. Testimonial advertising was entering a slow period that would last until around 1975. Endorsement ads were, of course, nowhere near absent in that time, they just had less prominence and were the focus of a lot less interest.

5

Endorsements Hit a Long Slow Period, 1940–1974.

We never ask prominent people to open Air-Wick bottles all over their establishments. What we do is suggest their domestics use it. Then we can say that it's popular in So-and-So's household.
— Jules Alberti, 1949

Your piano is the finest I ever leaned against.
— Denise Darcel, 1950s

For most people the athlete is still the all–American boy. Actors, on the other hand, are actors, and there is the suspicion that they are always acting.
— Steve Arnold, 1969

One thing that emerged at the beginning of this period was the middleman organization on a permanent basis. That is, an organization whose sole reason for being was to line up celebrities hoping they would be sought out by advertising agencies looking for endorsers for their accounts. Often these organizations were aggressive and actively sought out agencies or even national advertisers directly to try and get testimonial contracts for the names on their rosters. Such organizations had sometimes existed in prior years, but none seemed to have lasted very long. Larger ad agencies often had their own in-house personnel or department to line up celebrities and thus did not need a middleman organization but sometimes used one nevertheless. Most agencies, however, were not big enough to line up much of a celebrity roster themselves. Hence, there was room for such middleman firms to emerge.

One of the first of those concerns, and one that got a fair amount of publicity, was founded in 1946. Almost three years later the *New Yorker* did a piece on this unusual new enterprise, a company whose sole business was the lining up of testimonials for advertising purposes. Jules Alberti, who founded Endorsements, Inc., thought testimonials should be given for free. "The very keystone of a wholesome testimonial campaign is that no money change hands," he said. Take a product, he added, and match it up with an "outstanding" person. Then say to that person: "You're a human being, like the masses that follow you. Try this product for two months, three months, four months. If you like it, let us give the world your opinion." He was opposed to a then current Calvert liquor ad campaign in which ordinary men were portrayed as having switched to Calvert. In his view that campaign lacked dignity: "The endorsers have not been carefully screened." On the other hand he did like the Men of Distinction campaign for the Lord Calvert people. But he was involved in lining up the men for that series.[1]

To select and evaluate potential endorsers generally, Alberti's company maintained a research division which filed the names of people conspicuously mentioned in assorted periodicals and then investigated them to make sure no wife beaters, alcoholics, marijuana users, and so on were in the group. Also, Endorsements, Inc., did not want any celebrity who had spread himself too thin by endorsing "everything in sight." In its almost three years of operation, Endorsements, Inc., had accumulated a list of about 2,500 "experienced" endorsers; 50 percent were said to be from outside the amusement field. One of Alberti's most successful projects revolved around Air-Wick, a product designed to eliminate noxious odors—that is, an air freshener. As he wanted to be sure people who endorsed the product actually used it, he explained that "we never ask prominent people to open Air-Wick bottles all over their establishments. What we do is suggest that their domestics use it. Then we can say that it's popular in So-and-So's household." When reporters asked him who So-and-So might be, Alberti cited Charles Boyer, Guy Lombardo, Sonny Tufts, Jessica Tandy, Eddie Cantor, Jane Wyatt, George Raft, Joan Bennett, Fannie Hurst, and others. "All wholesome types," he added. And he said it was the same with Schaefer's beer, with endorsers including Al Jolson, Paulette Goddard, and Hedy Lamarr, "wholesome family types." Endorsements, Inc., was then said to be collaborating with 26 advertising agencies, but that left 2,800 more in America and, declared Alberti, "we're ready to give all of them endorsers. Wholesome types—Dana Andrews, Fred Astaire, Humphrey Bogart, Hoagy Carmichael, Rex Stout, Gene Tierney, Dinah Shore...."[2]

Endorsements, Inc., received another spate of publicity in the mid–1950s. Jules Alberti complained to business reporter George Moses that he thought one would not find a single celebrity testimonial in any farm magazine. Moses looked at two such publications, *Country Gentleman* and *Farm Journal*, finding therein only four and three endorsement ads, respectively, and those all used ordinary people, none used celebrity shills. Still, Moses thought those magazines had got it right: "In the first place, they showed real pictures of real people. They didn't use someone's name and then pose a picture with a professional model. To my way of thinking, that's the worst possible use of the testimonial." Alberti's firm had just completed a tour of the farm belt, during which they signed up 15 farmers in ten states for one of the most difficult of all products for which to secure endorsements—a laxative. Said Alberti, "Celebrities can and should have a more important place in farm advertising. Farmers today are not the backwoods bumpkins or hillbillies that so many ad men seem to think they are…. They know who the nation's celebrities are just as well as city people, and they're just as interested in them." Accepting the argument that testimonials were good if and only if they reflected the actual and bona fide opinion of the endorser, Moses wondered what connection farmers could have to celebrities. In response, Alberti said there were literally scores of famous people in the country who had an active and "burning interest" in farms and farming, and who were available to give "truthful, honest, and aboveboard endorsements." Cited as examples were Roy Rogers (he raised horses), author Louis Bromfield (he had a horse farm), and Bing Crosby (he had a cattle ranch).[3]

According to a *Fortune* account

Bandleader Paul Whiteman's wife endorsed wieners in this 1941 ad. Herein faint celebrity status (some supposed rub-off from Whiteman to his wife) met incongruity to produce a somewhat inane ad.

in 1955, Alberti had difficulty at first when he set up his company in getting advertising agencies to accept his service as legitimate. But in late 1946 the company got an assignment from Batten, Barton, Durstine & Osborn to round up endorsers for Schaefer beer. That got the company going. In 1946 billings by Endorsements, Inc., were $6,600; in 1947, $11,800; in 1948, $67,000; and in 1954, $850,000 gross. All of those gross figures represented fees from ad agencies. By this time, Alberti's organization had reportedly worked with over 400 advertising agencies. Endorsements, Inc.,

was sometimes, but not always, told by the agencies which celebrities were wanted. It was said to be the proud contention of the company that all of its testimonials were true. It was through Alberti that Fred Allen was matched with a shoe manufacturer and with Heublein's prepared cocktails. A further requirement of a good testimonial, besides truthfulness, remarked Alberti, was that the endorser and the product be "logically connected." However, the author of the *Fortune* piece then pointed out some Endorsements, Inc., matches that seemed to contradict that idea, Bert Lahr with Westinghouse refrigerators; flamboyant showman Mike Todd and Alsco storm windows; and boxer Jack Dempsey with Atlantic Bond Paper.[4]

Later that same year, an account said that Alberti's list of endorsers included the likes of Eleanor Roosevelt, Leopold Stokowski, General Douglas

Bing Crosby testified for chewing gum in 1946. So big a box-office star was Crosby at that time that he showed up all over the place endorsing a vast array of products. Not for the first time, nor for the last, was the idea of overexposure for an endorser raised. Could a superstar endorser be used too often by too many products in too short a time and thus dilute his value? The industry had an answer for that: pay the endorser even more (the extra being for some type of exclusivity).

MacArthur, Cornelia Otis Skinner, and Joe DiMaggio. Individual fees were described as a closely guarded secret but, as a rule, were said to range from $500 to $1,500. There were some exceptions. The highest fee ever paid was two Thunderbird sports cars plus an unspecified bundle of cash to a famous singer; the smallest payment made was a case of soap that went to a budding starlet. Over its first almost ten years in business Endorsements, Inc., was reported to have handled over 700 products.[5]

New York advertising man Walter Goodman called Alberti the "king of the Testimonial" in 1956. U.S. advertising people were estimated to have spent $500 million over the previous ten years on testimonials. Alberti lured customers by promising to "get the people you want, speedily, through our exclusive, intimate contacts with the great." Literature put out by the company declared that testimonials were only effective when believable and only believable when: (1) the endorsement was true; (2) the personality and product were logically connected; (3) the testimonial copy was simple, sincere and honest. Alberti then reportedly had files on some 7,000 more or less famous people. When an advertising agency called on Alberti, said Goodman, he immediately sent samples of the product to be plugged to potential and "believable" endorsers. A month or so later he asked the recipients if they could "sincerely" endorse the products they had been given to try out. One or more was said to be likely to respond in the affirmative, "their sincerity having presumably been whetted by the offer of $1,000, a large quantity of whatever they are prepared to enthuse over (Elsa Maxwell, Cobina Wright and Gracie Allen got a year's supply of Mazola oil) and gobs of free publicity." Alberti declared that "I'm critical of the endorsement that has obviously been bought and paid for without any attempt to disguise the fact." As examples of what he meant exactly, he said: "Don't show Marilyn Monroe waxing her own car. People won't believe it." The campaign of which Alberti was reportedly most proud of was the one he managed for Cyma watches. A series of ads for that timepiece brand in the previous few years had featured General Douglas MacArthur, Eleanor Roosevelt, J. Edgar Hoover, Robert Oppenheimer, Warren Austin, Carlos P. Romulo, Leopold Stokowski, Cecil B. DeMille, Helen Keller, and Joe DiMaggio.[6]

Bennett Cerf stated in 1956 that Alberti and his company had three guiding principles: (1) endorsers and the products they promoted had to be "solidly entrenched, unassailable successes"; (2) the celebrities' personalities had to harmonize with the products endorsed; (3) the endorsers had to "honestly" use the products they recommended. Alberti collected his fee from a piano manufacturer for the following endorsement from lounge singer Denise Darcel: "Your piano is the finest I ever leaned

You get Better Pictures, Greater Viewing Comfort and Finest Cabinet Beauty with

⑤ SYLVANIA TV

America's Fastest-Growing Television

No fewer than 18 citizens were gathered together to testify on this page in 1953, in an extreme example of the round-up style ad.

against." When Grace Kelly endorsed the virtues of a certain soap, only to turn around to tell an interviewer shortly thereafter that "no soap had touched her face," Alberti, though not personally involved, was reported to have been chagrined. Cerf reported that in the previous decade advertisers had spent some $500 million in having more than 6,000 products endorsed by the "world's outstanding personalities."[7]

Later in 1957 an announcement was made that Jules Alberti's Endorsements, Inc., was opening new representation offices in London, Paris, Rome, Australia, and South America.[8]

The FTC took a few tentative, hesitant steps toward the endorsement industry in this period. In 1945 the trade publication *Advertising & Selling* published what it described as a cautionary article to the industry. If a manufacturer was planning a sales campaign based on experts' "scientific" claims for its product, that company was urged to remember that the FTC had the final say in determining the reliability of the "authorities" that endorsed a product. As early as 1941, the U.S. Supreme Court had backed a lower court ruling that held that conflicts between testimony of FTC experts and experts testifying for a manufacturer were up to the agency to decide. It meant the FTC had the final right to determine whether experts were qualified to endorse a product. In a 1944 Circuit Court decision, on a petition for review, it was held the FTC had every right to determine which "experts" it would believe; that court refused to entertain the maker's claim that the opinion of Commission experts should be turned down because they had no clinical experience with the product. In that specific case the FTC issued an order prohibiting a seller from advertising that his product was valuable in treating arthritis, neuritis, and so on, although the manufacturer produced two osteopathic physicians who testified they had treated hundreds of patients with the product and effected cures in many cases. On the FTC's side, a chemist and three doctors of medicine, two of whom were specialists in arthritis, testified that the product had no value in curing these ailments. Such examples caused the article to advise readers that "cautious handling of 'expert' endorsements of your product is indicated." And if a manufacturer intended to make use of scientific opinions in its advertising, it had to be able to convince the FTC that its experts had authentic standing in their profession.[9]

Lawyer Morton J. Simon was a member of the Philadelphia bar who wrote, in 1950 and 1951, about legal points and testimonials, some involving the FTC and some not. Simon argued that the use of testimonial ads was a well-accepted practice which, from the early days of patent medicine through to when he was writing, had seen an increasing use of endorsements from public people. The buying and selling of testimonials, he felt, was then a well-organized business adjunct of advertising, with most such ads paid for, and "carefully controlled and handled through specific channels and techniques." He wondered whether such a situation gave rise to correlated duties or responsibilities. Cowboy star Gene Autry lent his name to a boy's garment, the "Gene Autry Cowboy Suit," which proved to be flammable. A child wearing it was severely burned. As a result a lawsuit was brought, then pending in Utah, against the store where the suit was purchased as well as against Autry himself. It was said to be the first case of a consumer attempting to hold an endorser liable for damages as a result of the association of an endorser's name with a product that proved defective. That case, said Simon, raised many questions.[10]

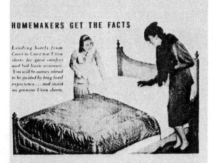

HOMEMAKERS GET THE FACTS

WHITE SALE TIP FROM HOTEL RECORDS
Utica Sheets Still In Use After 260 Launderings
...Equal To More Than 10 Years Normal Home Use

FREE "SNOWY" Picture Book

Hotel executives endorsed bed sheets in 1940.

Simon also argued that certain studios indicated that endorsement ads obtained better readership than any other types of advertising. "It has been shown by a Starch study of a few years back that the use of testimonials of celebrities, as against those of comparative unknowns, is effective in obtaining more thorough readership," he said. However, he warned that the FTC inveighed against "garbled and fictitious endorsements" and had an opinion of the U.S. Supreme Court to back it up. In many proceedings and stipulations it was said to have put a stop to the use of "fictitious" testimonials or "the exaggerating and garbling of those authorized." Simon also mentioned the 1932 case on paid endorsements lost by the FTC and cautioned: "But beware. One of these days an unhappy competitor is going to bring a falsified, paid testimonial case to the FTC and the outcome should make interesting reading." [The exposure of various falsified endorsements for Camel cigarettes, for example, indicated that nothing such as Simon suggested was likely to happen.] While advertisers had to get signed releases from endorsers those of film stars were more complicated. Film star testimonials had to be cleared through the publicity office of the film studio to which the actor was under contract and contained varied requirements that had to be met by the advertiser. Those covered items such as the size of the actor's photograph, size of type used in the ad for the star's name and the name of his current film, date of use of the ad, approval by the studio of the star photographs used, percentage of the total ad space devoted to the testimonial, and size of the ad. Failure to comply with one or more of those requirements could mean the withdrawal of the release and the resultant loss to the advertiser of a considerable preparation expense.[11]

Fake testimonials were common at the time, with much of the public well aware of the fact. Edwin F. Meier was president of the B. Meier & Son ad agency in 1945. One night at a dinner party, he related, he was razzed about all the famous athletes who endorsed food products in magazines, newspapers and on the radio when they did not actually eat the products. Meier argued that should not matter because if they caused children to eat a good hot breakfast based on some athletes' recommendation (even if the sportsman lied about eating the product himself) that was a positive outcome: "What is to be gained by kidding the champs and exposing their real eating habits in contradiction to their endorsements in newspapers and over the air? It's like telling a child there isn't any Santa Claus."[12]

In 1971 the FTC made another hesitant move in the direction of testimonial ads. It announced it planned to take a broad look at testimonial advertising where the endorsement was based primarily on "monetary consideration" and not personal use, preference, or familiarity with the product on the part of the endorser. A proposed complaint against Amstar Corporation, New York, contended that advertising for its Domino and Spreckles sugar brands falsely claimed they were different from other refined sugars in that they assimilated into the body faster and enabled professional athletes to perform better. Specifically the FTC referred to television and radio commercials in which the National Football League and Major League Baseball both endorsed the brands as their "official sugar." According to the Commission's proposed complaint, all ordinary refined sugars, including Domino and Spreckles, were essentially identical in composition and food value, consisting almost entirely of sucrose. Regarding the endorsements, the FTC said the sport groups had not selected the brands as their official sugar because of "superior quality and nutritional value, as represented, but because they were paid by Amstar." Referring to this case but speaking in more general terms, Robert Petoskey, director of the FTC's bureau of consumer protection, said it might be necessary for the FTC to "rethink the whole endorsement question" and possibly "develop guidelines." The agency was said to be concerned about "confusion" among adults as well as children because of the frequency of testimonial advertising, mainly on television. "The new interest in testimonials is understood to center on truthfulness and whether the spokesmen use or are authorities on the products they boost," concluded a media report. "Also, as in the Amstar case, there is the question of payment over familiarity with a brand and its uniqueness or lack of it."[13]

Nothing happened with the proposed Amstar complaint. Still, the FTC worried as seemingly more and more celebrities endorsed products on the air and in print. Finally, near the end of 1972, it proposed to do something about them. It issued a set of guidelines for endorsement ads that had the aim of avoiding misconceptions in those ads. Even the trade press described the FTC action as "not radical, just guidelines." Those proposed guidelines applied to all media and required advertisers, among other things, to disclose financial payments for endorsements and to require a relationship between the expertise of the celebrity and a product he was promoting. But, it was explained, when the endorsement was just

Seven famous athletes representing five sports touted cigarettes in this 1947 ad. Cigarette makers were always the ones who used endorsers the most. Left to right, bottom row: Lloyd Mangrum, Ted Williams. Second Row: Sid Luckman, Stan Musial, Nat Holman. Top row: Bobby Riggs, Adolph Kiefer.

"I like the taste of..." or something like that, "there would be no prob-lem." Interested parties had until March 1973 to send comments on the proposed guidelines to the FTC. Spokesmen for the advertising industry generally declared those guidelines "as avowing principles already in exis-tence in various advertising codes." There seemed to be a consensus that if the guidelines were made permanent, there would be no radical change in advertising practices. In a further weakening move, the Commission emphasized the proposed guidelines would not constitute rules; violators would be litigated on a case-by-case basis. "Advertising using celebrities who endorse a product because they like its shape or color or taste would not be considered violative," explained Gerald J. Thain, assistant director of the FTC's Bureau of Consumer Protection, "since the public is aware that they are being paid." According to the FTC, celebrity endorsements were taken more seriously by the public as the judgment of a broader group, rather than that of an individual, and that such endorsements were sometimes believed to imply that definite standards for the product had been established and met. A reporter noted that some organizations and associations had advocated more stringent control for endorsement adver-tising.[14]

Nothing came of those proposed guidelines, but in May of 1975 the FTC issued new proposed guidelines, this time applying only to television and radio ads. As issued, the proposed guidelines required anyone endors-ing a product in a television or radio ad to be an actual user of the prod-uct, and the commercial could remain on the air only as long as the endorser continued to be a user. Also prohibited were endorsements of drug products by laymen.[15]

Raised as an example of how these proposed guidelines worked was a well-known ad from the era that featured football star Joe Namath in an endorsement ad for Beauty Mist pantyhose — did it mean the guidelines required him to wear them if he was to be their endorser? The answer was no, because Namath did not claim to use [wear] them but only to like or admire them. *Time* magazine pointed out that the television and radio networks, in fact, already required that celebrities have at least some asso-ciation to the products they endorsed, as did many advertising agencies, with the implication being that the guidelines would change nothing. One example of those existing standards, and of how to meet the proposed guidelines of an endorser having to use the product, could be found in how ad man Jerry Della Femina, who handled the Teacher's Scotch account, dealt pragmatically with the problem. When Groucho Marx, Jimmy Breslin, Mel Brooks, and Tommy Smothers, among others, agreed to appear in Teacher's ads, his agency started sending them two cases of

Scotch a month. For *Time* magazine, in respect to the FTC's proposal, the real question was: "Does anyone care? The hype of advertising works on such a different plane from conventional truth.... It is edifying, perhaps, but hardly necessary that it be literally honest."[16]

Ordinary citizens (noncelebrities) were mentioned less and less often as the focus shifted more and more to the famous. One who still used citizen testimonials was Perry B. Johns, supervisor of Agricultural Advertising for the Caterpillar Tractor Company in 1944. He believed it was unrealistic to expect that many people would give an endorsement for nothing to help sell a cigarette, chocolate bar, or a bar of soap. However, he felt that did not apply to his firm's product, or to any other machines "capable of earning wealth." For around 50 years the Caterpillar concern, and its predecessor companies, had consistently used testimonials in its advertising and sales promotion program. The unsolicited letter from customers, he said, was welcome "if unexpected," but usually dealt too much in generalities to be of any use in Caterpillar advertising. They wanted testimonials that dealt in hard figures, in dollars and cents of operating costs and income, and so on. So they sent each tractor purchaser a Performance Report that asked for the specific facts desired,

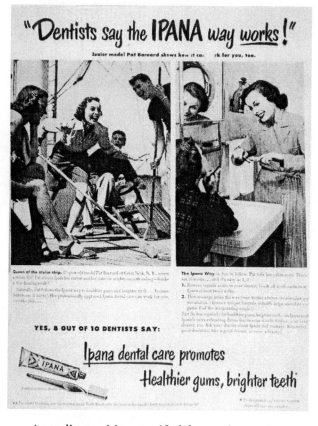

An ordinary citizen testified for toothpaste in 1949. Using ordinary citizens as endorsers had the advantage that no expense was involved for the firm. However, the worry was that they were not very effective in selling a product, perhaps no better than non-endorsement copy.

such as fuel costs, number of hours of operation per season, "and other such items around which we can build an informative display advertisement" Johns believed that Caterpillar had achieved a worldwide reputation for using only honest and accurate testimonials and "that non-purchased testimonials given by owners as a result of customer satisfaction are of much greater value than hired puffs of wind (not to mention the ethics of this issue)!"[17]

Conrad F. Stuhlman was with the St. Louis ad agency Krupnick & Associates in 1948. Over time, he felt, the style of the testimonial ad had changed. In the old patent medicine days the content of the endorsement message was of prime importance. It mattered little whether the endorser of that time was famous or obscure, while in 1948 it did not matter so much what was said as who said it; the effectiveness of the testimonial was pro-

portionate to the fame, prestige, or popularity of the testifier; "the closer this person comes to being a popular and respected public figure, the greater the value of this association" between product and shill. For example, when Prestone anti-freeze was first put on the market, it encountered considerable skepticism from the public because it was new and unfamiliar and people did not know if it was safe and effective. According to Stuhlman, "All those doubts were swept away by a campaign on the use of Prestone by Admiral Byrd on his first Antarctic expedition"—to protect his motorized equipment. Other examples he cited for using the "prestige" endorsement technique were the Parker Pen's Hands of Famous People series and the Calvert liquor "Men of Distinction" series. Although that latter series contained some film stars, most of the endorsers

Actor Ralph Bellamy for Lord Calvert whiskey, 1947. This alcohol maker tried to inject some snob appeal into its ads by featuring very well-dressed actors and business executives in their "Men of Distinction" series. The ads were made to look like portraits of CEOs that might be found hanging in corporate boardrooms.

were high-ranking executives of U.S. companies. All endorsers in that series were dressed in expensive suits and posed as though they were CEOs sitting for an official company photograph. No text was used.[18]

Stuhlman had recently run a prestige testimonial campaign himself for one of his clients, the Bank Building and Equipment Corporation of America (a designer and builder of banks). He decided he wanted bankers as shills because bankers were representatives "of that class of successful professional and businessmen whose names make the best 'who' testimonials." His advice to anyone contemplating a similar prestige campaign was to first of all make a list of names of desired endorsers and go after the biggest name first, even if it involved a trip across the country. Best results were obtained, he explained, by planning to get the first half dozen through personal contact. "With these secured, the balance frequently can be obtained by mail, because you can then show the biggest names in the profession or business are already committed." Also advised was that little information be given out in the phone calls or letters setting up those personal meetings and to "give the impression you are personally traveling all over the country just to secure the cooperation of one dozen or two dozen persons of his caliber." One was also advised to carry a layout or dummy of the ad to the meetings so the prospect could see exactly how it would look because "Their greatest concern is having their names used in a way to enhance their prestige." At the first interview Stuhlman advised telling the prospect that you would prepare the endorsement statement for him and submit it for approval. He emphasized that an already prepared statement not be submitted to the prospect at the first visit (even though it in fact was ready) because "you want to give your prospect the impression that you are studying his individuality and preparing a statement to suit his particular personality or experience. This obviously makes it impossible to write a statement to appear over his name until you have had some contact with him." The mere offer to write the statement for the prospect could mean the difference, he stressed, between success and failure in getting him to sign up.[19]

With respect to the subject of compensation for those prestige endorsers, Stuhlman argued that each case had to be studied individually: "Obviously some form of compensation is necessary, for you cannot approach busy name men and ask for a chunk of their valuable time without offering some special inducement. Nor can you offer to pay them outright for what you want. That smacks of bribery, and in most cases it would utterly defeat your purpose." He felt the best compensation was to offer them something special, "intrinsically valuable and so rare that they cannot readily obtain it elsewhere." For the series of banker endorsements the agency offered each endorser, a large scratchboard portrait of the banker with a brief extract from the endorsement letter. Those portraits were made by Sanford Rubir of Chicago, said to be one of America's finest scratchboard artists, and cost $300 to $400 each. The framed original was presented, free, to the banker. Stuhlman claimed that when he sought out these prestige endorsers he received one turndown for every three acceptances.[20]

One of the largest testimonial campaigns by an individual company was conducted by the Personna Blade Company just after the end of World War II. It was a year-long campaign that featured famous personalities Bing Crosby, William Bendix, Bert Lahr, Guy Lombardo, Gary Cooper, Xavier Cugat, Fred Allen, and Dorothy Lamour (the first time a woman had been used in a razor blade ad), to name a few. Those celebrity ads appeared in eight national magazines and in 197 newspapers, with a total circulation of 30 million, published in 185 cities.[21]

In 1948, several years after President Franklin D. Roosevelt's death, Eleanor Roosevelt teamed with her daughter, Anna Boettinger, in a five-a-week program for ABC Radio. She was on the broadcast twice weekly. Later, her son Elliott sold *Tea with Eleanor* to NBC-TV. Friends from show business, politics, the international diplomatic corps, and so on dropped by to chat with her on the air. Her assignment as a radio/television spokeswoman for Lever Brothers' Good Luck margarine came in 1959, three years before her death. Reporter Maurine Christopher commented that "some critics, such as my old friend Jack Gould of the *New York Times*, were horrified to find the 'First Lady of the World' in margarine ads on CBS-TV, NBC-TV and CBS Radio." Gould found the sight of Roosevelt "raising her eyes to the camera and linking her concern for the world's needy with the sale of a food product at a retail counter disquieting in the extreme." Although Gould excused her for a rare "lapse in judgment," he lambasted Lever Brothers and the agency involved, Ogilvy & Mather, for "taking advantage of her." Roosevelt, who had also appeared in print ads for Otarion hearing aids, said, in explaining her decision to be an endorser, that she wanted a television platform to talk about world hunger. At that time, said Christopher, writing in 1984, many successful, highly paid, in-demand actors in Hollywood and on Broadway criticized fading stars for "lowering" themselves to take commercial endorsement contracts. Roosevelt's appearance as endorser "helped puncture that hypocritical hot air balloon. Laurence Olivier and other theatrical luminaries can thank her for clearing the way for them to accept lucrative commercial assignments without shame."[22]

In the late 1940s and early 1950s it was generally understood, wrote

A society couple got married, thanks to Woodbury soap, in 1948. ("Her blonde-satin beauty is a tribute to the care of Woodbury Facial Soap.") By this time the fad for society endorsers had just about run its course.

journalist Susan Murray, that a television star's image had to be consistent with the image of the sponsor's product to successfully initiate viewer identification with the item and a desire to purchase a specific brand. Also, a star had to exude an honesty or "naturalness" that would engender trust in the audience. George Burns acknowledged the dual responsibility a star had when acting as a product spokesperson: "[Gracie and I] don't try to kid people, but we never forget we're supposed to sell Carnation milk. We make every effort to do it as honestly as possible. If we don't sell the product, we don't have a show." Hal Davis, a vice-president at the Kenyon and Eckhardt ad agency, warned in 1954 that "people will buy products pushed by personalities they like" and stars who refused to deliver commercials "won't be around long." During this period performer Arthur Godfrey was consistently cited by radio and television advertisers as one of their favorite pitchmen. Dozens of popular and trade press articles during the late 1940s and early 1950s, said Murray, acknowledged Godfrey's unique ability to generate unprecedented revenue for CBS and his sponsors, bringing the network about 12 percent of its overall revenue at one point.[23]

By 1952, Godfrey was producing 9.5 hours of live daytime and primetime television a week, on four separate programs, all of which ran simultaneously on CBS, to a total weekly audience of 40 million. His sponsors included Chesterfield cigarettes, Lipton tea, Pillsbury, Nabisco, and Lever Brothers, while his approach in his programs "was to enmesh the project of selling into his persona." Some observers thought that Godfrey's joking about his sponsor's products was the central factor in his believability as a product spokesman.

In another example of an incongruous pairing, screen tough guy Humphrey Bogart touted an air conditioner in 1952.

Humphrey Bogart

SLEEPS COOL

with a low-cost Fedders Room Air Conditioner in his bedroom!

HUMPHREY BOGART
starring in
"THE AFRICAN QUEEN"
Color by Technicolor
Released thru United Artists

SLEEP COOL in the hottest weather! This compact, handsome cabinet ... a real electrically refrigerated system ...sits on your window sill, plugs in like a radio. Cools and dehumidifies the air, filters out dust and pollen. Helps hay fever sufferers ... keeps room cleaner. No building alterations, no water connections. Exclusive twin evaporators offer more cooling power ...more comfort for you. Mail coupon today for facts.

New attractive window model in stunning Hawaiian Tan, from $229.95. Easy terms.

fedders
A GREAT NAME IN COMFORT

FREE! MAIL COUPON TODAY!

105

Murray felt that "Godfrey's viewers responded emphatically to his disavowal of blind participation in commercial process (even as they were purchasing many of the products he recommended)." Prior to Godfrey, Fred Allen was said to be even more outspoken in his criticism of American commercial culture. During the 1930s and 1940s on his radio show Allen acted as the perpetual outsider, attacking almost every aspect of the industry in which he worked. "Yet, even though an avid critic of commercialism, he was still able to move a sponsor's product," said Murray. "In part, by employing self-referential humor that poked fun at the sponsor's product without denigrating it."[24]

The automobile industry built its best known celebrity/brand relations with the arrival of television. Ford's Lincoln and Mercury brands were paired with Ed Sullivan for nearly a decade; it was a linking that made

In a logical match-up of endorser and product, superstar Marilyn Monroe testified for cosmetics in 1952.

something of a celebrity of Julia Meade, who delivered the spiels. Sullivan and Meade made routine appearances at the sponsor's annual corporate pep rallies and appeared, sometimes, as sidebars in the firm's print ads, although print and television were usually separate spheres as far as car advertising was concerned. When Texaco stopped sponsoring television legend Milton Berle and the *Texaco Star Theater* in 1954, it became the *Buick Berle Show* and reportedly carried the automaker to the largest sales in its history. Bob Hope united on television with Chrysler in the late 1950s and early 1960s. Chrysler's DeSoto division sponsored Groucho Marx on *You Bet Your Life* for years, while

Lawrence Welk and Dodge were paired for more than a decade. Reporter John McDonough remarked that the protocols were always the same, with the star mentioning the product and perhaps participating in the commercials, "but only within the context of the program, rarely if ever on a spot basis. No kept celeb could fraternize with the competition."[25]

McDonough reported in 1958 that singer Gordon MacRae, a big star in movie musicals, was offered a pair of DeSoto cars by Chrysler if he would appear in a couple of filmed commercials. The deal also provided for him to get 1959 and 1960 models when they came out. Happy with the deal, MacRae accepted it, apparently having forgotten the half-hour television special he had coming up for Oldsmobile later that year. When the DeSoto commercial hit the air, the issue of "sponsor conflict" arose and MacRae lost both the upcoming special and his $10,000 fee. In addition, he lost another $100,000 in slated guest appearance fees that were canceled. Reluctant to sponsor a Chrysler presenter, Lincoln-Mercury canceled a season's worth of MacRae guest shots on Ed Sullivan's *Toast of the Town* program and Oldsmobile canceled him from Patti Page's variety hour, *The Big Record*. Linked from 1951 through 1961 were Dinah Shore and Chevrolet with the slogan "See the USA in your Chevrolet," becoming one of the more famous closing lines in television history. Greg Taubeneck, an executive with the Leo Burnett Company ad agency, explained that pairing by saying: "Dinah was the embodiment of American values. It was such a natural tie between her personality and Chevy." He added that the selection process was simple then: "I want everybody to like my car, so find me a celebrity whom everybody likes." Another well-known auto match, in the 1970s, was actor Ricardo Montalban with Chrysler. He appeared in both television and print ads and declared in those ads that Chrysler's Cordoba had "rich Corinthian leather," while no one, said McDonough, "bothered to mention that there was no such thing."[26]

Athletes became more important as endorsers in this period, especially from the late 1950s onward. A fictional treatment of the subject appeared earlier, in the 1940 movie *Knute Rockne: All-American* (Pat O'Brien played the legendary Notre Dame player and coach). In the film, a businessman offered Rockne the coach $10,000 a year — very big money in those days— to endorse a new liniment to be called Rockne Rub. However, the coach tossed the offer into a wastebasket because he would never trivialize his sport or cash in on it.[27]

Toward the end of 1959 it was reported that endorsements by sports stars amounted to a gross of about $250,000 a year for the players, with athlete agent Frank Scott accounting for over half of that total (he got 10 percent of the endorser's fee). Scott had recently lined up baseball star

Mickey Mantle, football's Johnny Unitas, and seven other athletes for a Post cereal promotion; signed baseball's Casey Stengel to promote Skippy peanut butter, and arranged a television commercial in which New York Giants (football) Kyle Rote and Frank Gifford shilled for Colgate shaving cream. *Newsweek*'s account noted that sports endorsements were not new on the American scene. Under the management of Christy Walsh, for example, Babe Ruth lent his name to more than 100 products, ranging from breakfast cereal to underwear. But, except for the superstars, continued the report, the practice of athlete endorsements did not really blossom until Scott (a one-time road secretary for the New York Yankees) got into the act in 1950: "Since then, manufacturers of everything from cigarettes to cement products have scrambled to sign athletes." Deodorant makers, however, were said to generally avoid player endorsements. "It sort of makes you think of smelly locker rooms," explained Scott. At that point Scott reportedly had more than 90 big-name athletes in his stable. When Milwaukee's Lew Burdette pitched and won the seventh and deciding game of baseball's 1957 World Series, Scott netted the hurler $15,000 for endorsing such products as Camel cigarettes, Washington apples, and Colgate shaving cream. Don Larsen, of the New York Yankees, who pitched the only perfect game in World Series history, cashed in with endorsements (Camel cigarettes and Gillette razor blades, among others) to the tune of $25,000, all off the fame of that one game.[28]

Film icon Elizabeth Taylor endorsed candy in 1953. Later, when she had weight problems, the image of a candy-consuming Taylor became the butt of jokes.

Two years later, New York Yankee star Mickey Mantle was said to have endorsed a considerable number of products, ranging from Camel cigarettes to an antismoking pill called Bantron. Reportedly, Mantle led both baseball leagues in amount of endorsement money received, but his business agent would not reveal the exact sum. A couple of weeks earlier the FTC had advised the Yankee slugger to stop endorsing one product he admittedly did not consume: the milk marketed by Mid-West Creamery of Oklahoma. Oklahoma-born Mantle quickly agreed.[29]

Gay Talese reported in 1961 that Frank Scott then represented 60 baseball players, as well as an unspecified number of athletes from other sports. Some years earlier, when an Associated Press photographer caught Mantle blowing bubblegum in centerfield, some used the photo as evidence that the player was immature, not too bright. Turning a disadvantage into an opportunity, Scott called up the Bowman Bubble Gum Company and sold them Mantle's endorsement of their product for $1,500. "There's absolutely no limit to the amount of outside money big-name professional athletes can make," said Scott, "provided they're hot." In explaining how he entered the business, Scott related that part of his old job as road secretary for the New York Yankees was to check on the availability of players who were being sought as banquet speakers, television guests, or product endorsers. Sometimes when a Yankee player received money for one of those functions, the player asked Scott if he had been paid enough. But Scott did not know the answer, as there were then no standards to go by. "Sometimes the players received no money at all for endorsements—only some of the sponsor's products," recalled Scott. Soon thereafter he left the Yankees and founded Frank Scott Associates. "I never guarantee them a dime," he said, "I tell them only that I will represent their interest in negotiating off field deals and that they must sell themselves on the playing field if we're going to make any money off of it." Still, Scott's business did not really thrive until Mickey Mantle's superstar season of 1956. That year he got the slugger about $70,000 in endorsement deals (for a pancake mix, Lifebuoy soap, Ainsbrooke pajamas, Wheaties, and Viceroy cigarettes, among other products). Except for Mantle and New York Yankee Roger Maris, who commanded the highest endorsement fees of all athletes (the pair engaged in a highly publicized home run derby in 1961, with Maris breaking the long-standing mark established by Babe Ruth), Scott had established prices that were described as fairly rigid. If one of his client's won the Most Valuable Player award, then Scott demanded a minimum of $1,500 per endorsement on a maximum one-year deal; should his client have a good season, no less than $1,000; should the baseball player have a so-so season the minimum demanded was around $750. As for Mantle and Maris, Scott believed that each of them, coming off that record year, had the potential to make as much as $500,000 in endorsement deals over the following three years. Mickey Mantle, Roger Maris, and Yankee teammate Whitey Ford had just done an endorsement ad for Big Yank trousers, and received $5,000 each.[30]

In the summer of 1969, an article in *Forbes* reported that personal endorsement was the single most important source of outside income for many celebrities. Southern California football star O.J. Simpson, who was then holding out for an estimated $650,000 a year from the Buffalo Bills, was expected to make $500,000 on endorsements before he played his first professional game, according to his manager, Charles Barnes. Chevrolet alone had signed Simpson to a $250,000 testimonial deal. Barnes got 10 percent of Simpson's player contracts and 20 percent of his endorsement deals. Sports Headliners, Barnes's company, managed eight other sports figures, including football's Johnny Unitas and auto racing's Mario Andretti. In 1968 the sport of baseball itself—Major League Baseball (MLB)—hired Kinney National's Licensing Corporation of America (LCA) to sell its name to advertisers in a project that was hoped to generate $1 million over the coming two years; 33 percent went to LCA. Doing the same thing was the U.S. Lawn Tennis Association (USLTA). It hoped to generate $200,000 in the first year. LCA struck a deal to have the USLTA name on a new line of Uniroyal tennis shoes. In return Uniroyal paid a royalty of 5 percent of the wholesale price, half going to the USLTA, half to LCA. By then American Sugar had the MLB logo on its Domino sugar packages.[31]

Writing in *Sports Illustrated*, also in 1969, reporter Frank Deford declared that athletes had risen to a position of eminence in the testimonial world. Steve Arnold, one of the founders of Prosports, Inc. (an endorsement-arranging company), said the athlete provided recognition and image. "For most people the athlete is still the all–American boy. Actors, on the other hand, are actors, and there is the suspicion that they are always acting," he explained. "That's the last thing you want when you hire somebody to endorse your products. The athlete provides sincerity." So hot were athletes becoming that people rushing to sign them up had no knowledge of their situations. When football star Y.A. Title was at his peak with the New York Giants, a woman representative of an ad agency called up an agent and asked if Title would appear in a hair tonic commercial. Title was bald. Another new entry in the endorsement-arranging business was Lois Holland Callaway, Inc., led by George Lois—it was an ad agency that had branched out. One campaign Lois conducted was for the hot breakfast cereal Maypo. The campaign was said to have probably utilized more of the nation's best athletes than any other advertising effort. "The ads require that our greatest he-men must cry for Maypo," wrote Deford. "This gimmick has raised Maypo sales more than 10 percent." Willie Mays was initially skeptical about doing the ad because he thought it might damage his image. Professional athletes used in that campaign included: Willie Mays, Don Meredith, Mickey Mantle, Wilt Chamberlain, Oscar Robertson, Johnny Unitas, Ray Nitschke, Gil Hodges, Tom Seaver, and Carl Yastrzemski.[32]

Deford admitted that the black athlete did not do nearly as well in the testimonial field as did his white counterpart. "To this day Frank Robinson has never been approached for a national endorsement. Jim Brown did not get one until 1965, his final season," he wrote. "Less than 1 percent of Bob Gibson's outside income derives from national endorsements. Heavyweight Champion Joe Frazier has never endorsed a product." One exception to that generality was O.J. Simpson, whose aforementioned $250,000 deal with Chevrolet was one of the largest athletic endorsement contracts ever.[33]

That endorsement money was then going to more players than in the past was accounted for in large part, thought Deford, by the growth of the player agent, who aggressively sought and pursued such deals. In 1964, when Steve Arnold was acting as a lawyer for an ad agency, he went to negotiate with a top football quarterback for a commercial. He hoped to sign the famous athlete for something slightly under the several thousand dollars that had been budgeted, for a project that involved a couple of hours work on the part of the endorser. Arnold asked the player what he considered fair. "Does $100 an hour seem too much?" was the response. When Arnold returned to New York, he told the story to another young lawyer, and the pair formed Pro Sports, Inc. Even then few athletes who were approached turned down the testimonial deal. Basketball player Bill Bradley was one who had always refused. Nevertheless, only a relative handful of pro athletes could expect to make much money from endorsements because so few athletes had a high recognition factor. Commented George Lois, "On the other hand, the rare athlete who does gain a universal reputation is better known than any movie star or politician."[34]

Stuart W. Little reported in 1970 on an expansion of the testimonial business in general, with talent agencies such as Creative Management Associates and the William Morris agency having set up commercial departments while sports agents had also rushed into the field. In the case of sports figures, he believed there was a correlation between the popularity of the sport on television and the amount of money a player could command for endorsements. Golfers were reported to be the highest paid endorsers in sports. Arnold Palmer, in addition to numerous other inter-locking commercial activities, had a long-term contract with United Air-lines. Jack Nicklaus had a long-term deal with Eastern Airlines. Top stars such as those two derived most of their incomes from testimonial activity. The day after baseball's New York Mets won the World Series in 1969, an ad appeared in the *New York Times* announcing the availability of pitcher Tom Seaver and his wife, Nancy, for product promotion. According to Frank Scott, for a player at the top in any sport, such as an Arnold Palmer or a Johnny Unitas, television endorsements could mean an additional $25,000 to $125,000 a year, while for the "quick cash-in" or fleeting star — such as a World Series hero — it could mean anywhere from $5,000 to $25,000.[35]

Chuck Barnes, president of Sports Headliners, Inc., majored in economics at the University of Southern California. After graduation he worked for a time at Firestone Tire and Rubber, where he was employed in the public relations department. As one of his duties he helped set up some golf tournaments sponsored by Firestone, and learned how much money some golfers got for endorsing golf clubs and balls. That gave him the idea to merchandise race car drivers. Barnes felt those drivers had a certain advantage as endorsers over everybody else in sports. An O.J. Simpson could endorse a football, shoulder pads and helmet, but then you had to get him into other areas that were not traditionally associated with being a running back. "But with a fellow like Mario Andretti," he explained, "if you go from the front of his car to the rear and from the top to the bottom, you're talking about thousands of products that are directly involved in the way he makes his living." It meant, Barnes added, that someone like O.J. Simpson could expect to make perhaps $125,000 a year from endorsements, but for race car drivers it was more. His aim, he said, with respect to his clients, was "to double a player's dollars through wise use of his name and fame." As of late 1971 his roster included Johnny Unitas, Simpson, Calvin Hill, and race car drivers Mario Andretti, Bobby Unser, Al Unser, and A.J. Foyt.[36]

In a 1973 piece, *Time* magazine wondered if U.S. men actually bought the products endorsed by sports figures. According to Manhattan's Alan R. Nelson Research, Inc., the answer was no. After questioning 2,500 men on the product-promoting talent of 192 sports figures, the company concluded consumers were far more likely to trust endorsements by less flamboyant personalities. Ranked one-two-three in the "trustworthiness" category were Stan Musial, 53, who had not played for the St. Louis Cardinals in ten years; Mickey Mantle, 42, retired for five years from the Yankees; and New York Mets manager Yogi Berra, 48. Best known sports personalities were, in order, retired baseball star Willie Mays, football's Joe Namath, and ex-heavyweight boxing champion Muhammad Ali. But when asked which athlete's endorsements respondents would trust most, they ranked Mays 31st, Namath 156th, and Ali 190th, out of 192. Nelson Research concluded that an athlete's potential success as an endorser depended not on his skill or fame but on his "likeability" by the public. And what the public appeared to like, argued Nelson, was "the quiet, comfortable, old-shoe personalities— not the abrasive or swinging types."[37]

When a reporter visited the U.S. Open tennis tournament at Forest Hills, New York, in 1974, he was struck by all the endorsements by tennis stars he had seen there, for rackets, balls, clothing, suntan oil, cameras, luggage, airlines, and so on. Tennis star Rod Laver was reported to have some 50 separate endorsement deals.[38]

Endorsement fees received by non-sports celebrities included the following: around 1960 the Old Crow whiskey company offered novelist McKinlay Kantor $2,500 to sign a paragraph praising their liquor. Kantor declined, saying he liked the whiskey "but had a prejudice against signing his name to another man's words." Author Robert Ruark had no such qualms and signed up in place of Kantor. In 1969, entertainer Edie Adams reportedly got nearly $500,000 in cash and stock from Cut & Curl, Inc., over the following five years for lending her name and image to a string of beauty salons and beauty products. Television personality John Cameron Swayze (television shill for Timex watches) received $60,000 plus stock options worth an estimated $15,000 to endorse Robot-guard, a telephone alarm security company franchiser. Actor Orson Bean spent three days of intensive shooting, taping 18 spots for Wallachs Clothes, and received $25,000. Raquel Welch spent five hours in 1970 in a New York studio videotaping a commercial for Motorola televisions. Said Stuart Little, "For introducing herself, for wearing the red dress, for walking up to the Motorola model, and for speaking her two lines of dialogue, Miss Welch was paid between $30,000 and $40,000."[39]

A study of the sales influence of endorsements that were stamps of approval from organizations (such as the Good Housekeeping seal of approval) was made by *Good Housekeeping* magazine. It was based on 2,459 personal interviews conducted nationwide with women between 15 and 65 years of age and done in December 1944 and January 1945. Respondents were asked if, when they read about such seals or saw them on packages, they felt they were influenced by them; 62.4 percent said yes, 36.7 percent said no, 0.9 percent did not answer. Disclosed by the survey was that women in the 20–44 age bracket and in the upper income groups were most influenced by such stamps of approval. Respondents were also asked which such seals of approval they could think of — no prompting was given, no checklist provided. Good Housekeeping's seal led with 47.5 percent naming it, don't know was second at 37 percent, American Medical Association was third at 10.9 percent, the U.S. meat stamp fourth with 2.6 percent, and the American Dental Association was fifth at 2.1 percent.[40]

Ethical aspects of testimonials were rarely mentioned in this period. One exception occurred in 1948, when the National Better Business Bureau issued a bulletin, "The Use of Testimonials in Advertising." It argued there could be no valid endorsements unless they conformed to the eight principles and standards set forth in the bulletin. Those principles were: (1) an endorsement must be genuine; (2) it should represent the "honest and sincere" opinion of the testifier; (3) the author should be competent and qualified to express an opinion; (4) the testimonial should contain no "misstatement" of fact; (5) it should reflect the current opinion of the author; (6) any extracted portion of an endorsement should fairly represent the "spirit and content" of the complete testimonial; (7) endorsements that were purchased should meet the same test of good faith as "free-will" testimonials; (8) when photographs of professional models were used to illustrate testimonials, that fact should be stated in the ad.[41]

Corey Ford produced a hilarious satire for the *New Yorker* magazine in 1949, mocking the number of endorsers on the go in the previous year. At his mythical meeting of the Endorsers' Club, Ford said, of the Lady Iris Mountbatten, that "she said that for years the advertising pages of the American magazines have represented a virtual 'Social Register' of all the best people and that nobody is anybody today unless his or her photograph has appeared alongside a cake of soap or a box-spring mattress, or a corn plaster." Lady Mountbatten went on to remind the membership to be mindful of its inherent responsibility in shaping the tastes of the lower classes.[42]

Effectiveness was another aspect of testimonials that was only rarely touched on. Monroe Dreher, president of the Monroe F. Dreher, Inc., ad agency, argued in 1953 that the testimonial was one of the most effective elements of persuasion. In mail response, he added, testimonials led all other types of approaches (except those offering recipes) in pulling returns through keyed ads. A study by Harold J. Rudolph in the late 1940s was said to have found that endorsement copy ranked first in his read-most index, while a study by Daniel Starch indicated an advantage of from 8 percent to 26 percent in noters per dollar for the testimonial ads over the nonendorsement ads. "Wheaties rocketed to No. 2 position in the ready-to-eat cereal field behind Kellogg's Corn Flakes, on the wings of a testimonial campaign," Dreher explained. "This is the Breakfast of Champions campaign.

Until Wheaties began to obtain and exploit the endorsements of athletic stars, Wheaties was an also ran." According to him, the success of testimonial campaigns had been documented in studies by Starch in graphs showing such things as the lead held by testimonials over no testimonials. Another survey, a continuing one by the Newspaper Publishers Association, was said to further support the effectiveness of well-known personalities in attracting readers.[43]

When Daniel Starch completed a magazine study of endorsements for Endorsements, Inc., he concluded the results reaffirmed the findings of previous studies—that celebrity endorsement ads were seen and read on average to a much greater extent than nontestimonial ads. Analysis was conducted on ads in five consumer magazines (*Collier's, Life, Saturday Evening Post, Look,* and *Ladies Home Journal*) over the period 1951 to 1953. One hundred endorsement ads were matched with 100 nonendorsement ads on variables such as size, color, and so on. "Both well-known and lesser-known celebrity testimonial ads produce on the average a much higher noted and read-most score than nontestimonials," concluded Starch. "The closer the celebrity is pictured in relation to the product, the higher the read-most scores."[44]

Ronald Reagan's brother Neil was commercials production head at the McCann ad agency in Los Angeles in 1962. Neil had the assignment of handling the television program *Death Valley Days* for Borax and needed a spokesman. Ronald was a likely choice since he had just finished eight years for General Electric in that capacity and as a speaker to GE employees. After making test ads, Neil ran them against several existing commercials for Borax before a panel of women brought in for the test. The only commercials those women wanted to talk about, recalled Neil, in 1981, were the Ronald Reagan ads. "It's true and I'll say it again. Those women told us that not only would they buy anything from him, but that they'd vote for him, and we hadn't even asked them that."[45]

Regarding the psychology of testimonials, Dreher felt people took the word of someone whom they trusted before making a purchase: "As a rule, there is a natural reluctance to acquire something with which we are not familiar, and a familiar person who vouches for a product renders a definite service. The likeness of an admired celebrity confers a mark of approval on an advertisement — wins confidence for its contents." For Dreher, possession of the endorsed item formed a sort of subtle connection with that personality. He also argued it was well established that there was a desire on the part of the average reader to identify himself with the image observed, and the more easily that was achieved, the more effective was the advertisement. More ad readers, he continued, could identify themselves with a baseball player than a diplomat, more with a movie star than a great musician. Important in the testimonial area, Dreher declared, was "the endorsement counselor"— the middleman. In linking celebrities with products, "the endorsement counselor maintains a sixth sense in out-guessing that fickle damsel, Fame." Concluded the ad man: "Multi-faceted and awe-inspiring, the testimonial is a valuable adjunct to the advertising profession, and the fine edge of its integrity should not be blunted by heavy-handed use."[46]

As the testimonial ad industry limped along over this period, it seemed to have become stuck in a rut, in a minor role within the advertising world in general. But a few signs emerged late in this period to indicate that might not remain the case; a slight increase in endorsement use seemed to be visible by the beginning of the 1970s, and the fees paid to endorsers rose significantly through the 1960s. Also, more middlemen worked the area. Athletes in particular seemed to benefit from these changes more than any other group of endorsers. Then, starting about 1975, a real endorsement boom got underway, a boom that has continued up to the present.

6

Testimonials Boom in the Modern Era, 1975–2003

Have name, will huckster. —*Saturday Evening Post*, 1980

The celebrity is the message. —*Forbes*, 1986

Most celebrity ads are preposterous, with no reason for being. Most of the guys who make them don't know what a consumer looks like. —Steven Levitt, 1985

As a bit of Madison Avenue wisdom has it: if you have nothing to say, have a celebrity say it. —Stratford Sherman, 1985

I never said a thing about the product.... You never hear me say "Eat a Dorito and it'll make you beautiful." —Mario Cuomo, 1996

After a long period in which endorsements in advertising maintained a low profile — playing a relatively small role in advertising overall while drawing only minor media attention — things changed suddenly and dramatically as the testimonial field experienced a renewal and rapid growth, beginning around 1975. Reflecting that boom was the television situation. Late in 1974 business reporter James Forkan reported that no less than 64 performers on the television networks' new and returning series and specials had worked in or were then doing commercials. More than just a source of extra income, those commercials were also said to be a way for performers to stay visible to the public, and to producers who might want to use them in the future. A year later Forkan observed that some 70 actors then in network prime time television programs were doing testimonials. Confirming the count of 70 plus for 1975, another journalist commented that once upon a time having a celebrity appear in a print ad or on a television commercial was uncommon enough to guarantee some visibility but that in recent years advertisers were finding it increasingly difficult for their well-known testifier to stand out in a sea of "celeb clutter."[1]

In a 1977 piece Forkan explained that actors belonging to the American Federation of Television and Radio Artists (AFTRA) and the Screen Actors Guild then earned more than $100 million yearly from their work in television and radio commercials. About $25 million of that total was from radio spots alone, according to an AFTRA source. However, there was no breakdown as to how much of the total dollar amount went to stars, lesser television regulars, and the "neutral presenters" who specialized in commercials (actors unknown to the public except from ads—that is, not celebrities). Non-star union members could make several thousand dollars in a year's time for one television spot (depending on the number of times it was broadcast, and so on), while celebrity fees for such a spot often began at $100,000 a year. Forkan said that no fewer than 150 stars and regulars on network series had done commercials or print advertising. Of those, by his estimate, 80 were featured in 44 prime-time series that season, while another 40 appeared on the three networks' specials, mini-series, and made-for-television movies. "As for the established tv stars, none of them need be ashamed of commercials work," concluded Forkan, "since movie colossus John Wayne took his Duke-size headache to the great outdoors for Datril 500 and stage demigod Laurence Olivier almost lost his majestic cool over the 'breathtaking' color of the Polaroid SX-70."[2]

Further evidence of the growth in testimonials came in 1976 from the trade publication *Advertising Age*, which had taken it upon

"IN TODAY'S BUSINESS CLIMATE, I COULDN'T SURVIVE WITHOUT THE WALL STREET JOURNAL."
JAMES J. CASEY, PRESIDENT, EDDIE BAUER, INC.

"For over sixty years, Eddie Bauer has outfitted customers to function in all kinds of rugged wilderness environments. And for years, I've seen to it that Eddie Bauer, Inc. can function in another kind of rugged environment, thanks to The Wall Street Journal.
"I depend on the concise information and thorough background The Journal gives me every business day. The remarkably accurate economic forecasts that appear in The Journal make it the most important source I have for reading the future economic picture. I might easily wander into difficult terrain without The Journal to guide me.
"That's why, whether I'm in my Seattle office or out field-testing new equipment, I read The Journal every business day. It's the most important piece of survival gear I've got. With the possible exception of my Eddie Bauer goose-down parka." **THE WALL STREET JOURNAL.**
All the business news you need when you need it.
Subscribe today, call 800-345-8540 except Hawaii or Alaska, PX 800-662-5180. Or write: 200 Burnett Rd., Chicopee, MA 01021

Yet another example of any expert endorsing an item, in 1984. Even the background was geared to reflect what might be exected for the CEO of the Eddie Bauer company as the ordinary folk were again urged to emulate their "betters."

itself to develop a kind of Oscar for the advertising celebrity performer field, or as they called it, a Star Presenter of the Year. Following a review of the field, the editors selected actor Karl Malden for the first Star Presenter award. Malden won for his commercial work with American Express Travelers Cheques. He topped what was said to be a long list of celebrities who were evaluated on the basis of credibility, persuasiveness, sales effectiveness, image and "merchandisability." The actor was then in the third year of a three-year contract with Amex. In the opinion of *Advertising Age* editors, "Mr. Malden dominated by coming across as a forceful presenter without overshadowing the sales message." And "he manages, in his few wrap-up seconds on camera, to blend sincere concern with his lawman image" simply by wearing the hat he used as Det. Lt. Mike Stone on ABC-TV's *Streets of San Francisco*. He emerged as an "authority figure" that was presold to the more than 20 million weekly viewers of that series. Sales of the traveler's cheques reportedly had risen every year since Malden had begun pitching, and he had just signed on for three more years.[3]

Before Malden signed on with American Express he got a call from his agent with the firm's offer. But the actor told his agent that he did not do commercials. "And then," explained Malden, "he quoted the figure and how much work it would involve and somehow I just feel anybody would be a fool if he didn't do it." Initially American Express wanted him to wear his Mike Stone coat and hat, and to shoot the ads in front of a police station. The indignant actor replied by asking them if they wanted to use Stone or Malden. A compromise was reached: he wore the hat but not the coat and the ads were shot in front of the American Express building.[4]

When the editors of *Advertising Age* announced their second annual Star Presenter of the Year, in 1977, the recipient was football star and actor O.J. Simpson. He ranked highest on the same five traits that Malden had topped a year earlier. Specifically, Simpson was recognized for his advertising and promotion work for RCA's Hertz Corporation, Tree-Sweet Products, plus endorsements for Acme Boot Company's Dingo Boots and Hyde Athletic Industries' Spot-Bilt athletic shoes. Since 1968, when he left the noncommercial world of college football to turn pro with the Buffalo Bills, Simpson had been a national advertising spokesman for General Motors Chevrolet Division, Foster Grant sunglasses, Schick shavers, Royal Crown Cola, and PepsiCo's Wilson Sporting Goods. Hertz cited consumer surveys that showed a 23 percent increase in awareness for the Simpson commercials, a 41 percent increase in unaided recall, and a 35 percent hike in the firm's rating as the "best" car rental agency. In the opinion of reporter Louis Haugh, "Whatever it takes to be a superstar, O.J. seems to have it. Acclaimed in the sports world for his speed, he's now gaining ground in the performing arts as he has on the gridiron. And as an ad spokesman, he has boosted product sales."[5]

Bill Cosby was named Star Presenter of the Year for 1978, particularly for his work for Del Monte, Ford Motor Company, and General Foods' Jell-O. A year later James Garner and Mariette Hartley were named joint winners for their television commercials for the Polaroid Corporation. Over the years Garner had received numerous offers, but none he felt he should accept. A brewer wanted him to do a beer commercial, but he declined since he did not drink beer. Another time he rejected an offer simply because he did not like the product.[6]

Rodney Dangerfield was selected as the *Advertising Age* Star Presenter for 1983, especially for his work on the long-running Miller Lite beer campaign, for Sterling Drug's Lo-Sal antacid tablets, and for a Pilot Pen campaign. Over the years other Star Presenters have included Wilford Brimley, 1988; Bo Jackson, 1989; Ray Charles, 1990; John Cleese, 1991; Candice Bergen, 1992; and Michael Jordan, 1993.[7]

Other evidence of an increasing use of celebrities in testimonials could be found in articles that mentioned who was not doing endorsements— virgins, as they were sometimes referred to in the trade — a list said to be small and shrinking. In 1975, *Harper's* contributing editor Barry Farrell mentioned that two stars in that group were Paul Newman and Marlon Brando, who both reportedly saw nothing but compromise in tying themselves to a product.[8]

A few years later the editor of *Advertising Age* listed Newman, Robert Redford, and Richard Widmark among the decreasing list of celebrity holdouts. Dick Reibold, an executive with the Motivators, a Los Angeles-based celebrity advertising packager, had done a survey of prime-time television spots and found that some 60 percent of commercials featured name talent.[9]

Steve Pinkus was a talent agent in 1986 who worked with ad agencies in signing up celebrities for commercials. In the world of testimonial ads, he believed, nobody was unreachable "because money talks." He added that "if you're in touch with what the person believes, and the money is right, you shouldn't be ashamed to go to anybody." However, Pinkus did make an exception to that rule for holdouts Barbra Streisand and Bruce Springsteen because "it's just a matter of their image of themselves."[10]

One place American celebrities were popular was in Japan. In 1986, at least 30 Western actors, musicians, and sports stars were advertising Japanese and foreign products on television in Japan, with most of them earning between $300,000 and $600,000 a year. For the biggest celebrities, such as Sylvester Stallone (Kirin beer), Paul Newman (Nissan), and

Madonna (Mitsubishi Electric), the payoff was closer to $1 million a year. As early as 1970 Charles Bronson showed how effective U.S. stars could be in Japan when he appeared in a series of highly successful hair tonic television commercials. Foreigners were then used primarily to introduce unfamiliar products. "The easiest way to transmit the Western style of life was to use foreign personalities," recalled Akio Nakamura, a manager in ad agency Dentsu's creative department. As a result, Kirk Douglas drank instant coffee in Japanese ads, Orson Wells sipped whiskey, and Alain Delon modeled men's suits. More than half of all television commercials in Japan reportedly then used shills immediately recognizable to the public, said to be a much higher ratio than in the United States. Said Barrington Hill, the Tokyo-based vice-president of McCann-Erickson Worldwide, "It's cheaper to spend money on a major talent than on additional TV exposure." He added that "in this country, if you have unknown people marketing your product, you're going to lose."[11]

Mitsubishi Electric reportedly paid $650,000 for the right to use fragments of Madonna's "Virgin Tour" rock video in a Japanese television ad for its videocassette recorders. After that ad debuted in May 1986, sales of Mitsubishi's VCRs doubled in the coming three months while the sales of competing products rose only 15 percent. Reportedly the highest endorsement fee to that date went to actor Faye Dunaway. On behalf of Parco, a Tokyo department store, Dunaway spoke six words in English, for which she was paid $900,000. Those half-dozen words were; "This is an ad for Parco."[12]

Ten years later reporter Stephen Rae observed that American visitors to Japan were often startled to find big-name celebrities on billboards and in television ads; Sylvester Stallone hawked canned meat, Arnold Schwarzenegger pitched noodles and vitamins, Charlie Sheen promoted Tokyo Gas, Sigourney Weaver shilled for Nippon Steel. Stars that Rae felt people would not believe would do those ads— Jodie Foster, Woody Allen, Paul Newman, and Richard Gere — all did them, with contracts that started at $1 million for a single ad. According to journalist Jeff Jensen, the film studios wanted their stars to do the ads because it boosted their visibility in the Far East: "Increasingly, the market for films is global, and the more recognizable the star, the better the picture will do in the Asian market." The studio and the celebrity both benefited.[13]

With the increase in celebrity testimonials came a parallel rise in articles about the ethics of the area and opinions pro and con. One of the first to comment was author Russell Baker, who recalled in 1975 that he still remembered "the sorrow and dismay" with which he first saw actor Edward G. Robinson selling coffee in television ads. Although that had been several years earlier, the memory persisted, perhaps, said Baker, because "it was a cultural milestone of the modern age." He viewed it as a fall from grace because "the great people of the world simply did not hawk consumer goods on television in those days." But with the increase in celebrity endorsements, Baker worried, ironically, that we were approaching "a time when an invitation to perform in a sales pitch will be the most distin-guished accolade American society can bestow on its citizens."[14]

More openly satirical was another article that year. Writing in the *New Republic,* Roger Rosenblatt mentioned the large number of celebri-ties, and the products they endorsed, that he and his family encountered as they went about their lives. When the children asked mom and dad why they always bought products recommended by celebrities, Rosenblatt explained it was because celebrities were famous. In an article that was a bit less than a page in length he mentioned some 40 celebrities: Joe DiMag-gio (Mr. Coffee); Catherine Deneuve (Chanel cologne); Lee Radziwell (a Korean hotel); Chuck Connors (Speed Queen washing machine); Peter Duchin, Margaux Hemingway, Miles Davis, the Duke and Duchess of Bed-ford, Andy Warhol, Carol Channing, S.J. Perelman, and John Lindsay (Air France); Karl Malden, Mel Blanc, and William E. Miller (American Express traveler's cheques); Paul Lynde and Rod Serling (National City Bank); Joe DiMaggio (Bowery Savings Bank); Lorne Greene (Alpo); Mark Spitz (Schick razor); Catfish Hunter (Ford trucks); Ricardo Montalban (Cor-doba cars); Domenico Modugno (Volare cars); Rex Harrison (Aspen cars); Yul Brynner (Lauder's Scotch); Dinah Shore (Chevrolet); Tom Seaver (Sears clothing for men); Joe Namath (Hanes pantyhose); Allen Ludden (a private school); O.J. Simpson (Hertz car rental); Dick Butkus, Rosey Grier, Mickey Mantle, and Whitey Ford (Lite beer); Andy Griffith (Ritz crackers); Bill Cosby (Jell-O); Bing Crosby (orange juice); Danny Thomas (Maxwell House coffee); Bill Russell (long-distance phone calls); and Julie Eisenhower (an embroidery kit).[15]

Harper's contributing editor Barry Farrell remarked in 1975 that so many celebrities were then doing testimonials that no longer were any stars show business innocents. "I used to be," he added, "but I grew up around the time that Willie Mays quit baseball to become a full-time armpit. Now I am beyond embarrassment or shame." Farrell argued that endorsements would be better seen for what they were, confessions of per-sonal greed by the testifier, and that the public would be better served by seeing every endorsement as a "useful little fiction" that did not reflect the tastes of anyone involved. "For while the false enthusiast is merely turning a well-paid trick, the person who actually believes that his status as the lead-ing actor in the English-speaking world or the top rebounder in basketball makes his personal choice of a flea collar a matter of public concern is suffering from serious delusions and is someone the law should punish, not reward," he concluded.[16]

When Lloyd Kolmer of Lloyd Kolmer Enterprises (a middleman firm that brought celebrities in contact with advertisers and their ad agencies) talked about celebrity virgins, he used the term in a slightly different way. For him, a virgin celebrity was one who had not done any endorsement ads on television, although he may have done print ads. Virgin celebrities were said to be in demand because their credibility was high. Among that group he counted, in 1976, Jimmy Stewart, Kirk Douglas, and Glenn Ford. Using a celebrity to promote too many products was wrong, argued Kolmer, because the person's credibility went down with every commercial. Over the years, he continued, actors' perceptions of commercials had changed, with endorsements being a source of income actors could not afford to pass up: "It may have been an embarrassment to do commercials 15 years ago, but not now." Ten years earlier, $100,000 was the top price a superstar could expect for doing an ad, but by 1976 that maximum fee stood at $1 million for celebrities in the A-list. Clint Eastwood and Burt Reynolds were described by Kolmer as "untouchables," with Reynolds said to be an actor who "will not do advertising for any price right now." Carol Burnett also then vetoed all ad offers and had turned down $1 million to do a Jell-O campaign. Although the William Morris Agency had signed actor Steve McQueen to do a Suzuki campaign in Japan "for a huge fee," Kolmer advised the Japanese ad agency involved, Dentsu, to "stop offering such unrealistic sums" before they got out of hand in that country.[17]

Maxine Marx, casting director at the New York–based ad agency Cunningham and Walsh, and daughter of Chico Marx, remarked that the use of celebrities in ads boiled down to whether or not an advertiser client was oriented toward spending a great deal of money for a big name. In her opinion the star pitchman was not worth it, except under extraordinary circumstances. She felt celebrities were fussy about what products they associated with and tended towards beer, wine, automobiles and corporate image. Marx mentioned a high fee of $250,000 but said that many stars were willing to appear in spots for a price ranging from $25,000 to $150,000, depending on whether their careers were waxing or waning. Stars could do a good job for a particular kind of commercial, she felt, although she did not define it, but other than that it was a waste of money and unknown actors could be employed at scale wages who could do the job just as well.[18]

Not concerned with the rise in product endorsement, or with the ethics of the issue, in 1977, was the *National Review*. It argued that people did not care much about the issue one way or another: "Like professional wrestling, everyone knows it is phony; and nobody appears to care. Laurence Olivier can move from playing Coriolanus, and disdaining the imperfections of human nature, to shilling for Polaroid: so what?" The situation could be summed up as follows: "Art is for hire."[19]

Helen Van Slyke had been a creative vice-president at an ad agency but left Madison Avenue around 1972 to become a successful novelist. Five years later she delivered an address at the annual meeting of the Association of National Advertisers in which she was critical of advertising for its lack of originality and for its reliance on the celebrity endorsement personality cult. "In some cases it works. In more, it does not. Why on earth should I bank where Joe DiMaggio tells me to? Just because he's rich? He's an ex-ballplayer, not a financial genius, as far as I know," she explained. "Andy Griffith does not motivate me to buy crackers, or Angie Dickinson vermouth. I don't believe they care about those things anymore than I think Duke Wayne ever has a headache, even though he's touting its remedy."[20]

More and more articles commented on the celebrity boom as the 1970s neared an end and it became apparent that a boom was indeed underway and that it would last for some time — that it was not just a sudden spike that would disappear as quickly as it surfaced. When *Business Week* asked itself in 1978 why there was a boom, it talked of an intensifying competition for consumers' attention and a proliferation of new products. According to one study it mentioned, the number of television spots featuring a celebrity had jumped to one in three from one in five during the previous five years. Demand for stars had grown so much in just a few years that several new firms in the "celebrity brokering" (middlemen) industry had opened. Commercially active stars like Bill Cosby reportedly made from 25 percent to 33 percent of their annual income from ads. Along with that trend to more endorsement ads was a decline in the number of virgins. With superstars like John Wayne succumbing to big advertising dollars, the stigma of making commercials had waned. Just one month earlier, Steve McQueen, a longtime holdout in the U.S. despite his previous ad work in Japan, announced he was willing to make commercials for $4 million. However, his asking price was so high that no one expected any takers. It was acknowledged that no firm using celebrity endorsers could directly relate sales performance to the star's efforts, but all seemed convinced the effort and extra expense did pay off. Great Western Savings & Loan Association in Los Angeles, which paid John Wayne $350,000 a year for ads that appeared in California only, claimed it saw an "immediate and dramatic" influx in savings when the Wayne campaign began in December 1977.[21]

Writing in 1979, business reporter Ainsworth Howard declared the boom had started five years earlier, when large numbers of celebrities started showing up in television commercials. Fees paid to endorsers were said to total $10 million a year. According to a study done by the research firm Gallup & Robinson in 1972, one in six television commercials featured a celebrity. Paul Lambert, of Lloyd Kolmer Enterprises, said, of the boom: "It's incredible. It just keeps growing by leaps and bounds." Lambert stated that no one knew why there was a boom, with some attributing it to a much broader national mania for celebrities, nurtured by a boom in mass communications while others claimed it was due to the rising cost of media advertising, which made it imperative to get more impact for advertising dollars. Still others traced it to a proliferation of almost identical consumer products, making it increasingly difficult for a marketer to distinguish his own brand. What was widely agreed upon, though, concluded Howard, "is that the use of celebrities has been successful in moving many products, sometimes phenomenally so." If fees for endorsers were mostly high, Howard observed that at least the odd company got off "dirt cheap" by convincing celebrities of the value of the exposure they would get by appearing in a commercial. For example, *U.S. News & World Report* magazine paid dozens of celebrities, such as Dick Cavett, designer Diane Von Furstenburg, and Andy Warhol, just $1 each to appear in its well-known ad campaign.[22]

In the movie *The Electric Horseman* Robert Redford played Sonny Steele, a former champion rodeo rider who had signed on as a celebrity spokesman for Ranch breakfast cereals. His duties, including appearances at industry shows and supermarkets, did not suit him, nor did the marketing people he had to associate with. Eventually he opted out and went off in pursuit of a more meaningful life in the wilds of Utah. In real life, as of 1980, Redford remained a refuser (except for public service ads for conservation and other causes). Reporting on the continuing boom, reporter Arthur Bragg related the story of the Olympus Camera firm. In the struggle for dominance among 35mm camera manufacturers, Olympus was an also-ran until it hired Cheryl Tiegs, spokeswoman for Cover Girl makeup and Clairol's Clairesse hair coloring, to also appear on its behalf. After Tiegs signed on, sales of Olympus cameras were said to have increased by 229 percent. At Olympus the decision to use Tiegs was made by company chair Robert Brockway and his aides after they studied a list of 30 celebrities who had "high consumer appeal" (Redford was on the list). Her contract called for $500,000 a year, with extra money for additional duties. Tiegs had recently accompanied Olympus executives on a sales call to the J.C. Penney department store in New York.[23]

With few exceptions, noted Bragg, stars that endorsed were also available to appear at their employers' sales meetings, industry shows, conventions, and so on. American Express had just flown tennis pro Bobby Riggs to New York City to exchange volleys, one at a time, with 30 of the firm's most important restaurant customers. Riggs later appeared at a cocktail party attended by around 100 of American Express's customers. Those events were arranged by Jack Drury, a middleman agent described by Bragg as "one of the hundreds" who specialized in that field. Black & Decker (B&D) used ex–Dallas Cowboy Bob Lilly to speak at its sales meetings as well as to circulate and act as a greeter at trade shows. These duties were outgrowths of the television commercials Lilly did for B&D's circular saws, sanders, and other products. Avis Rent-a-Car System had just hired former Oakland Raider football player George Blanda to lend his name to an internal program for Avis salespeople. Letters over Blanda's signature urging the recipients to exceed sales goals were mailed out. Other sports celebrities who made appearances at their employers' sales meetings and in some cases went on sales calls with them included former New York Yankee greats Mickey Mantle and Whitey Ford (both for American Beauty Macaroni, a Pillsbury subsidiary), the Pittsburgh Steelers' Rocky Bleier (Uniroyal), University of Arkansas coach Lew Holtz (Cory Food Services), former Kansas City Chiefs' quarterback Len Dawson (Indiana Oil Jobbers), Miami Dolphins' quarterback Bob Griese (Catalytic), and ABC-TV sportscaster Keith Jackson (A.B. Dick). Former Dallas Cowboy quarterback Don Meredith, color commentator for *ABC Monday Night Football* and Lipton Tea spokesman, was available for appearances also, at a fee somewhere between $5,000 and $10,000, according to his agent David Burns, president of the Chicago-based middleman firm Burns Sports Celebrity Service. "In fact," Burns continued, "I have 300 stars available, all absolutely willing to make it to a sales meeting or make sales calls with a salesman."[24]

Bragg reported that agents insisted that celebrities were effective at motivating a sales force or getting accounts to sign sales contracts because salespeople and buyers were "every bit as susceptible to their charms as the general public." According to the account there were thought to be over 500 middleman agents representing sports celebrities alone. In offering advice to marketers on how to pick a celebrity, Bragg observed that unless a company could afford to pay extra to sign the celebrity to an exclusivity clause in the endorsement contract the advertiser had to expect to share the name, that is, he would endorse other types of products. A warning was given to avoid stars that "oversold" their names. Another piece of advice was for the advertiser to carefully probe how the celebrity was viewed by the public. David Schwartz, of Consumer Response Corporation, had recently conducted just such a survey. He found the celebrities most liked by the public were; James Garner, Bruce Jenner, O.J. Simpson, and Cheryl Tiegs. Least liked stars were; Cathy Rigby, Suzanne Somers, Farrah Fawcett, and Robert Conrad. Schwartz said Rigby was on that list because respondents were not comfortable with the main product she was associated with — sanitary napkins. For companies that could not afford the often high cost of a full celebrity campaign, there was a low-cost alternative. For $15,000, Dycon International, of Dallas, would find an appropriate celebrity to make a recorded sales talk for a company's product. Dycon then put together telephone lists targeting a selected audience and even furnished a "telecomputer" programmed to dial up to 100 calls per hour. Arthur Godfrey had been used in that fashion by Dycon, "calling" the public to sell a pension plan, and Zsa Zsa Gabor had similarly sold flowers for a Texas florist.[25]

In a humorous, mocking article in the *Saturday Evening Post* in 1980 about how celebrities in all areas were doing testimonial ads, Harry Stein commented, "Me, I got over being shocked years ago — when Sir Laurence Olivier began telling me, using all the skills honed by 50 years of playing Shakespeare, to buy a Polaroid."[26]

Writing in *Black Enterprise* in 1981, journalist Stephen Gale observed that while Bill Cosby was one of the biggest endorsers, he was also one of the few black entertainers who had managed to "transcend" being black. Cosby said, "In this business many of us are well paid but we are not all that wealthy ... remember, everybody takes a cut — the lawyer, the agent, the publicist." He added that "A great bit of our careers depends on keeping ourselves in the public eye. I think performers should take advantage of commercial offers if they're satisfied with the product." Gale argued that although white stars had been in demand for years as endorsers, it was only recently that blacks had been solicited as celebrity shills. As recently as 1971, he said, research showed that many whites had trouble accepting advertising with black spokesmen and that even if that problem had disappeared many advertisers still lived with that fear. Waynett Sobers Jr., an executive with Earl G. Graves Publishing, said there were certain industries that just did not use blacks in their ads or place ads in black media. They did not want to have any black image associated with their product. As a prime example, Sobers cited the fragrance industry — colognes and perfumes: "This is particularly true for men's fragrances, yet studies show that, proportionately, blacks use two to three times more fragrances than whites." New York celebrity broker Lloyd Kolmer remarked that commercials were pretty conservative and that television advertising had stayed behind television itself in terms of morality. "Many companies want no ethnic identification of their product at all because they feel there are only a limited number of black people who don't cost advertisers white business," he stated.[27]

The idea of using show business celebrities and name athletes to advertise financial institutions had also grown in popularity in recent times. Banking industry observer Richard Miller declared that most banks and thrifts that had hired celebrities, such as comedian Bob Hope or baseball star Carl Yastrzemski, reported substantial gains in new accounts and/or public acceptance. Selecting an endorser who had "integrity" was even more important for banks than for other advertisers: they required someone who would present the right image over an extended period of time. An example of such an endorser, one who was a widely used spokesman for financial institutions in the early 1980s, was television's Ed McMahon (announcer and sidekick to Johnny Carson on *The Tonight Show*). McMahon then represented ten banks and thrifts in local markets around the country.[28]

Four years later Miller returned to reiterate that celebrity spokespeople worked for financial institutions. George Burns was then doing ads for United Virginia Banks. For the previous two years Glendale Federal in Glendale, California, had been using Dinah Shore in both print and video as its spokesperson. The bank wanted to build an upbeat image and personality for the institution. Glendale wanted somebody who projected a feeling of honesty and integrity. Research by the Fleet National Bank in Providence, Rhode Island, revealed that character actor James Whitmore was one of the top five people in the country, on the trait of credibility. He had been appearing in the bank's ads for two years. Jackie Gleason was one of several endorsers used in a campaign for MasterCard International. It was reported that Gleason received $850,000 for about three hours' work. The Bowery Savings Bank in New York had used baseball legend Joe DiMaggio for many years, and still did, as of 1986. Great Western Savings was sponsoring a 13-week revival of a campaign that featured John Wayne as the company's spokesman. When those commercials were originally run in the late 1970s they won several awards, but they were pulled when Wayne died. Miller could cite only one failed campaign. A couple of years earlier, at the start of the 1984 Olympics hype, Carteret Savings Bank in New Jersey began to use former gold medal (decathlon) winner and ex-congressman Bob Mathias as its spokesman. However, observed Miller, "Carteret found that not all that many people remembered Mathias— or cared about a Californian speaking for a New Jersey institution." As a result, after several months, the savings bank changed to a different campaign.[29]

Someone not enthused about the celebrity endorsement boom was Sam Kaplan, editorial director of *Beverage World* magazine, who wondered if personalities selling soft drinks were worthwhile. He worried that a lot of money was being paid to these people to sign them up to endorse when all that might be accomplished was "to further promote a prominent entertainer."[30]

One of the longer, negative articles on the boom appeared in 1985 in the pages of *Fortune* magazine. Journalist Stratford Sherman declared flatly that spending to put a famous face in a commercial rarely worked. For one thing, he felt, viewers believed the stars were only doing it for the money. A major objection was that celebrity advertising was not cheap. From Coca-Cola and General Foods Jell-O, Bill Cosby made an estimated $1.5 million in 1985. Back in 1983, actor Alan Alda of the television series $M^*A^*S^*H$ signed an estimated $2 million-a-year deal with Warner Communications's Atari division to pitch home computers. Months after the first commercial went on the air, Warner sold Atari, which dropped the campaign. However, under the terms of the contract, Alda was then still getting paid. Sums of $100,000 or less, reported Sherman, would buy perhaps three days of work by lower-level celebrities such as actor Rita Moreno. But that was just for television commercials; print ads cost extra. To stop the endorser from pitching all other products, competing or not, required an exclusivity contract, and that cost up to three times the usual endorsement fee. In the United States Pepsi-Cola signed deals estimated at $5 million each to get singers Michael Jackson and Lionel Ritchie to appear in commercials.[31]

Another objection Sherman had was that evidence suggested that viewers did not believe what a star said. According to a 1984 survey of 1,000 adult television viewers by the New York advertising and research company Video Storyboard Tests, half of all viewers assumed that celebrities who appeared in ads were just doing it for the money. "Certainly Bill Cosby's claim that he likes new-formula Coke better than the original version he had been touting for four years has come to seem strained," he remarked. Choosing the right celebrity was an art, but according to Steven Levitt, president of Marketing Evaluations, a research company, few ad agencies did it well. Catherine Deneuve had failed for Whitehall Laboratories' Youth Garde moisturizing lotion because women were said to have found her intimidating, while John Wayne flopped for the Datril headache remedy because few people believed he was an expert on headache remedies. Levitt saw so much similar miscasting that he concluded that "most celebrity ads are preposterous, with no reason for being. Most of the guys who make them don't know what a consumer looks like." According to Sherman, U.S. advertising spending in 1985 was $96 billion in total, with

23 percent of that amount going to television. And roughly 10 percent of the ad dollars spent on television then went for celebrity ads. Burton J. Manning, chief executive of the J. Walter Thompson USA ad agency, remarked, "What you get from a celebrity at a bare minimum is audience attention." Some pairings, felt Sherman, were incomprehensible in any other light. Examples he cited were "low-brow" comedian Dom DeLuise for high-tech NCR personal computers and sequined actor Suzanne Somers for Ace Hardware stores.[32]

Cited as virgins by Sherman were Clint Eastwood, Robert Redford, Eddie Murphy, and Walter Cronkite. Jay Schulberg, the top creative executive at the Ogilvy & Mather ad agency, figured that only about one celebrity ad in five was effective. Sherman concluded that celebrity advertising would never be a sweet proposition for advertisers, although the rare combination of the right star, a relevant ad, and "brilliant execution" could yield an effective pitch. "But a celebrity campaign is more likely to be remembered — if it's remembered at all — for its dazzle, not its substance. As a bit of Madison Avenue wisdom has it: if you have nothing to say, have a celebrity say it."[33]

Ties between stars and automakers also strengthened in the boom years. In the old days Dinah Shore promoted Chevrolets; Chuck Connors shilled for Dodge Trucks; Bing Crosby and Lowell Thomas pushed Oldsmobile; Bob Hope spoke for Chrysler; and race car driver Jackie Stewart pitched Ford automobiles. As of late 1987, Audi of America had in its stable rally champion Michele Mouton; basketball player Oscar Robertson, pilot Dick Rutan, and actor Joanne Woodward (all for the Audi 5000). Chrysler had brought back actor Ricardo Montalban after a one-year absence; he had first appeared in Chrysler Cordoba ads in 1974. James Earl Jones provided voiceovers for Chrysler LeBaron ads while Richard Crenna could be heard in Jeep commercials. Professional golfers Chi Chi Rodriguez and Lee Trevino promoted Toyota cars and trucks. Detroit Piston basketball star Isaiah Thomas had been signed to a one-year deal to pitch Toyota vehicles. Fred Gwynne did voiceovers for Hyundai ads. For 1988, Honda replaced actor Burgess Meredith (its spokesman for the previous ten years) with Daniel Travanti, from the NBC-TV series *Hill Street Blues*. James Coburn did voiceovers for Acura commercials, while Mazda continued to use James Garner to hawk its car line. On the other hand, some celebrities had been axed. Buick discontinued its one-year relationship with Hal Holbrook for more product-related advertising, and Oldsmobile limited the use of golfer/spokesman Fuzzy Zoeller in 1988. Chrysler dropped Renault shill George C. Scott and his $1 million-per-year contract when it purchased American Motors. Celebrities who promoted cars could expect to earn from $25,000 to $1 million annually, according to Sandra Joseph, president of the Los Angeles–based talent agency Joseph Heldfond & Rix. And that did not include the free use of a car, a perk often given to the automobile celebrity endorsers.[34]

Early in 1990, a Houston teenager received a life sentence for slaying a 16-year-old. Demetrick James Walker, 17, wanted the $125 pair of Nike Air Jordans that Johnny Bates was wearing on April 1, 1989, so badly that he shot and killed the victim with a pistol and walked off with the shoes. On the day Walker was sentenced, *New York Post* columnist Phil Mushnick likened basketball star Michael Jordan (who endorsed Nikes—and for whom the shoes were named) and other prominent athlete endorsers to drug dealers because they had sold their names and images to the sneaker manufacturers and were taking the marketers' ad money. Reebok International (number two company in the $5-billion-per-year branded athletic shoe market at 23.7 percent; Nike had 24.8 percent), which marketed a $150 shoe, agreed with Nike in arguing that it was unfair to blame the shoe companies. Reebok said it was considering requiring its endorsers to speak to kids about staying in school and about how long the odds were against having a professional sports career. Ted Ewanciw, director of public relations at ProServe, said client Patrick Ewing of the New York Knicks basketball team purposely arranged a sneaker contract with Phoenix Integrated, a subsidiary of sportswear marketer Champion Products, that would price the shoes within kids' reach. "They're going to retail at $50 to $60 a pair because Patrick thought shoes already cost too much and this will send a different message," explained Ewanciw.[35]

So robust was the celebrity endorsement boom that by the mid–1990s it had spread to encompass politicians, to an extent never before reached. Ad writers Andrew Dalsass and Ward Packer were hired by Air France to design a spot promoting the airline's special weekend rate to Paris. Half-jokingly, they proposed putting the Air France pitch over a picture of Bob Dole (this was just weeks after he had lost the November 1996 presidential election to Bill Clinton) waving. Those ad writers had expected that no one — their boss, Air France, or Dole — would go for the ad, but surprisingly they all did. One year after her failed bid for the vice-presidency, Geraldine Ferraro was shilling for Diet Pepsi. Dan Quayle had endorsed Wavy Lay's potato chips, while Mario Cuomo and Ann Richards had endorsed Doritos. Bill Taylor, a then-retired creative director at advertising agency Ogilvy & Mather, blamed himself for starting off the trend to use politicians as endorsers. He was the person behind the "Do You Know Me" campaign for American Express. Taylor broke an unwritten rule of advertising back in 1975 when he used a politician, William E. Miller (Barry

Goldwater's vice-presidential running mate in the 1964 election), in that campaign's most successful spot, Dole said he donated his $3,000 Air France fee to charity. In a 1995 Super Bowl spot Cuomo and Richards (one-time governor of Texas) were munching on Doritos as they packed up her office. Cuomo explained his role thusly: "I never said a thing about the product.... You never hear me say 'Eat a Dorito and it'll make you beautiful.'" Ferraro was considered a little more honest, by reporter Stephen Glass, in explaining that she did the Diet Pepsi ad because she needed the money, but then constructed a defense that included mentioning "she never actually touched the product" in that ad. Glass did not accept Dole's excuse that he gave the money to charity: "Dole's demurral — the fact that he's donating his fee — may be the lamest of all ... playing the spot as a charity stint is insincere. It acknowledges that it's unbecoming for a presidential candidate to turn himself into a shill for an airline, while insisting that donating the money transforms the pitch into a virtuous act."[36]

After the celebrity boom started in the mid–1970s, it remained strong for decades and showed no signs of slowing down as the 1990s neared their end. M.A.C., the trendy Toronto-based cosmetics company, assembled the media to introduce its first celebrity spokesperson. It was RuPaul, the six-foot-three cross-dressing man. Frank Toskan, M.A.C. founder, explained that "She's perfect. And besides, we couldn't find anyone who wore as much makeup." That campaign, with RuPaul saying ironically, "If M.A.C. can make me beautiful, imagine what it can do for you," was enjoyed by some and found offensive by others, but it did gain a good deal of attention. *Time*, the *Wall Street Journal*, and many other publications ran stories about the promotion. Sales of the cosmetics reportedly soared. "These days, everywhere you turn, the rich and famous are selling things. They're putting their names on inexpensive clothing lines in the Wal-Marts and Kmarts of the nation as well as on pricey athletic sneakers and are fronting the entire telepsychic industry," observed journalist Stephen Rae. "Remedies for every bodily ailment imaginable have celebrity spokespeople: Kim Alexis is the public face of hemorrhoids; fifties screen star June Allyson extols adult diapers." It was estimated that 25 percent of all ads used celebrities. Rae also mentioned what he called the star-of-the-day concept. Three years earlier no one had heard of any of the actors on the television program *Friends* yet they then endorsed "everywhere." Pepsi, in a bidding war against Coca-Cola, spent an estimated $10 million for the right to use the cast members — in character — in their soft drink ads. Still, observed Rae, overexposure or the wrong exposure could damage a big star's credibility, as Cher, "the queen of cheesy infomercials," found out. One industry analyst said that appearing in all those infomercials nearly destroyed Cher's acting career. Cher admitted as much when she told *Entertainment Weekly* that the infomercials had been "just devastating to my career." "By and large, somebody with a prominent film career doesn't want to go out and put his or her face on a packaged good or even an automobile," said Charles Cowing, vice-president of the J. Michael Bloom & Associates talent agency in New York City. Doing so, he felt, downgraded the viability of major stars.[37]

When selecting celebrity endorsers, explained Rae, many companies used Q-ratings—an index of a star's commercial value put out by Marketing Evaluations, Inc., a Manhasset, New York, research company. Each year, the company polled 7,000 consumers nationwide on the recognition and likeability of around 1,500 celebrities, whose names were submitted by clients in advertising and entertainment. By dividing the number of people who say a star is "one of my favorites" by the number who said they had heard of the celebrity, a Q-rating (Q stood for quotient, as in IQ) was obtained for each celebrity. Subscribers to the service could also check to see how a certain star rated within certain demographic groups: teenage males, women aged 18 to 34, and so on. Among those with the highest Q-scores in 1997 were Tim Allen, Bill Cosby, Will Smith, and Whoopi Goldberg. Video Storyboard surveyed 4,000 people annually and from the results generated a list of the most believable celebrity endorsers. Ranked high then were Cindy Crawford, Candice Bergen, Michael Jordan, Bill Cosby, Elizabeth Taylor, Whoopi Goldberg, and Jerry Seinfeld. Among those ranked low in believability were Cher, Shari Belafonte, Chevy Chase, and Susan Lucci. Perhaps most bizarre of all in the star-of-the-day field, reported Rae, was the fact that the company Benetton wanted to put Subcommander Marcos, the masked Mexican leader of the Zapatista guerrilla uprising in Chiapas, in an ad; Marcos turned the offer down.[38]

7

Athletes Dominate the Field, 1975–2003

First come touchdowns, then endorsements.
—*Advertising Age*, 1982

He shoots! He scores! He sells!   —*Canadian Business*, 1983

Talent, character, and style: the Nike athlete.
—*Harvard Business Review*, 1992

I'm tired of hearing about money, money, money, money, money.
I just want to play the game, drink Pepsi and wear Reebok.
—Shaquille O'Neal, 2002

No group of endorsers benefited more from the celebrity endorsement boom of this period than did professional athletes. When ad agency Ted Bates & Company was looking for a way to help people remember Hertz Rent-A-Car's new slogan, "superstar in rent-a-car," it did not take long to settle on O.J. Simpson. He signed with Hertz for an endorsement fee widely believed to be $250,000 a year. Television viewers began to watch Simpson dash through airports and leap over baggage to get to his Hertz rental car in the fall of 1975. Two years later tens of millions of viewers had seen the spots, with public awareness of the company reportedly having risen by 40 percent. Hertz said it had broadened its market share over main rival Avis to 14 percentage points in major airports. So successful was that campaign that Simpson was able to renegotiate his endorsement fee a year before his original contract expired. Reporter Nils Howard observed that the use of athletes had increased so much that the 1970s had been called the decade of the athlete in marketing because of the number of companies that had used sports to sell a wide variety of products.[1]

Howard, though, felt some of that claim was exaggeration. David Burns, who formed Chicago's Burns Sports Celebrity firm (a middleman concern) said he got at least one phone call a day from sports agents who wanted to know the chances of their clients getting some fat endorsement contracts. Lately Burns had been telling them, "Almost zero." Lloyd Kolmer, who headed another middleman firm, got a call from the business manager for Mike Thomas, a Washington Redskin running back who was named Rookie of the Year in 1975 by several news agencies. The manager wanted to get Thomas into television commercials. But, grumbled Kolmer, being rookie of the year only meant, "Nobody will even know his name." Said Howard, "The truth is, the chances were never as good as newspaper headlines and the frequent repetition of commercials led people to believe." He felt two or three dozen athletes would get $5,000 to $10,000 each for lending their names to manufacturers of bats, gloves and hockey sticks, but not much more. Baseball players received an average of $600 for posing for Topp's baseball trading cards. Ever since the days that Ty Cobb let the old American Tobacco Trust name a cigarette after him and Babe Ruth lent his name to Quaker Oats, said Howard, the big sports endorsement money had gone to those durable few whose reputations transcend their particular sport, making them celebrities in their own right. "Today the collection of superstars who can routinely command more than $100,000 for a TV commercial numbers perhaps thirty, or less than 1 percent of the professional athletes in the United States," he wrote. For Kolmer the key to success for an athlete endorser was consistency. Faberge was said to not be worried about paying football great Joe Namath $250,000 on an eight-to-twenty-year contact to promote its Brut line of toiletries because it believed Namath would "be around forever." For the same reason, Sears, Roebuck & Company had no trouble justifying the six-figure fee it paid golf pro Johnny Miller.[2]

Back in 1974, before Hertz signed Simpson, research the company commissioned in that year revealed that businessmen, the heaviest users of rental cars, perceived little difference between Hertz and Avis. Other research indicted that what businessmen looked for most in a car rental company was speed of service. Hertz instructed the Bates agency to produce a commercial that would appeal to businessmen and to emphasize speed. Bates came up with the slogan "superstar in rent-a-car," and then went out looking for a superstar. According to Howard, the Bates agency attributed the success of that campaign to, among other things, "a certain flamboyance and credibility that Simpson brought to the job. Those qualities, as much as athletic prowess, mean the difference between a department store commercial in Hoboken and a six-figure national advertising contract." Reportedly, it was widely agreed, for example, that while Simpson had such charisma, Walter Payton, the Chicago Bear running back who nearly outran Simpson for the National Football League rushing title

the previous year, did not. Payton had received few offers to endorse anything, and he had done no commercials except a radio spot for Nutra-
ment, a food supplement for athletes, and a television spot for Chicago
Buick dealers.[3]

In 1973, a New York market researcher named Alan Nelson persuaded
20 national advertisers to contribute around $6,000 each to finance a
research project to discover what American men thought about television
sports in general and about individual athletes in particular. He surveyed
2,500 men across America, using a questionnaire designed to measure how
well athletes were known, respected, liked and trusted. The athlete most
widely trusted and liked turned out to be Stan Musial, superstar first base-
man for the St. Louis Cardinals who had retired ten years earlier. The best-
known athlete was baseball star Willie Mays, out of the sport since 1973.
Yet those qualities, Howard pointed out, did not seem to be sufficient by
themselves to produce an outstanding pitchman, as neither Musial nor
Mays had a very successful career in television endorsements. On the other
hand, Joe Namath, who showed up in the survey as one of the least
admired, least liked, and least trusted of the top athletes, was one of the
most sought-after and most effective shills. After his research, Nelson
offered the following conclusion as a rule of thumb: "If you're dealing with
a mundane product, often the only way you can draw attention to it is to
get some flamboyant athlete spokesman who doesn't necessarily have
trust."[4]

Writing in *Sports Illustrated* in 1977, Melissa Ludtke wondered why
so many athletes, both active and retired, were then doing ads. She concluded that sports television programming, which long had consumed
weekend afternoons, then stretched into prime time. So advertisers, citing the proliferation of sports shows and studies that indicated the growing appeal of athletes as salesmen, were grabbing up star athletes as
endorsers. Joe DiMaggio got $1 million for signing a three-year deal to
become Mr. Coffee. For selling Magnavox television sets for two years,
Henry Aaron, baseball's home run king, received $1 million. In 1975
Namath agreed to lend his name to Faberge for ten years at $500,000 annu-
ally. Ludtke argued that Simpson's race was never an issue for the Hertz
campaign, and "In fact, more and more black athletes appear in advertisements, which 10 years ago featured neither blacks nor athletes." Alan
Nelson had found that the more congenial an endorser appeared, the more
credible he would be as a salesman. Ability on the field was felt to be valuable to the athlete only in gaining the exposure necessary to attract an
advertiser's attention. For example, of the 192 athletes evaluated by Nelson, boxer Muhammad Ali ranked third in public awareness but, because

many people neither trusted nor liked him, finished 190th in commercial appeal. Miller Lite beer then used 16 retired athletes in its campaign because Miller had to comply with a Federal Communication Commission (FCC) regulation that prohibited active athletes from endorsing alcoholic beverages. Miller's use of athletes was said to have helped to increase its annual sales by 43 percent.[5]

Business reporter Dick Reibold predicted in 1979 — erroneously as it turned out — that one trend for the coming years would be less use of famous athletes in ads. One reason he believed that would happen was the huge salary increases athletes were receiving. It meant to him that, whereas in the past an advertiser could have signed many of them for a year for slightly over union scale, by 1979 an advertiser had to talk in six figures with their agents, managers, and attorneys. Many ad budgets, Reibold reasoned, could not cope with that.[6]

Back in the early 1960s, Valvoline decided to go into auto racing with its motor oil. By 1979 Valvoline was the leading motor oil in racing, was number three in off-track use among independent motor oils, and had hundreds of drivers joined to the product, according to Len Manley, advertising and sales promotion manager for Valvoline. Two of racing's biggest names— A.J. Foyt and Mario Andretti — then served as the company's ad spokesmen. Those two were the prime presenters for Valvoline in the United States. Valvoline also supplied complimentary motor oil to hundreds of drivers on the racing circuit. When the drivers accepted the oil, they were also under contract to allow their names to be used in print ads. More prominent drivers worked under personal services contracts and received remuneration beyond free motor oil. The choice of Foyt (used since 1964) and Andretti (1976) was based not just on their driving records, said Manley, but on research that showed they were the top two names in consumer awareness among Valvoline's target audience, males aged 18 to 54. Ron Miller, an executive with Valvoline's ad agency, said one of the challenges in using a driver's endorsement was in convincing the skeptics that a driver could not and would not endorse a product he did not use or believe in. Manley said that 31 of the 35 drivers at Indianapolis that year ran on Valvoline. A driver signed to use one product exclusively within a category but could also endorse a variety of products from noncompeting categories. Product endorsements by drivers were reflected in the product patches to be seen on racing uniforms. In Europe, race drivers then wore emblems for everything from cameras to cigarettes.[7]

The day after Joe Montana quarterbacked the San Francisco 49ers to a 26–21 victory over the Cincinnati Bengals in the 1982 Super Bowl, his personal appearance fee went from $400 to $7,500, one of the highest in

the league. Also that day, observed journalist Robert Raissman, the selling of Joe Montana began. He was felt to have an excellent chance of land-
ing in the legend category of four other notable quarterbacks that went to
commercials. In the previous 15 years those four — Joe Namath, Fran
Tarkenton, Roger Staubach, and Terry Bradshaw — were said to have cap-
tured the minds of people who had no interest in professional football and
to have parlayed their athletic abilities into careers pitching for Madison
Avenue. At his peak Namath made about $560,000 a year off the field (from
endorsements and personal appearances); Tarkenton nearly $700,000;
Bradshaw approximately $425,000, and Staubach about $570,000. The key
for any athlete, according to several agents, was to transcend the audience
for his particular sport and reach the general audience. That was what
attracted advertisers.[8]

On the eve of the 1982 heavyweight title fight between Gerry Cooney
and champion Larry Holmes, the former's manager, Dennis Rappaport
(anticipating a Cooney win), had a concept about how Cooney would be
marketed. He explained that his fighter was not going to be just a
spokesman for a company and then be discarded when his recognition factor faded. "We're going to take small- or medium-size companies, get
equity positions— stock — plus a guarantee against a percentage of gross
sales. He could help them grow from a mini to a mighty," Rappaport
explained. "We want the right of prior approval of the sale of the company, et cetera. That's the route we're going to take." To that point Cooney
had made just one endorsement, a commercial for Norelco razors. Other
boxers had also not been busy. Muhammad Ali was best remembered for
his pitch for a roach killer, after more than 15 years in the public eye.
Holmes had held the crown since 1978, during which time he was involved
in 11 successful title defenses, 10 by knockout, but "no commercials."[9]

Number one-ranked tennis pro John McEnroe won at Wimbleton in
1981 using a Dunlop Maxply Fort tennis racket. By the end of that year
sales of that racket had shot up 170 percent. Dunlop then paid McEnroe
$600,000 a year to use the new Maxply McEnroe racket every time he was
on a public tennis court, even when practicing. Additionally, he made
$300,000 a year for wearing Sergio Tacchini clothes and $100,000 plus per
year for wearing Nike shoes. Doing even better among the tennis players
was Bjorn Borg, whose yearly endorsement fees included $600,000 from
Donnay rackets, $220,000 from Diadora shoes, and $500,000 from Fila
clothes. Borg also endorsed Bancroft rackets in Australia, Jockey clothes
in Scandinavia, and 50 or so nontennis products. Number three-ranked
player Ivan Lendl made $200,000 to $250,000 yearly from Adidas rackets
and endorsed Superga shoes and Adidas clothes, but wore L'Alpina outfits

in Italy and Japan. Jimmy Connors was paid between $100,000 and $200,000 annually by Wilson rackets and $30,000 plus for endorsing Robert Bruce clothes and Converse shoes.[10]

Among the female tennis players, Chris Evert Lloyd had a $1 million multi-year contract with Ellesse Clothes, although she wore G.T.O. in Japan; $250,000 from Wilson rackets; and $150,000 plus from Converse shoes. Tracy Austin received $200,000 a year from Spalding rackets and about $750,000 annually for endorsing Pony shoes and Gunze clothes. Martina Navratilova earned between $200,000 and $250,000 year from Yonex rackets plus unknown amounts from Kim Moda and Spalding shoes. Andrea Jagger got between $100,000 and $200,000 a year from Wilson rackets and also endorsed Fila clothing and Bata shoes. Tennis was said to have become big business when major tournaments began admitting professionals in 1968, but even in the days of amateur tennis, players would wear somebody's clothes and they would be slipped some money under the table, according to player agent Bob Kain of International Management Group. Wilson's vice-president of national racket sports promotion, Gene Buwick, remarked that no company could expect the endorsement investment to come back in terms of added sales or dollars. Rather, he continued, it would probably be judged in terms of the kind of visibility the player would give that company's product and the company itself. Sexism was said to prevail at that time, with more male tennis players doing endorsements than women players, and also getting paid more. "Worldwide, men's tennis enjoys much greater stature than women's. Women's events are not covered as broadly and that's a fact," said Buwick. He added that the bottom line was that "a woman probably sells fewer rackets than a man."[11]

Less than three years later, in 1985, women's tennis was said to be booming, with its two biggest stars being Martina Navratilova and Chris Evert Lloyd. The latter estimated she made $1.2 million a year from tennis tournaments and special exhibitions, but that endorsements brought $1.8 million more. One of Navratilova's many endorsement contracts was with Thorneburg Hosiery Company of Statesville, North Carolina. For around $40,000 a year Navratilova wore and promoted a special padded sock called Thor-Lo. Thorneburg company president James L. Thorneburg said he could not be happier and that "the deal was a bargain."[12]

In Canada in 1983, Lanny McDonald made an estimated $300,000 annually as a hockey player for the Calgary Flames, plus another $100,000 from commercial endorsements. However, the king of Canadian athlete endorsers was Wayne Gretzky. The Edmonton Oiler hockey superstar had a contract with the team that ran for nine years and guaranteed him a total of $8 to $10 million. But as a shill he made around $1.6 million plus in 1983. Athlete testimonials got their start in Canada when Gerry Patterson approached Montreal Canadiens hockey star Jean Beliveau in 1969, two years before the player's retirement. At 38, Beliveau was earning a then huge hockey salary of $55,000 a year. Canada's premier athlete of the time was felt to be the perfect candidate for endorsements, an idea that was gaining popularity in the United States with sports figures such as golfer Arnold Palmer becoming a pitchman. Patterson's first deal was arranging Beliveau's endorsement of International's Pure-Pak milk cartons. "As I expected Jean underestimated his worth in the marketplace," recalled Patterson. "He offered to do it for $5,000. He was surprised when I said, 'Jean, multiply that sum by four.'" Other companies signed him up, and soon Beliveau was collecting $100,000 a year for endorsements. Later Patterson orchestrated deals worth a total of $700,000 for skier Nancy Greene, by having her endorse a variety of products ranging from Mars chocolate bars ($30,000) to a sportswear line ($100,000). By 1983 there were about a dozen athlete managers/endorsement arrangers in Canada. Father of those managers in the United States was said to be Mark McCormack (he took 25 percent of the endorsement fee — high in a field where the agent usually charged 10 percent to 15 percent). He started his International Management Group (IMG) around 1958 when a young golfer named Arnold Palmer asked him to handle his affairs. Palmer's endorsements since then had earned him an estimated $70 million, while McCormack's IMG expanded to 16 offices around the world. In Toronto, IMG's office was headed by Peter Smith. Deciding not to do business with hockey players any longer, Smith sold IMG's Toronto stable of hockey players in February 1983 to Frank Milne's agency in St. Catherines, Ontario. Hockey players were "not really interested in pursuing the big endorsement money," Smith explained.[13]

Wayne Gretzky, in 1983, needed a business manager and two marketing agents to handle the business of being Gretzky. Endorsements were handled by Mike Barnett, who heard from as many as two dozen corporate sponsors a week who wanted to make deals with the superstar. Barnett responded to every request courteously, politely rejecting such ideas as Wayne Gretzky's Down-Home Country-Style Sizzling Hot Chili. Screened out by Barnett were any endorsement proposals that might have tarnished the player's image. A reputable manufacturer of baseball equipment was rejected because of a worry that baseball fans might be offended, explained Barnett, just as hockey fans might grumble if a baseball star such as Pete Rose tried to promote hockey sticks. Gretzky signed on with Nike athletic footwear and thus became the first athlete shown wearing

Nike shoes, although he did not perform professionally in Nike products, as the firm did not make skates. The image, signature, and hockey number (99) of Wayne Gretzky turned up on a variety of household items, many seemingly improbable, from Bic razors to Ultima wallpaper, from Stanford Art mirrors to Lady Sandra bedspreads, sheets and pillowcases. Worried about overexposure, Barnett explained his strategy to minimize that risk, saying: "Over a 13-week period, we make sure that no more than three of our endorsers use TV as their ad medium. Now we hope to have a voice in suggesting the hours when the commercials can be shown." Estimated annual endorsement incomes for some other Canadian superstars were: Steve Podborski (skier, $300,000); Ken Read (skier, $300,000); Gary Carter (Montreal Expos catcher, $250,000); Bobby Orr (retired from hockey, $250,000); John Anderson (Toronto Maple Leafs forward, $200,000); Phil Esposito (retired from hockey, $200,000); Jim Nelford (golfer, $150,000); Sharif Khan (squash player, $100,000).[14]

Evidence of the increasing use of athlete endorsers could also be seen in the fact that by the mid–1980s tennis players, for example, were being used more and more to endorse non-tennis-related items. It was said to be a prime example of how corporations, attracted by the high-income demographics of tennis players and viewers, were using top tennis names as shills. Jimmy Connors had a lucrative contract with McDonald's, and Sandy Silver, director of national marketing at the company, spoke of the player as a "permanent family member of McDonald's." Connors also wore a patch on his shoulder that bore the McDonald's logo and that was visible every time the camera showed him serving. "I'll be honest," said Silver. "It is a free way to get advertising on television," where 30-second network spots during tennis tournaments averaged $30,000. Television executives were reported to not be happy about the patch but felt they were unable to regulate what a player wore. McDonald's had less luck in baseball, where a program to have players wear wristbands with the logo was so controversial with league owners that it was dropped. Silver added, "We go beyond using Connors as a billboard." That is, he visited Ronald McDonald Houses in whatever city he was touring. Although Chris Evert Lloyd had been a spokeswoman for Lipton Tea for four years, her role had been lately increased, according to Lipton's marketing vice-president, Gerald Boycks, who added, "She is learning the tea business," and "there's nothing more natural than iced tea and tennis." Lloyd also did print ads and made personal appearances for Cirrus Systems, whose independent bank card enabled travelers to use the automatic teller machines of 820 member banks in 40 states. Cirrus president Bruce A. Burchfield explained that tennis was a good sport for the market his firm was trying to reach.

"There are two basic markets among business travelers: middle-aged men and younger women. This may sound sexist, but middle-aged men love to look at young women, and the women identify with her." Computer-Land Corporation had just signed up Martina Navratilova, who had agreed to make several ads and to wear a shoulder patch.[15]

Nike sales moved from $14.1 million in 1976 to $867 million in 1983. For 1983, the athletic shoe maker's promotional budget was $26 million plus. Almost half of all the professional basketball players in America were Nike endorsers and wore Nike shoes (135 of the 273 players in the National Basketball Association). Dominance of the $2 billion-a-year sneaker market by Nike was said to result from the company's promotional strategy of paying the athletes highly. Reportedly, that 1983 Nike promotional budget, for example, was around ten times the amount spent on promotions by the top ten (after Nike) sneaker makers combined.[16]

Barely four weeks into his rookie season in 1984 as guard for the Chicago Bulls basketball team, Michael Jordan had drawn a huge audience while improving dramatically the Bulls' winning percentage and generating their first sellouts in three years. Also, he was said to be the cause of cable television ratings for Bulls' games to have increased 20 percent over a year earlier. He was becoming one of the hottest endorsements in pro sports. However, warned Thomas M. Collins, an agent for several athletes both black and white, "Basically, white American advertisers are not looking for black kids." Jordan's contract with the Bulls, a $4 million, five-year deal, paid him about $600,000 for the 1984–1985 season, his first in the NBA. Already he had a five-year $500,000-a-year contract with Nike, which planned to create a new line of footwear bearing his name — a signature shoe for the first time in the company's history. As well, Nike planned to introduce apparel and accessories called Air Jordan. Said David H. Smith, general counsel of Nike's Demand Group: "Jordan is the most exciting player to come into the league in six years or more. I'd like to envision this as a lifetime relationship." (The Demand Group was the division that created demand for company products through advertising, marketing and promotion.) Jordan was expected to sign a three-year deal with Wilson Sporting Goods momentarily, worth $200,000 in total. Although Michael was then just 21 years old, he had 16 suits even then. "Meeting people in the market arena, I feel I should have a business attitude," he explained. Described as genial and soft-spoken and displaying none of the arrogance often found in modern athletic stars, this account predicted he was likely to charm any businessmen and advertising executives he was introduced to. Jordan was only the third pick overall in the previous NBA draft, behind the Houston Rockets' Akeem Olajuwon and the Portland

Trailblazers' Sam Bowie. Drafted fourth was Sam Perkins, then with Dallas. Yet, observed journalist Maria Recio, all of them lacked the charisma that made Jordan an endorsement superstar. During that first professional year Jordan was expected to double his $600,000 player salary from his off-court enterprises.[17]

On October 6, 1993, Jordan announced his retirement from the game [his first retirement]. David Falk, his agent, remarked that Jordan would no longer be seen on a basketball court for 100 or so games a year, "but he's with a group of blue-chip companies that will work to maintain his image around the world." In the summer of 1993 Falk had told those companies that it was time to prepare for the 30-year-old superstar's eventual retirement. Falk then renegotiated most of the endorsement deals—set to expire over the following few years—extending them out ten years, regardless of how long Jordan remained in the game. Guy E. Thomas, Wilson Sporting Goods' marketing director for basketball, commented that "the goal was to try to maintain the public fascination with Michael Jordan for a long period of time."[18]

At the time of that first retirement, Jordan made some $30 million plus per year from endorsements: Nike (basketball shoes, $18 million); McDonald's (restaurants, $3 million); Sara Lee (Hanes, Ball Park Franks, $3–$4 million); General Mills (Wheaties, $2–$3 million); Quaker Oats (Gatorade, $2 million); Wilson Sporting Goods (basketballs, less than $1 million); Chicagoland Chevrolet Dealers (automobiles, amount undisclosed); Electronic Arts (videogames, sum unreported). Reporter Julie Liesse thought his unparalleled success as an endorser could be attributed to the confluence of three items: Nike, seeking to become the world's number one sports company; the NBA, looking for a player to lead it away from near bankruptcy; and Jordan himself.[19]

According to business reporter Jeff Jensen, the Air Jordan phenomenon did not really take off until the late 1980s, when the Bulls began winning playoffs and championships, and when Nike paired Jordan with filmmaker Spike Lee in an ad and Gatorade got America humming with "Be Like Mike." David Falk remarked that "Michael wasn't manufactured; he reached his level of marketability by being who he is and by his play." When Falk shopped his client around as a rookie, he was not looking for mere endorsement deals but long-term commitments to spend media dollars on Jordan and use him as a vehicle to drive sales. Falk acknowledged that companies were reluctant at first: "Such deals were reserved for white athletes in upscale, individual sports, like golf and tennis, not those in team sports—and not African-Americans." Still, some firms saw the potential to sign him to long-term deals. "We wanted to create a slow burn around Michael," explained Scott Bedbury, Nike advertising director. "It was three or four years before Michael Jordan uttered his first words in a Nike spot. And by that time, with the Spike Lee commercials, we had created a myth around Michael but not from Michael."[20]

For 1998, Jordan earned $45 million as an endorser, plus $35 million as a basketball player for the Chicago Bulls. (He had returned to the game and had just retired for the second time, but not the last time.) Rick Burton, director of the sports-marketing center at the University of Oregon, observed, "He's the most amazing endorser ever. He's handsome, articulate, classy. He had a purity to his performance on court and off. It's hard to find the perfect celebrity these days." Jordan made millions for non-sport businesses like MCI WorldCom and McDonald's, and that success reportedly changed the way companies looked at athletes: boxer George Foreman sold mufflers, while tennis star Martina Hingis hawked shampoo. Black athletes were said to have been helped to become used more as endorsers due to the success of the Jordan example. "He helped advertisers become colorblind," said Bob Williams, president of Burns Sports Celebrity Service. Number two among endorsers in 1998 was golfer Tiger Woods, who made abut half of what Jordan took in from endorsements. However, Reebok cut its endorsement roster at that time from 70 players to about 12 — dropping such high profile names as basketball's Shaquille O'Neal and Dallas Cowboy Emmitt Smith. Nike chairman Phil Knight blamed "sports negativism," such as the incident in which basketball player Latrell Sprewell had choked his coach, for hurting business and causing a retrenchment in athlete endorsements. Jordan's 1998 $45 million endorsement total broke down thusly: Nike sportswear, $16 million; Gatorade sports drinks, $5 million; Bijan cologne, $5 million; MCI WorldCom, $4 million; Rayovac batteries, $2 million; Hanes underwear, $2 million; Ball Park franks, $2 million; Wheaties cereal, $2 million; Wilson Sporting Goods, $2 million; Oakley sunglasses, $2 million; AMF bowling, $1 million; CBS Sportsline, $1 million; and Chicagoland Chevrolet, $1 million.[21]

Automotive reporter Laura Clark pointed out the connection in 1988 between cars and golf by mentioning five golfers as doing endorsement ads for automobiles, with an even longer list of 14 golf tournaments sponsored by car makers. That much interest existed, explained Clark, because of the demographics. According to the National Golf Foundation in Jupiter, Florida, the average golfer was 38 years old and earned $42,000 a year. Buick's target buyer, for example, earned between $40,000 and $75,000. Rick Slifka, director of marketing for the Tournament Players Club of Michigan (Dearborn), commented that golf appealed to sponsors also because it was "a clean, respectable sport." When was the last time, he wondered, you heard of a professional golfer being charged with drug use or drunk driving? Also, it was felt to be politically astute for an executive to play golf. An executive could play golf with a senior manager 20 years older than himself, a much less likely prospect with a sport like tennis.[22]

Conflicts sometimes erupted between team rights and individual player rights. Writing in 1989 reporter Scott Donaton mentioned the 1984 conflict between Major League Baseball (MLB) and Steve Garvey's Garvey Marketing Group. In that case, MLB ordered Garvey and some other players to stop wearing wristbands carrying McDonald's golden arches logo, saying the bands were part of the players' uniform. The league feared that if they allowed the wristbands it might open the door to the sale of other parts of players' uniforms to advertisers. There was also the potential conflict of a player wearing the sweatband of one company while one of its competitors was the exclusive sponsor of the team's television broadcasts. The players argued, unsuccessfully, that the bands were not part of their uniforms and to deny them the right to wear the bands prevented them from maximizing their income potential. Such

So popular did athletes become as endorsers that many continued on as testifiers after their career ended, sometimes long after. Former Chicago Bear football star Gale Sayers endorsed this exercise machine in 1984.

conflicts were not new. For example, athletes often appeared in endorsement ads minus their uniforms when the products competed with one of the team's sponsors. Professional athletes appearing at the Olympics had to wear the official clothing and shoes, not the ones they may have personally endorsed. Jordan, for example, had to wear Converse shoes, not Nike. Said Mike Moran, director of media relations for the U.S. Olympic

Committee, "Michael Jordan would be forced to wear, at the opening and closing ceremonies and all media events, the official leisurewear of the U.S. Olympic team. His competitive wear would be chosen by his sport's governing body. For that two-to-three week period, the athlete's sponsors might as well not exist. All individual contracts are moot."[23]

The *Wall Street Journal* estimated that in 1989, advertisers spent over $100 million on endorsements by sports celebrities: more than double the $50 million spent in 1984. Twenty-seven different celebrities (in addition to 31 NFL football players appearing as a group) were used by Coke and Diet Coke during 1989.[24]

Ian Hamilton was Nike's director of tennis sports marketing in 1992. One of his duties involved scouting the junior tennis circuit for athletes with a combination of talent, character, and style. Talent was the most important ingredient for a Nike athlete, he explained, but character was also important. In getting to know the prospects in their early teens, Hamilton had to determine if they were the type of people who would work well with Nike over the long term. Things he looked for included a commitment to the sport, a sense of humor, and "an attitude the public will embrace." Hamilton met the prospects' parents, coaches and agents to decide if a relationship with Nike was in everyone's best interests. According to Hamilton, there were plenty of players who met the talent and character requirements, "but only Nike athletes meet the third: a distinctive sense of style. People expect Nike to perform to a high standard and to make a statement at the same time. Our athletes do the same thing." When Hamilton started at Nike, John McEnroe was the most visible player in the world, already part of the Nike "family." He was said to have epitomized the type of player Nike wanted as one of its endorsers—"talented, dedicated and loud. He broke racquets, drew fines, and, most of all, won matches. His success and behavior drew attention on and off the court and put a lot of people in Nikes." By the end of the 1980s, McEnroe was ready to hand over the angry young man mantle to become more of a tennis elder statesman. That meshed perfectly with the emergence of Andre Agassi, whom Hamilton first saw as a 15-year-old. "From a marketing standpoint, Andre was the perfect vehicle for Nike. Like us, he was anti-tennis establishment and he was different," explained Hamilton.[25]

Touted as the overwhelming choice to take over from Michael Jordan (in the wake of the 1993 announcement of his first retirement) as the top athlete endorser was Orlando Magic basketball center Shaquille O'Neal. He pulled in $8 million as an endorser in his NBA rookie year. Deals with Reebok International and Pepsi brought in a combined $6 million, while contracts with Scoreboard trading cards, Spalding sporting goods, Electronic Arts videogames, Tiger electronics, and Kenner Toys brought in another $2 million in total. According to his agent, Leonard Armato, O'Neal had a wide appeal: "He's like a combination of the Terminator and Bambi — he can rip down backboards, but he also likes to play with kids. He's the kind of person that women love and men don't find threatening."[26]

Even before signing a seven-year $40 million contract with the Orlando Magic in August 1992, O'Neal and his agent Armato went to work. They turned down Nike, choosing instead Reebok's offer to make O'Neal "The Man" (the biggest fish in a smaller pond concept). If Reebok did not spend $50 million over three years promoting its Shaq Attaq sneakers and athletic wear, O'Neal could walk away from the long-term deal. He received royalties based on sales of the apparel but was guaranteed at least $3 million a year. Coca-Cola offered O'Neal a part in its "Always Coca-Cola" campaign, but number two soft drink company Pepsi signed him by offering a package that made O'Neal the centerpiece of his own spots. That deal was worth about $12 million to the player and ran for five years. To generate consistency, Armato had a Shaq logo designed. The logo, along with the name Shaq and the phrase Shaq Attaq, was copyrighted. All O'Neal-related products, from shoes to basketballs to electronic games, contained the logo and paid a royalty to the superstar. "It's like the Mickey Mouse logo," explained Armato. "People know what it stands for." Jordan became synonymous with the "Air Jordan" logo, but it appeared only on shoes and sportswear, and Nike owned it.[27]

Reporter Randall Lane felt O'Neal's persona was a gold mine that was built around a physical image of power combined with a boyish quality. Said Brian Murphy, publisher of the *Sports Marketing Letter*: "As huge as he is, he comes across as a guy with a profound gentleness. There's even a sense of sweetness about him, in the most masculine and commercially acceptable kind of way." Lane argued that as a marketer and businessman Jordan was a basketball player first, earning his celebrity on the court. On the other hand, O'Neal became a celebrity first, lining up major endorsements before he played his first professional game. Other endorsement contracts and books, movies, and music soon followed. "Put it this way: O'Neal was the league's first prepackaged multimedia superstar," he concluded. In the summer of 1993, Reebok, which sold internationally, took O'Neal to Japan, Singapore, Australia, Spain, Italy, and France. Shaq's 1993 income broke down as follows: basketball salary, $3.3 million; Reebok, $3 million; Pepsi, $2.2 million; Scoreboard cards and memorabilia, $2 million; movie salary, $1 million; Skybox Shaq Exchange advance (cards and memorabilia), $1 million; rap record royalties, $500,000; Spalding sporting goods, $600,000; autobiography royalties, $500,000; Kenner action figures and toys, $300,000; Tiger electronic games, $300,000; Electronic Arts videogames, $250,000; Shaq Attaq video royalties, undisclosed; for a grand total of $15.2 million.[28]

Moving on to the Los Angeles Lakers in 1996, O'Neal expressed frustration, in 2002, about the constant questions asked him about his huge $121 million contract with that team. "I'm tired of hearing about money, money, money, money, money. I just want to play the game, drink Pepsi and wear Reebok," he grumbled. That caused journalist Ross Diamond to remark, "That there is still something shocking and comic to our ears about O'Neal's internalization of his paymasters' values is, sadly, probably only temporary."[29]

Saturation celebrity endorsement reached one of its higher levels during the telecast of Super Bowl XXVIII on Sunday, January 30, 1994, when 43 ad spots were aired. Most of the advertisers paid a record $900,000 for each 30 seconds of airtime. Athlete and celebrity endorsers appearing on that broadcast included basketball players Charles Barkley, Larry Johnson, Shaquille O'Neal (two separate spots—Pepsi and Reebok), Larry Bird, Michael Jordan (McDonald's and Nike); model Cindy Crawford; comedians Chevy Chase, Rodney Dangerfield, Steve Martin, Michael Richards; former football coaches Mike Ditka and Bum Phillips; sportscaster Marv Albert (Anheuser-Busch and Nike); actor David Carradine; musicians John Sebastian, Country Joe McDonald, and the Jefferson Airplane; athlete Bo Jackson; and personalities Regis Philbin and Kathie

Basketball star Kevin Johnson endorsed Converse athletic shoes in 1991, as the fad for jock endorsers continued.

Lee Gifford. Actresses Christine Lahti and Linda Hunt were heard, but not seen, doing voiceovers. And a spot aired during the halftime show, in which Dan Quayle ate a Wavy Lay's potato chip, had "the dubious distinction," said an account, of being the first endorsement ad by a former vice-president of the United States. In the opinion of reporter Stuart Elliott, mostly "the celebrities were poorly used." He felt that a lesson Super Bowl advertisers should heed was that the name to emphasize during a commercial was the brand's, not the celebrity's. Including the two who did voiceovers, Elliott counted 23 celebrity endorsers on that telecast, nine of whom were sports or sports-related figures.[30]

A 1994 survey of marketer executives revealed that 75 percent of them were opposed to selling advertising space on baseball players' uniforms on the ground that the game was then overly commercialized.[31]

Tennis star Pete Sampras signed an $18 million five-year endorsement deal with Nike in 1994. Yet, according to author Donald Katz, a year earlier senior Nike executives decided to pass on Sampras because they figured his "bland" and "robotic" style were not big selling points with the public. Nike already had under contract the "equally colorless" tennis player Jim Courier, mainly to offset its other big tennis name — Andre Agassi — whose flamboyance disturbed older consumers. It meant that Nike talent scouts saw Sampras as a needless expense. However, Nike founder and CEO Philip Knight overruled his executives, according to Katz, based on his gut feeling that the three strongest male U.S. players would create excitement.[32]

When Steiner Sports Marketing conducted a 1994 survey of the most sought-after sports endorsement properties, they found the top-ranked people to be, in order: Shaquille O'Neal, Nancy Kerrigan (1994 Olympic figure skating silver medalist who was expected to have three to four years of marketability), Frank Thomas (Chicago White Sox), and Pat Riley (coach of the New York Knicks). Those four were all Reebok athletes, while the men who ranked sixth through ninth were all Nike athletes: Troy Aikman (Dallas Cowboys), Ken Griffey Jr. (Seattle Mariners), David Robinson (San Antonio Spurs), Michael Jordan (Birmingham Barons — he briefly played baseball for this team during his first retirement from basketball). Tenth ranked was Adam Graves of the New York Rangers, the only hockey player to make the list. Although Graves had no endorsement deals at the time, he was felt to have "much potential." Polled for that survey were senior-level marketing executives at 250 American companies.[33]

Research released by American Sports Data in 1994 declared the athletes most influential in influencing consumers were, in order: Michael Jordan, Joe Montana, Shaquille O'Neal, Nolan Ryan, Magic Johnson, and

Larry Bird. Nine of the top 20 most influential athletes for advertising purposes were retired. Those people were: Ryan, Johnson, Bird, Arnold Palmer (number 10); Jack Nicklaus (11); Kareem Abdul-Jabbar (13); Joe Namath (15); George Foreman (17); and Chris Evert (19).[34]

In 1995, an ESPN Chilton Sports Poll surveyed 20,000 people and asked them to name the athletes they would choose for endorsements and the ones they would avoid using for testimonials. Athletes chosen (by sports fans only, less than the full 20,000) were: 1. Michael Jordan, by 25.1 percent of the respondents; 2. Joe Montana, 5.6 percent; 3. Shaquille O'Neal, 5.0 percent; 4. Troy Aikman, 3.8 percent; 5. Emmitt Smith, 2.4 percent; 6. Charles Barkley, 2.0 percent; 7. Dan Marino, 1.7 percent; 8. Steve Young, 1.5 percent; 9. Magic Johnson, 1.3 percent; Larry Bird, 1.0 percent. Athletes to avoid were: 1. Charles Barkley, 8.3 percent; 2. Dennis Rodman, 7.9 percent; 3. O.J. Simpson, 7.8 percent; Michael Jordan, 6.2 percent; 5. Mike Tyson, 5.9 percent; 6. Deion Saunders, 4.1 percent; 7. Shaquille O'Neal, 3.7 percent; 8. Darryl Strawberry, 2.1 percent; 9. Magic Johnson, 1.3 percent; 10. Tonya Harding, 1.2 percent. The list of athletes chosen by the overall population was said to be fairly consistent with those picked by sports fans (for example, Jordan was chosen by 24.5 percent of the overall population). But the list of athletes to avoid differed a little more; number one on the overall list was Simpson at 8.5 percent, with Barkley number two at 7.9 percent.[35]

Another piece of research looked at which of two groups of endorsers had more ad believability: athletes or entertainers. For 1986, entertainers were rated believable by 45 percent of the respondents, athletes by 38 percent. For the following years the numbers were, respectively: 1990, 40 percent, 52 percent; 1994, 40 percent, 60 percent; 1995, 33 percent, 64 percent. According to the results, basketball players almost always outscored baseball and football players—perhaps, thought industry observer Dave Vadeha, because they were not hidden from view under caps and helmets.[36]

On the afternoon of August 28, 1996, 20-year-old golf sensation Tiger Woods held a press conference to announce the start of his professional career. The first Nike television commercials starring Woods started being broadcast less than 12 hours later. By the fall of that year the golfer had two huge endorsement deals. The one with Nike ran for five years and was estimated to have been worth $31.5 million, or more. The other deal was with golf equipment maker Titleist for three years and was worth either $3.5 million in total, or $3.5 million per year. Reportedly those deals made Woods the biggest rookie endorser ever. Nike spent nearly as much to secure Woods as an endorser as its entire golf division generated in sales the previous year. It planned to build a line of clothing around Woods, much as it had with Andre Agassi and Pete Sampras. Being described as young and good-looking with a beaming smile, a natural stage presence, charisma, and so forth, Woods was touted as a prime candidate to become the next athlete endorser superstar.[37]

After the Los Angeles Lakers traded player Eddie Jones to the Charlotte Hornets in March 1999, Nike docked him $300,000 on his endorsement deal. (Details of his Nike endorsement contract became public as part of a lawsuit he filed against his former agent.) As a Laker, Jones played for what Nike called a Group A NBA team, one of the marquee franchises at the top of a three-tiered system the company used to assess the marketing value of NBA players. The Chicago Bulls, Boston Celtics, Miami Heat, and New York Knicks were the other A teams. Jones's deal with Nike paid him $950,000 a year as long as he remained with a Group A team, but that sum automatically dropped to $650,000 when he was dealt to small-market Charlotte, one of 19 league franchises that lacked even the Group B status given to the Atlanta Hawks, Detroit Pistons, Houston Rockets, Philadelphia Sixers, and Seattle Supersonics.[38]

Individual deals continued to escalate upward. Reebok and Philadelphia Sixers basketball star Allen Iverson inked a deal in 1996 for ten years and $50 million. Philadelphia coach Larry Brown once remarked: "the company Allen's with is Reebok, not us." Titleist and golfer Davis Love III signed a deal for the same terms as Iverson's, in September 2000. Basketball star Grant Hill and Fila reached agreement in September 1997 for seven years and $80 million (it was a resigning for Hill). Then Tiger Woods and Nike did a new deal in September 2000 — $100 million over five years. Ex-boxer George Foreman was resigned by Salton (maker of the George Foreman Grill) in December 1999, for $137.5 million over five years. Woods's deal was said to be the largest ever offered to an active athlete (Foreman was, of course, retired). Said Ravi Dhar, a professor of marketing at the Yale School of Management, "There were three people for whom the American public has broad powerful associations: Bill Cosby, Colin Powell and Michael Jordan. Now there are four." Woods was the fourth. Reporter Michael Bamberger said, of the new deal, that the sneaker maker had gotten a bargain: "Tiger's a steal." In May 2000, Nike had just 1.3 percent of the $1.5 billion-per-year golf ball market. Then Woods won several big tournaments using a ball with the familiar swoosh stripe on it. By July Nike's share of the ball market was 2.3 percent and rising. That 1 percent increase translated into a rise in sales of $15 million in those few months.[39]

Working in conjunction with the players' union, the National Football League (NFL) in September 2001 added ephedrine (a stimulant often found in diet pills) and related "high-risk stimulants" to a list of banned substances headed by anabolic steroids. At the same time, the NFL barred players from endorsing companies that made products containing any substances prohibited by the league. Stefan Fatsis reported that "the NFL grew so perturbed a few years ago by Denver Broncos players conducting Super Bowl interviews in hats and T-shirts bearing the logo of supplements company EAS that it banned such attire on game days." By compiling what amounted to a blacklist that incorporated 49 firms, he argued, the NFL had struck back at the growing $1.5 billion athlete-supplement business, and the promotion of it by players. NFL players had been earning anywhere from a few thousand to $150,000 a year hawking supplements — in ads in fitness magazines, through trade-show personal appearances, and by wearing logos during television interviews. A few sports stars reputedly made as much as $500,000 a year pitching those products. Such endorsements were said to be crucial to the companies; those Denver Broncos — including then-retired quarterback John Elway, who was still an endorser — had made EAS famous.[40]

Even though endorsement deals seemed to be sky-high for some highly publicized talent ready for, or in, their rookie year, those deals continued to rise. Eighteen-year-old Ohio high school basketball star LeBron James signed an unprecedented multi-year, $90 million endorsement deal with Nike in the spring of 2003. That was before he was drafted and signed by the NBA's Cleveland Cavaliers, and long before he played his first game as a pro — in October 2003. Other notable first endorsement deals for NBA rookies included: Allen Iverson (1996 deal with Reebok, multi-year, $50 million in total); Tracy McGrady (1997, Adidas, six years, $12 million); Kobe Bryant (1996, Adidas, multi-year, $5 million); Michael Jordan (1984, Nike, five years, $2.5 million); Chantique Holdsclaw (1999, Nike, five years, $1 million — she played in the women's pro basketball league, the WNBA); Yao Ming (1999, Nike, four years, $200,000).[41]

Later in 2003, but still before the NBA season started, endorsement deals signed by James had surpassed the $100 million mark. His contract with the Cavaliers was worth $10.8 million over three years. "I've been around the game for 40 years," said Cleveland coach Paul Silas, "and I've never seen anything like it. It's scary." Sportswriter Jack McCallum observed that James was already "an economic system as much as he is an athlete." Other deals signed by the teenager included a $12 million, six-year deal to endorse Sprite and Powerade, both Coca-Cola products; he also had a $5 million contract with the Upper Deck company. Bob Williams, the president of Burns Sports and Celebrities, remarked that no one had more expectations put on him than did James at that time. Aaron

Goodwin, James's agent, said his firm's accountants handled the young star's money while his marketing people worked on his endorsement deals—three were assigned to LeBron's account. A former high school teammate, Maverick Carter, had been hired by Nike for the sole task of taking care of their high-priced endorser.[42]

British soccer star David Beckham was described by one journalist in 2003 as "more than an icon; he's a brand." Vodafone and Pepsi each paid him £2 million per year for endorsing their products, while Adidas had recently been paying him between £2 and £4 million annually. On top of that, Beckham's team Real Madrid (after his 2003 transfer from Manchester United) paid him £4.2 million per year to play football for them. Beckham was in Tokyo when the transfer was announced. There he reportedly earned £5 million for just four days of work as a shill for auto lubricants, chocolates, and a chain of beauty salons.[43]

8

Legal Points, Government Agencies, Medical Men, and Scams, 1975–2003

The [American Medical Association] endorsement deal was a scandalously bad decision and the organization must get rid of the people responsible for this program.   — Sidney M. Wolfe, 1997

Where was Hollywood when regulators insisted, and respectable marketers accepted, the principle that phony testimonials are beyond the pale?   —*Advertising Age*, 2001

The ad copy read: "Liza introduced us to white rum and soda at an Andy Warhol party," while photos accompanying the 1978 ad showed a trendy couple that explained how entertainer Liza Minelli introduced them to the drink. However, the events depicted were fully fictional. That couple were models Minelli did not know and there had been no Warhol party. Using a twist in celebrity endorsements, the Kenyon & Eckhardt (K&E) ad agency decided to use only the names of the celebrities along with photos of models in imaginary short stories. "Ordinary testimonials don't turn me on," observed K&E executive Steve Frankfurt. With questions raised about the propriety of the method a request was issued by the Federal Trade Commission (FTC) that K&E furnish it with proof that the celebrities actually endorsed the rum. Apparently they did, receiving a fee of from $15,000 to $25,000 for the use-of-name-only endorsement. If their photos had also been used the fee could have been as high as $75,000. K&E chairman Ron Moss explained that "Sure the event depicted by the models is fictional, but the impression the ads give is that the celebrity drinks the product — and they do." At least one celebrity, though, was unhappy. Dick Cavett's endorsement ad featured a model telling how Cavett introduced him to the rum when "we were both in a wacky off-Broadway play in a theater so small the cast outnumbered the audience." Although K&E claimed Cavett had approved the copy, the entertainer returned his fee and asked K&E to withdraw the ad. "What wacky off-Broadway play?" he asked. "The fact that people took something to be true that isn't, disturbs me." Because of the controversy, K&E changed the campaign for the rum. Henceforth the ads were to feature the celebrities' real friends and colleagues.[1]

As of May 1978, in a separate development, some new rules were introduced into the celebrity endorsement field when the FTC announced that henceforth it would try to hold celebrities personally liable for any false claims made in the ads they testified for—and would make them pay out of their own pockets part of any legal penalties that might be assessed against such a company. The first target for the FTC under that philosophy was singer Pat Boone. With daughter Debbie Boone, he appeared on television to claim that all four of his daughters had found a preparation called Acne Statin a "real help" in keeping their skins clear and blemish free. A claim had been filed against the preparation's maker, Karr Preventative Medical Products, Inc., of Beverly Hills, by the FTC, contending the product did not really keep the skin free of blemishes. That month it got Boone to sign a consent order in which he promised not only to stop appearing in the ads but to pay about 2.5 percent of any money that the FTC or the courts might eventually order Karr to refund to consumers. Boone said, through a lawyer, that his daughters actually did use Acne Statin and that he was "dismayed to learn that the product's efficacy had not been scientifically established as he believed." Commenting on the order against Boone, the director of the FTC's Bureau of Consumer Protection warned of "some basic obligations" which other celebrities would be advised to follow in the future if they wanted to avoid the same kind of trouble. A celebrity, said the FTC, had to verify the claims made in any commercial before it appeared, hiring reliable independent analysts to study them if the celebrity had no personal expertise in the subject.[2]

Almost a year after the Boone case, James Forkan reported that some sponsors and ad agencies were being more careful in securing various affidavits from their star endorsers—that is, attesting that they used the products. For their part, the celebrity endorsers were said to be "extremely judicious" regarding getting indemnification clauses in their deals so they could not be subjected to financial penalties, as had happened to Boone, and potentially be out-of-pocket. At that time actor James Stewart was the television spokesman for Firestone Tire and Rubber company. He made sure he learned a lot about the Firestone 721 tire at testing plants.[3]

Somewhat at odds with that account was a piece by business reporter

Marie Krakow, who said that a year after the Boone case it had no effect in the signing up of celebrities. That case produced a minor stir in the field for a time, she conceded, with the only lasting effect being more legal work in the form of indemnification clauses being added to the paperwork. Lloyd Kolmer, of Lloyd Kolmer Enterprises, New York, remarked that he had found the case had not even dented the celebrity buying market. "I just think they're being a little more careful about the kinds of products they ask celebrities to do. Celebrities in turn are being more careful about what they'll do. And everyone's asking for indemnification." Everyone, from ad agencies to the FTC, pointed out to Krakow that the U.S. government went after Boone largely because of the unusual business arrangement involved in his endorsement for Acne Statin. Instead of receiving a flat endorsement fee from the manufacturer, which was how the vast majority got paid, Boone received a commission of 25 cents for every $9.50 bottle of the Acne Statin product that was sold. "The FTC confirmed that it singled out Mr. Boone because he was getting a piece of the action in the Acne Statin deal," she said. Also working against Boone was that Acne Statin was a relatively unknown mail order remedy. One advertising executive, who pointed out Boone's predicament was "unique," added that "Pat got himself involved with a fly-by-night pimple cream." Most celebrities endorsed products that were already popular or which were made by well-known companies and sold at the retail level.[4]

Around 1954 the U.S. Bureau of Alcohol, Tobacco and Firearms (BATF) had prohibited the use of active athletes in beer and wine ads. As a result, all the beer commercials, for example, that used athlete endorsers in their ads were actually using retired players or those in management positions to sell the product. Hearings were held in December 1980 by the agency as part of its proposal to revamp its advertising and labeling regulations for beer, wine and distilled spirits. Theoretically, BATF could have tightened or loosened the rules for athlete endorsers. The National Football League Players Association argued that any move to tighten the rules would be unfair because the average NFL player's career lasted just 4.6 years, which meant he had "a very brief time" to gain financial rewards from any celebrity status he may have achieved while playing. And, it argued further, the players had the right to commercially exploit their names and identities in the advertising media. Agreeing with the players' lobbying for loosening the rules was the Association of American Vintners, who maintained the BATF should "abolish its hitherto archaic and discriminatory advertising prohibition." Some brewers opposed any loosening of the rules at all. The G. Heileman Brewing Company felt the product should sell itself, without the aid of nonactive athletes, and the government agencies should impose more stringent rules. Taking a similar position was the Joseph Schlitz Brewing Company, which felt the current BATF ban "is most appropriate ... but is too limited." Schlitz wanted the ban expanded to include former athletes "readily recognizable" and extended to include coaches and managers of athletic teams, many of whom, it argued, were also readily recognizable or former athletes.[5]

Nothing came of the 1980 hearings but BATF — the government agency with primary jurisdiction over alcohol advertising — was back into the endorsement area in 1985 when it prepared to release a rulemaking that proposed restrictions on beer and wine advertising. The bureau had authority under the Federal Alcohol Administration Act of 1935 to regulate alcohol advertising that was false, misleading, obscene or indecent — the FTC was concerned with unfair and deceptive ads. In the early 1950s the bureau had ruled against the use of active athletes in alcohol advertising. It felt that the appearance of active athletes in ads was misleading because "it implied that alcohol somehow contributed to their athletic skill," explained BATF Director Stephen E. Higgins. Since then, he continued, the regulation had been criticized for being arbitrary. "What's the difference between an active athlete and the impression that that gives and a retired athlete?" wondered Higgins. "The distinction between those somehow got kind of blurred." BATF began re-examining the role of athletes in ads in 1980.[6]

One thing BATF was considering was extending its existing ban on active athletes to include retired players as well as stars from stage, screen and music. Some agency officials regarded revisiting the issue as not worthwhile, describing it as a "can of worms" — for example, how did one define a celebrity, and so forth? Apparently fueling the revisitation was, said reporter Steven Colford, the fact that BATF "also felt the political need to examine an issue whose significance has risen in union with the drive to rid tv and radio of beer and wine advertisements." Reportedly the agency was looking especially to remove people in those wine and beer ads that had special appeal to youngsters, such as cowboys, race car drivers, rock stars and amateur or professional sports celebrities, past or present and, said Colford, "the agency is almost ready to raise the question of whether it is proper for beer and wine ads to feature any celebrity."[7]

An editorial in *Advertising Age* declared that much of that controversy involving BATF centered on the ads for the Miller Brewing company's Lite beer, which, over time, had used a host of retired athletes. Those long-running ads were very popular and were considered classics by their supporters, but critics saw them as celebrities hawking beer to susceptible youth. "The campaign has been so successful, you see, that these ex-jocks are today's heroes rather than yesterday's," explained the editorial. "This perception was much in evidence during the recent Senate subcommittee hearings on beer and wine advertising."[8]

Finally, in May 1986, BATF announced it was relaxing its restrictions on the use of active athletes in ads endorsing alcoholic beverages. Bruce Weininger, chief of the agency's industrial compliance division, said that BATF then considered it permissible for beer and wine advertising to feature athletes— active or retired — as long as the athlete was not shown consuming the alcoholic beverage and did not link its consumption to athletic prowess. The catalyst for BATF to rethink the rules was the battle a year earlier between the agency and Miller Brewing and Anheuser Busch over their use of race car drivers in television and print ads. BATF sent memos to both brewers expressing concern about the ads— which featured brewery-sponsored drivers Danny Sullivan (Miller High Life) and Darrell Waltrip (Anheuser-Busch's Budweiser)— running prior to the Indianapolis 500 race. However, other obstacles remained. Major League Baseball rules, for example, barred its players from appearing in ads for tobacco and alcoholic beverages. The major roadblock to athlete endorsements, though, may have been the television networks. An NBC spokesman said the network had just amended its standards to include a provision stating it would not approve the use of "active professional or prominent amateur athletes" in commercials for beer and wine. For years the network had no provision because it was believed BATF had a strict prohibition against the use of active athletes, said Richard Gitter, vice-president for standards and practices at NBC. "But when we detected some ambiguity in that policy and wanted to be specific ourselves, we added a provision to our regulations forbidding the use of active pros or prominent amateurs." A spokesman for CBS said they had not analyzed the new BATF rules, "but I'm not sure that a change in their policies would lead to a change in ours. We don't allow active athletes whatsoever for those ads."[9]

Testimonials for prescription drugs became a problem issue in the 1990s, not long after such ads began to appear before the general public for the first time, having long been prohibited. After receiving a series of FDA complaints about its prescription drug advertising practices, a large pharmaceutical firm announced late in 1991 that it would stop using celebrities to promote its prescription drug products. The announcement by Ciba-Geigy Corporation of Summit, New Jersey, came after three months of discussion with the FDA. The agency regarded celebrity endorsements of prescription drugs to be frequently deceptive because consumers tended to assume that the celebrities were giving objective endorsements of a product when, in fact, they were typically paid to provide the endorsement, and also because the celebrities usually did not provide balanced information about the risks and benefits of the product. In the past Ciba-Geigy had used baseball great Mickey Mantle and actors Shirley Jones and Debbie Reynolds to promote its arthritis drug Voltaren.[10]

But the trend continued. *Consumer Reports* noted in 1999 that celebrities then endorsing prescription drugs included Denver Broncos running back Tyrell Davis testifying for Novartis's Migranal for migraine headaches, while former *Good Morning America* television host Joan Lunden touted Claritin for allergies, the most heavily advertised drug on the air. NBA star Karl Malone testified that Rogaine Extra Strength got rid of his bald spot, and Bob Dole enthused that Viagra had transformed his marriage. Gavin Macleod of *Love Boat* fame endorsed Muse and its ability to correct erection dysfunction. It was a trend that underscored the boom in prescription drug television ads. During the first six months of 1998, drug firms spent $306 million on television ads, $5 million more than they had spent in all of 1997. That rapid growth took place because in August 1997 the Food and Drug Administration Modernization Act relaxed advertising guidelines. Prior to that date mandatory disclaimers that had to accompany such ads made them difficult to place on television. But with the new act, only important side effects had to be mentioned (the television ads also had to provide a website address, toll-free number, or print ad where consumers could learn more). Said Dr. Matthew Hollon of the University of Washington, "The use of celebrities plays on people's hopes and expectations." He added that many of those ads were inaccurate and incomplete. Since the rules had been relaxed the FDA had sent 18 letters to drug advertisers, objecting to overstated benefits or understated risks.[11]

In a rare interview, actor Lauren Bacall appeared on the NBC *Today* program in March 2002 and told of a good friend who had gone blind from an eye disease. Then she mentioned a drug called Visudyne, a new treatment for the eye disease known as macular degeneration. Bacall never revealed that she had been paid to tell the story, and neither did NBC. Dr. Yvonne Johnson, medical affairs director for a division of Novartis (the Swiss drug manufacturer that sold Visudyne) admitted, "We compensated her for her time.... We realized people would accept what she was telling them." According to reporter Melody Petersen, in the previous year or so dozens of celebrities, from Bacall to Kathleen Turner to Rob Lowe, had been paid big money to appear on television talk shows and morning news programs and to disclose the intimate details of ailments that afflicted them or people close to them. "Often, they mention brand-name drugs without disclosing their financial ties to the medicine's maker." Said Dr. Joseph Turow, professor at the Annenberg School for Communication at the University of Pennsylvania: "It is highly problematic and maybe even unethical. We admire these people and that is why drug companies pay for their time and services." He added that when it came to issues of health, especially medicines, "transparency is an ethical concern. People should be clear about the reasons they are making certain recommendations." Allison Gollust, a spokeswoman for *Today* agreed that NBC might have made a mistake in handling the interview: "In hindsight, and with more information about celebrities and their connection to drug companies, we may have handled that differently."[12]

Drug companies, observed Petersen, could then avoid federal drug advertising regulations by hiring celebrities for what they described as campaigns to raise awareness about a disease. Regulations required that all prescription drug ads disclose the medicine's adverse effects and refrain from overstating its effectiveness. But as long as the celebrity did not mention a prescription drug by name, the FDA considered the event educational, not promotional, and did not regulate it, according to an agency official. Petersen noted that Bacall had crossed that line when she named the drug. Amgen was another drug company that had recently hired celebrities to help promote its products. Actor Danny Glover was paid by Amgen to help market Aranesp by raising awareness about anemia. Also, the company sold Enbrel for rheumatoid arthritis, and paid Kathleen Turner to discuss how she was coping with that disease. Rob Lowe was paid to raise awareness about neutropia, a side effect of chemotherapy that was treated by Amgen's drug Neulasta. Gollust, at NBC, said *Today* declined an interview with Rob Lowe after learning of his Amgen ties. In April 2002, talk show host Montel Williams, who suffered from multiple sclerosis, devoted an entire show to a discussion of the disease. On the show Williams told his audience that he took the drug Copaxone and that "Copaxone has been what has kept me running." Yet he never discussed the drug's possible side effects or his financial ties to the firm that sold the drug, Teva Pharmaceuticals.[13]

Even the Securities and Exchange Commission (SEC) got involved in the endorsement advertising area; in 1992 it sanctioned the Franklin Group, the mutual fund company that San Francisco 49er quarterback Joe Montana represented. The SEC opposed six different ads in which Montana, his wife, and three daughters appeared. Those ads promoted mutual funds for retirement planning, college planning, and equity investments. A 1940 law prohibited testimonials for investment advisors. Mutual funds were required by law to hire investment advisers, so by extension the SEC applied the ban on testimonials to funds also. A way around the problem was to make certain the celebrity was the representative of an investment firm as a whole and did not just endorse a particular product. That was why actor John Houseman, from 1979 to 1987, could do testimonial ads for investment firm Smith Barney and not draw any wrath from the SEC.[14]

A furor that arose in 1997 involved the august American Medical Association (AMA). Stung by charges of a conflict of interest and commercialism, top executives of the AMA decided in August of that year that the organization should abandon plans to endorse health care products. Those executives recommended that an exclusive endorsement deal with one such manufacturer — Sunbeam Corporation (best known for its kitchen appliances) — be sharply scaled back. Under the proposal, which revised a deal announced a week earlier, AMA would no longer accept royalty payments from Sunbeam, estimated to be worth millions of dollars. And while Sunbeam products would continue to carry the AMA seal, the medical group asked to be released from its exclusivity agreement. By that action the group was responding to criticism not only from consumer advocates and editorial pages but also from some of its 300,000 members and even some of its trustees. The Sunbeam deal would have been the first product endorsement by the AMA in its 150-year history. Under the new proposal, the association would give no product endorsements in the future but would put its name on informational literature intended to be placed in the packaging of health care products. Instead of paying royalties, the manufacturers availing themselves of this service would pay to the AMA fees just large enough to cover the cost of writing and printing the brochures. According to critics, the original plan called into question the group's credibility as an independent organization. The new proposal also meant the AMA name would not be exclusive for such Sunbeam products as blood pressure monitors, heating pads, thermometers, humidifiers and vaporizers. Under the old plan, the Sunbeam heating pad, for example, would have carried the AMA logo and no other heating pad would have borne the seal, and the company would have paid the medical group a fixed royalty on each one sold. With the revised plan no heating pad maker would be allowed to use the logo exclusively, but all whose pads were acceptable in quality could enclose AMA literature in their packaging, after paying a limited fee designed to only cover the actual costs. Even that change was not enough for Dr. Sidney M. Wolfe, executive director of the Public Citizen's Health Research Group, who argued the new proposal was not acceptable: "If they don't make money off the transaction with the companies, the A.M.A. is still using the idea to market its logo. It's still a marketing scheme." Calling for the resignation of all the AMA executives involved in the original deal, Wolfe asserted that "the endorsement deal was a scandalously bad decision and the organization must get rid of the people responsible for this program."[15]

What prompted the AMA to consider endorsements for money in the first place was its need for cash for new public health campaigns on smoking and violence, according to journalist Christine Gorman. The original program promptly set off a storm of criticism, with a *New York Times* editorial calling it "an appalling decision." Gorman then recalled similar forays into endorsements by other health-related organizations. Back in 1990 the American Heart Association (AHA) launched an ambitious nutritional-labeling program that could have netted it as much as $600,000 annually from the endorsements of commercial products, depending on market share. Backed by a public-spirited goal, the AHA wanted the labeling to help consumers better understand the nutritional content of the foods they bought. However, the FDA objected and the AHA eventually dropped the program; a few years later the FDA itself started requiring more explicit food labels. Later the AHA began a more modest "food certification" program. In 1996 the American Cancer Society (ACS) entered into an exclusive deal with the Florida Orange Growers Association, under which the society received $1 million per year for cancer research in exchange for allowing the ACS logo to appear in ads and on juice cartons. "We do walk a fine line," admitted ACS spokesman Steven Dickinson. "But what we're doing is not a formal endorsement. We make it clear that orange juice is only an example of the kinds of foods in a healthy diet." Less controversy was stirred up by the ACS deal than by most of the other arrangements. Gorman felt the model commercial setup for a health group had been devised by the American Dental Association (ADA). For years it had put its seal of acceptance on products that it had tested — at its own expense. Two years earlier, in 1995, the ADA began charging modest application fees that covered about one-third of its $1.2 million annual testing budget. To that point the ADA had certified 1,300 dental products, including 65 toothpastes in all, Crest and Colgate among them. Fees charged for ADA endorsements included $900 for professional products for the first year, $9,000 for consumer goods for their first year. The AHA had certified a total of 577 products, including Kellogg's Frosted Flakes, for a product fee of $2,500 for the item's first year. Orange juice was the only product endorsed by the ACS, while the total was nil for the AMA, excluding the Sunbeam deal.[16]

Commenting on the general situation, business reporter Phillip Longman remarked that nonprofit organizations were selling their logos to commercial products all the time. In most of those cases, he argued, those organizations protected their integrity with a fig leaf that it was a "partnership" rather than a "product endorsement," a distinction he felt to be without much foundation. "The roster of offenders is long and distinguished."

The American Lung Association had sold its logo to the makers of American Sensors carbon monoxide detectors and Nicotrol nicotine patches; the Arthritis Foundation lent its name to "Arthritis Foundation" brand aspirin, manufactured by a company that donated $1 million annually to the foundation. Government regulators ended the latter pairing.[17]

Since the American Heart Association changed its charter in 1988 to permit product endorsements, an arrangement it had prohibited from its founding in 1924, it had raised millions of dollars through 1997. According to the nonprofit AHA, the money was used to support research and education programs and helped spread its message promoting heart health. Critics worried such arrangements confused the public into thinking that a food endorsed by the group was better than one that was not. Brigid McHugh Sanner, AHA senior vice-president for communications, said she objected to the world "endorse" because "we don't endorse products. We call those food-certification programs or corporate relationships. None of this constitutes an endorsement." Yet the AHA charged varying fees for the use of its name. For example, for $2,500 for the first year a company like Kellogg could put the association's heart check symbol on, for instance, a package of Fruity Marshmallow Krispies. The yearly renewal charge was $650. The National Cattlemen's Beef Association paid $25,000 for its arrangement with the AHA, the promotion of lean cuts of beef. A Heart Association brochure said the heart-check certification program, established in 1992, was "designed to help consumers easily select foods in the grocery store that can be part of a balanced heart-healthy diet."[18]

By this date, August 1997, the AHA had certified 636 products. To be designated "heart healthy," a product had to meet nutrient requirements established by the Food and Drug Administration or the U.S. Department of Agriculture; it had to be low in fat, saturated fat, and cholesterol. Also required by the heart association was a written assurance from the company that its nutritional labeling was correct. All foods were eligible except those manufactured by a tobacco company or its subsidiaries. Excluded by that provision were all products from Nabisco (a unit of the RJR Nabisco Holdings Corporation) and Kraft, Post and Jell-O (all owned by Philip Morris). It meant that Post's Raisin Bran could not carry the heart-check symbol, but Kellogg's Raisin Bran could, and did. Dr. James T. Bennett of George Mason University wondered whether the group's arrangement with the Florida citrus group meant that "California citrus won't help you with heart disease — only Florida can." Bennett, a political economist, called such endorsements "ludicrous." His views were echoed by Dr. Michael Jacobson, executive director of the Center for Science in the Public Interest, a Washington, D.C., advocacy group. An endorsement "deceives people into thinking one product is better than another," he said. No matter what form the endorsement took, argued Jacobsen, it was still dangerous territory for nonprofits because there was a risk that if they got money from a specific industry they would be unable to criticize that industry if the occasion arose. "They are compromising themselves, particularly when word gets out that they are getting big bucks," Bennett declared. "Over time they will lose their credibility. They become a shill for corporate interests and there is no way you can dress that up as a charitable activity. It is unethical."[19]

Consumer Reports wondered, in June 1998, how a cereal that was 42 percent sugar and had just one gram of fiber could carry an AHA logo. It could, said the magazine, because Kellogg's paid the AHA fees to use it on Frosted Flakes, Cocoa Krispies and other cereals that might contain a lot of sugar but were low in total fat, saturated fat, and cholesterol. General Mills paid the same fees and put the logo on boxes of Cookie Crisp cereal, among others. According to this article, a serving of a "truly" healthful cereal had five grams or more of fiber and three grams or less of fat. Post Grape-Nuts and Nabisco Shredded Wheat both met those requirements and were lower in added sugar, but got no heart logo. That was because both were made by Kraft, which was owned by cigarette maker Philip Morris.[20]

An endorsement scam surfaced when several major Hollywood film studios admitted in June 2001 that paid actors had been appearing in television commercials praising movies in what were purported to be man-in-the-street interviews. Those admissions came on the heels of a revelation that the Sony Corporation's Columbia Pictures used two studio employees to rave about Columbia's film *The Patriot* in television spots in which they portrayed a couple on a date who had just seen the movie. All of these actions by the studios shed an unwanted light on the studios' use of testimonials, or audience reaction, television spots. Those commercials featured supposed moviegoers who gave thumbs up reviews. In many cases, the use of testimonials by paid actors were mingled in the same spot with that of real cinema patrons, although there was never any disclosure that some of the people were receiving compensation for appearing in the commercial. A spokeswoman for Columbia said the studio was reviewing its advertising procedures, but had abandoned the use of testimonial advertising. Using studio employees to praise one of their own movies was "probably a mistake," acknowledged Robert Levin, head of marketing at Columbia when *The Patriot* was released in 2000. Nevertheless, he defended the practice of using actors in testimonials, as long as they were expressing their honest opinion. Business writer John Lippman suggested that testimonial ads were usually used by studios only when a movie was in trouble. Considered to be a last resort, such ads were produced within hours of being commissioned so they could be rushed on the air. Although the actors were supposed to express their own opinions, observers in the industry contended they were coached and even fed lines by the producers of those spots. There was even an agency that specialized in finding actors to do testimonial commercials for movie releases: the Morgan Agency of Costa Mesa, California. Lois Morton, a Morgan agent, said she got one or two calls every few months from commercial producers making television spots and looking for actors. Typically the agency sent out eight to 15 people per assignment, with the actors being paid anywhere from $60 to $200 per movie plus a free ticket. Other recent movies that utilized the practice of including actors paid to give testimonials in television spots were *Blair Witch Project II* (from Artisan Entertainment) and Fox's *Anna and the King*. A spokeswoman for Universal studio said the company sometimes hired actors to appear in testimonial ads. But, she said, their responses were not scripted and the actors typically appeared alongside real moviegoers who were also giving endorsements. Universal stated it did not use its own employees in those ads. Paramount Pictures said it did not use testimonial ads, while a Walt Disney studio spokesman said the company did not hire actors for such ads, nor did it use Disney employees in them.[21]

In response to the revelations about Hollywood's fake testimonial ads, an editorial in *Advertising Age* declared, "In the current mess over Sony's testimonial movie ads, Hollywood deserves no sympathy. The do's and don'ts of testimonials have been firmly established. Where was Hollywood when regulators insisted, and respectable marketers accepted, the principle that phony testimonials are beyond the pale?"[22]

Amid growing controversy over celebrity endorsements, a tentative decision late in 2002 by a California federal court judge found ex-baseball player Steve Garvey did not have to surrender profits he made from shilling for a weight-loss supplement in an infomercial. The Garvey case had been a test for the FTC and stemmed from the agency's pursuit not just of company principals but also Garvey, who made several infomercials and appearances for two products of Enforma Natural Products, "Fat Trapper" and "Exercise in a Bottle." In television spots and public appearances from 1998 to 2000, Garvey made untrue statements about the products, according to the FTC. The ruling against the agency was made by U.S. District Court Judge Gary Allen Feess. Both the FTC and the advertising industry regarded the case as a test of how far the agency could go in pursuing product spokespeople who profited from the marketing of dubious products.[23]

Earlier the FTC had settled its complaint against Enforma, but it also took the unusual step of demanding that Garvey and a co-host of the infomercial put their earnings toward a fund to compensate consumers. It argued that Garvey, whose management company got $7,500 plus royalties to make the infomercial (the final amount he received exceeded $1 million), went too far in the spots, making statements such as "You can eat what you want and never, ever, ever have to diet again." Also, charged the FTC, Garvey misled consumers and crossed the line between being an actor in a spot and becoming a product promoter. Citing appearances Garvey made on talk shows and elsewhere, the FTC declared he showed "a reckless indifference to the truth," a legal standard that could have made him liable. Heather Hippsley, FTC assistant director of advertising practices, said "Our view is he wasn't just a paid actor. He should have realized that the claims he made were so outrageous they couldn't possibly be true." Garvey, though, claimed he was merely an actor reading a script. In response to that claim, the FTC pointed out he had written part of the script. Judge Feess ruled the FTC had not shown that Garvey was sufficiently involved to warrant a money seizure and that his occasional appearance on talk shows outside the infomercial were not sufficient to make him an endorser, nor to make his statements knowingly false.[24]

9

Mistakes, Pitfalls, and Bad Boys, 1975–2003

A personality used by too many advertisers is not a spokesman.
He's a shill.   — Bourne Morris, 1979

Athletes, drugs and very nervous advertisers.
                                                   —*Business Week*, 1988

Advertisers must play the obnoxiousness game with great care....
Finding a long-term company spokesman is a different matter.
Gimmicks are okay, serious controversy is not.
                                                   — Peter Newcomb, 1990

Most articles on endorsement ads left the impression that they were mostly successful, that there was little that went wrong. In particular that was the case prior to 1975. But in the modern era a few more pieces surfaced that outlined mistakes, pitfalls, and failed campaigns. Celebrity testimonials were a long way from being a marketer's panacea.

One of the all-time legendary mistakes in the endorsement field went back to Olympic swimmer Mark Spitz. Arriving home from the 1972 Summer Olympics with seven gold medals, Spitz was besieged by companies that wanted his endorsement for their products. Happy to oblige, Spitz collected, by one estimate, about $5 million worth of endorsement and related contracts before falling suddenly and dramatically from public view. Said one recruiter of athletes for Madison Avenue, bluntly, "Spitz had no personality." Another remarked that "it was the biggest fiasco in the history of sports."[1]

In the opinion of Bert Randolph Sugar, senior vice-president at the Baron, Costello & Fine ad agency, Schick, Inc.'s tie-in with Spitz was "the worst sports promotion of all time." To promote its Flexamatic razor in competition with Remington's Mark III, Schick signed Spitz to a lifetime contract, $100,000 a year for five years and then $50,000 a year for life.

Schick, explained Sugar, over expanded its marketing efforts, lost $6 million, had to borrow $40 million to finance current operations, "and wound up with Mark Spitz for life, but not for long in commercials." Later an agreement was reached between Schick and Spitz to terminate the contract. Another bad deal that Sugar recalled was when Magnavox signed baseball star Hank Aaron to endorse its television sets. In an attempt to capture headlines, Magnavox signed the slugger to a five-year $1 million contract in 1973, as Aaron closed in on, and passed, the all-time mark for home runs set by Babe Ruth. Aaron's retirement shortly after eclipsing the long-standing record dictated against Magnavox getting their money's worth out of him, especially as he precipitously dropped from public view after his exit from baseball. Additionally, the media attention to the race served to make Ruth the large legend rather than Aaron. When Sugar visited Aaron at his home in Atlanta, a full year after he signed his Magnavox deal, he found the slugger had a Zenith television set in his den.[2]

Reporter John Emmerling noted that a marketer should always check the health of a prospective endorser. Actor Bert Lahr died in the middle of what was called an "outstanding" campaign for Lay's potato chips. Emmerling also advised advertisers to check on a star's after-hours behavior since a firm did not want to spend big money to sign a celebrity, and then spend more on the production of spots only to have the endorser turn up drunk on a talk show, for example.[3]

Stars could also lose credibility by being overexposed and overpaid. Some advertising executives doubted that old standby endorsers, such as Joe Namath and Bing Crosby, were worth their $1 million contracts. The whole idea of using celebrities to sell products offended the creative vanity of some ad agencies, noted reporter Lynn Langway. It brought up a copywriter's old cliché that "if you can't think of something sparkling to say, get somebody famous to say it." A newsletter published by Marstellar, Inc., an agency in New York, charged that celebrity endorsements were often a "creative copout" to disguise weak ads. Chicago's Leo Burnett USA agency, for one, was said to be using fewer famous faces than before, believing they had lost their glow. "Sometimes a big name overwhelms the message," explained a Burnett spokesman. George Lois of Lois Holland Callaway said celebrities paid off at the cash register — but only if they came across as believable. "The trouble is not with the stars, but with people misusing them," he said. "They shouldn't look like they're doing it only for the money, even when they are." At that time even actor Broderick Crawford could command $25,000 for a ten-second stint in a commercial. Candice Bergen, a proven spokeswoman, took in $125,000 a year from Polaroid for its camera spots, and was due to receive at least $1.5 million for a forthcoming series of fragrance ads. Some overexposed stars worked themselves out of future ads. Chanel fragrances, annoyed at its endorser, actor Catherine Deneuve, for doing Mercury Monarch spots, was then shopping around for a new French actress to replace her.[4]

Bourne Morris, managing director with ad agency Ogilvy & Mather, was another in the industry who thought the biggest problem in using celebrities was overexposure. The best answer to that problem, said Morris, was still money. That is, a firm could tie up a celebrity with a contract that prevented the famous name from working for a competing concern, or any company for that matter. But those celebrities expected, naturally enough, to be paid more for exclusivity, and some of Morris's clients were reluctant to spend the money. "That's foolish thrift. A personality used by too many advertisers is not a spokesman. He's a shill," explained Morris. "The fact that some famous stars seem bent on ruinous overexposure, and some famous clients seem willing to lease their services anyway, baffles me. If after a while I forget what Catherine Deneuve is purring about, how can I expect the consumer to remember?"[5]

Anita Bryant was the spokeswoman for Florida orange juice in the 1970s but did little for her employer because of her highly publicized criticism of homosexuals. Texaco had to ask its endorser, Bob Hope, to stop telling gay jokes after angry customers began cutting up their credit cards and returning them to the company.[6]

Another campaign that bombed was a 1975 promotion for Trans World Airways (TWA) that featured actor Peter Sellers as the celebrity endorser. In the ads, Sellers portrayed several eccentric characters that flamboyantly listed the advantages of TWA's vacation packages to Europe (the tight-fisted Scotsman Thrifty McTravel, upper-crust Englishman Jeremy Peake-Tyme, and so on). The campaign was attacked for containing supposed ethnic slurs and for promoting "an extravagant lifestyle" during a recession. Some also questioned the use of Sellers, as they failed to see his relevance to the airline. According to TWA, the basic problem with the campaign was negative employee reaction, especially from in-flight personnel. Many employees thought the ads were silly and took exception to Sellers's stereotypical characters; others felt the ads were in bad taste. Scheduled to be an 18-month campaign, it was halted by TWA after just three months. Overall, that campaign was assessed as a dismal failure.[7]

Still another failure involved Schlitz's choice of actor James Coburn in 1979 to be a spokesman for its Schlitz Light beer. It was a campaign that proved nothing but trouble. International Creative Management delivered the star for $250,000, but Coburn's macho image in television commercials turned off distributors, who felt he was "cold," even abrasive. Also, the actor's contract stipulated that his association with the product was limited to making television commercials. Coburn's one-year contract with the company was not renewed.[8]

Industry executive Sid Bernstein admonished advertisers to make sure a celebrity endorser fit their product in terms of personality, appearance and general ambience. He felt that such "harsh" admonishment needed to be delivered "due to the fact that John Houseman and Lauren Bacall have let me — and their sponsors — down recently." Just a couple of years earlier, *Advertising Age* had selected Houseman as Presenter of the Year, because of his "magnificent" work for the Smith Barney investment firm. But then, he added, "he brought that magnificent voice and dominating presence to McDonald's spots. Smith Barney's spokesman, exuding honesty and integrity and financial responsibility at every pore, turning up as a vapid chronicler of the wonders of dining at Mac's! Shame on all of you." Bacall was deemed a failure when she was hired to pitch coffee.[9]

When Vanessa Williams appeared nude in *Penthouse* magazine in 1984 she was stripped of her Miss America title (the photos were taken in 1982 before she won the crown). Four months earlier, *Madison Ave* magazine had run a cover story on the marketing potential of Williams. She was described as a natural and one holder of the Miss America crown who could last beyond a year — most Miss Americas were one-year wonders at best, in terms of marketing ability. At that time she had already appeared in an ad for Diet Coke. When Williams's scandal was unveiled, Coca-Cola was quick to say it had no intention of running her Diet Coke spot again. American Greeting pulled out of an expensive promotion it had planned with the beauty contest winner. Gillette withdrew its proposal that she be one of their spokeswomen, and Kellogg's stopped a special edition of Corn Flakes boxes featuring her picture. The real surprise, to the writer of one account, was not in the treatment handed out to Williams by advertisers, who were "notoriously skittish people who bolt at the first sign of controversy," but that advertisers blithely continued "to opt for celebrity spokesmen instead of original campaigns that have some relation to the product." This writer firmly believed that using a celebrity spokesman was a lazy way to do advertising "and one that can easily backfire."[10]

Promotion Watch (PW), a Livonia, Michigan-based unit of GFV Communications, began a new service in 1984 it said would provide a company contemplating a celebrity spokesperson with advice and assurance on their choice. Explained Barry Hoffman, president of Promotion Watch: "Discretion is everything — people are very sensitive about this." For a fee Hoffman said was "nominal," his company would investigate just about any celebrity a marketer was considering as a spokesperson. However, before any investigation was started PW would approach the celebrity or his or her agent with a release form that would keep PW clear of any legal ramifications. If the celebrity would not sign the release, PW would do no investigation and simply tell the marketer so, implying, of course, that there must have been a reason why the person would not sign the release. Using a network of private investigators described as "former FBI and Secret Service agents," the company stated it would check potential endorsers for criminal records or drug and alcohol abuse. Then it would check the candidate's past record as a spokesperson, if there was such a record, looking into issues such as reliability, perks demanded in the past (like expensive hotel suites) and the person's effectiveness as a spokesperson. Many celebrities, especially sports stars, did not have well-known track records in dealings with companies, explained Hoffman. "It's most important in sudden celebrity," he added.[11]

For *Fortune* magazine writer Stratford Sherman, one of the pitfalls in celebrity testimonials was the over-reliance by an advertiser on a single star. General Foods was said to have made that mistake by "almost indelibly" associating its Sanka decaffeinated coffee with Robert Young, best known for his television portrayal of Marcus Welby, M.D. Though he was likable and convincing, Young reportedly had little appeal to younger adults who were then the fastest growing group of decaffeinated coffee drinkers. "Our product had a medicinal image and sales were up only marginally," said Stephen Morris, general manager of the General Foods coffee division. Sanka dropped Young as a spokesman in 1981 and, four years later had not used another celebrity. Sherman was another who mentioned the Houseman flop, after many years of stellar work as a Smith Barney spokesman. Procter & Gamble were also apparently happy with his work as an endorser for its Puritan cooking oil. But his work for both McDonald's and Chrysler was considered to have flopped. "I worked my ass off in the theater for 45 years. God knows this isn't as complex as playing King Lear," said Houseman. "It is less work for the money than any other theatrical work."[12]

Failures reported at the end of the 1980s by researcher Grant McCracken included Mary Tyler Moore for vacuum cleaners, and Bill Cosby failing as an endorser for the investment firm E.F. Hutton, despite his recent successes for Kodak and Coca-Cola. Actor George C. Scott was the wrong choice for Renault cars, as was Ringo Starr for the Sun Country Classic wine coolers.[13]

In 1986, when E.F. Hutton used Cosby to try and get people to buy their stocks through Hutton, no one listened. The campaign that starred

Cosby (with an estimated cost of $6 million) was dropped after nine months even though Cosby's contract extended into 1990. Hutton had hoped that the comic's clean, good-guy image would help repair the firm's reputation after it was tarred by a check-kiting scandal. Observers felt the Cosby problem was almost certainly overexposure. "When Bill speaks, who are people listening to?" asked Gary Stibel of the New England Consulting Group. "Is it E.F. Hutton or Coca-Cola or Texas Instruments or any of the multiplicity of advertisers who have used him?" Hutton's big mistake, argued reporter Christy Marshall, was in abandoning a 14-year campaign that had tremendous recognition and credibility with the public. The focus of that campaign's ads was on the slogan "When E.F. Hutton talks people listen." With regard to the Houseman 1983 debacle, Marshall said that when the distinguished actor tried peddling Big Macs and French fries on television, "he provoked giggles." Said Jay Chiat, chairman of the ad agency Chiat/Day: "I can't imagine John Houseman ever having been in a McDonald's." Bill Younclaus, McDonald's vice-president of marketing at the time of the Houseman campaign, commented that "it seemed like a good idea at the time."[14]

Burt Reynolds was dropped as endorser of the Florida Citrus Commission (for Florida oranges) and by Quaker State Corporation (for Quaker State motor oil) in August 1993, as events surrounding the Reynolds and Loni Anderson divorce continued to make news, especially in the tabloid press. Both sides gave their version of the story to the media. Ivy Leventhal, public relations director for the Florida Citrus Commission, explained, "We just feel that our message has been overshadowed by the intense media and public interest in Mr. Reynolds's affairs." Scott Chickering, vice-president of marketing for Quaker State, denied Reynolds's personal problems had anything to do with the company's decision to stop using him as a spokesman. He insisted that the contract was up and Quaker State did not renew it as it intended to focus more on product than on personality. Reportedly there were difficulties in working with Reynolds that went beyond his personal life. "He insists on directing his own commercials," remarked one executive. "That's why they look so cheesy."[15]

Failed campaigns usually involved a company choosing the wrong celebrity. Typically the endorser did not engage in inappropriate behavior or, as in the case of Reynolds, engaged in a behavior many others had been involved in — getting a divorce — but had coverage of the behavior get out of hand in the media, becoming loud, long-lasting and ugly. Going beyond that was the behavior of the bad boy group of endorsers. These were celebrities that engaged in behavior all the way from the fairly mild and innocuous (but perceived as having a bad effect on the endorsed product) to the very serious, where the endorser faced criminal charges. Throughout the history of endorsement advertising the idea came up from time to time that an endorser's bad behavior could do harm to the product endorsed and that advertisers should make efforts to minimize the chances of hiring a celebrity endorser who might turn out to be a bad boy. Still, such articles were rare. It seemed that in the past either almost no endorsers turned into bad boys, or any such behavior stayed out of the media and thus never had a chance to taint the advertiser and his product. In any case, celebrity bad boy behavior has flourished in the modern era, and been reported on at length. This has caused no end of grief for advertisers— very conservative and nervous about anything remotely regarded as controversial in the first place — in their search for the perfect endorser. By the time the modern era began, most endorsement contracts between stars and advertisers provided for immediate cancellation in case of moral turpitude, but that protection was often inadequate. Invoking a moral turpitude clause allowed a company to stop paying the endorser but did not take into account the money expended, such as on ad production costs, and so forth. Ideal Toy Corporation, for example, invoked such a clause in 1978 to end its association with celebrity Evel Knievel in the wake of the daredevil's jailing in California for assault. It discontinued its Evel Knievel lines in the United States after their sales dropped off because of the incident.[16]

As blacks became more accepted as endorsers, journalist Stephen Gale observed, in 1981, that the future in endorsing looked good for those black celebrities "who have not stepped on corporate toes, but some celebrities have ruined their chance to do an ad because of injurious acts." New York celebrity broker Lloyd Kolmer said that Jayne Kennedy "must have lost her mind" when she did a spread in *Playboy* magazine because that took her right out of the business. "You can't go sticking your tongue into someone else's mouth in a major magazine, even if it is your husband, and expect everybody to want you for commercials." He added that Richard Pryor — the comedian did a lot of blue material and had been mentioned in connection with drugs—"also can't do commercials."[17]

A Japanese company picked musician Boy George to sell its sake (rice wine) on television in that country shortly before the pop star's drug problem became public. The advertisement was quickly withdrawn.[18]

By the late 1980s, celebrity involvement with drugs had reached the point where some advertisers were urging agents to adopt some type of drug testing policy for their clients prior to signing athletes and celebrities to endorsement contracts. That came in the wake of the assignment of New York Mets pitching ace Dwight Gooden to a drug rehabilitation clinic in 1987. Agents representing athletes and other celebrities were said to have conceded that drug testing was inevitable, especially as the issue had become urgent. Robert Briner, senior vice-president at ProServ, commented there was no longer any question that athletes "will be forced to look at a major sponsorship offer contingent on empirical evidence that the athlete is not involved with any illegal substances." William Stankey, an agent at Greater Talent Network, worried that the great concern over drugs in general could lead to drug-testing requests from any endorser. "When an advertiser asks us if our client uses drugs—if I can be held liable—the only answer can be supplied by drug testing," explained Stankey. His advice to advertisers was that if a celebrity did not want to take a drug test they should not use him. Stankey acknowledged that such advice could raise serious civil liberties issues. Gooden endorsed products for Nike, Spalding, and Polaroid, as well as a line of equipment under the Doctor K brand for Toys R Us. Luckier than most endorsers in a similar position, Gooden managed to hold on to all of his testimonial contracts.[19]

Advertisers and their lawyers were reported in 1987 to be preparing new ground rules to protect clients and brands from athletes who endorsed products and took drugs. They were pushing for new morality and reimbursement clauses in sports endorser contracts that specifically defined drug use, according to advertisers. Many advertisers were considering requiring athletes to take drug tests and to pay back the cost of producing a commercial if the athlete's drug use became public knowledge. Leah Collins, a spokeswoman for the Milford, Connecticut–based Bic Corporation, which for four years used tennis star John McEnroe to represent its disposable razors, said the company would consider requiring drug tests of endorsers and including that as a provision in future endorsement contracts. John Stitzell, advertising director for Amoco Oil, Chicago, which used golfer Lee Trevino, and other celebrities, in ads, said Amoco was seriously considering establishing a new drug policy. Steven Rotter, president of Towne, Silverstein, Rotter, the agency for Canandaigua Wine Company's Sun Country Wine Cooler, was pessimistic. "Let's face it," he said. "If you asked more celebrities to take a drug test, they'd tell you to get lost."[20]

Although the advertising industry had united behind a massive public service anti-drug ad campaign, observed reporter Larry Collins, it was not united over a policy to prevent hiring drug users as endorsers. The Association of National Advertisers (ANA) and the American Association of Advertising Agencies (AAAA)—both of whom sponsored the anti-drug campaign—had not recommended to their members a single unified policy on the problem of signing endorsers who used drugs. The ANA said its members had not yet requested such a policy, while the AAAA maintained that it must be decided by individual agencies. Some advertisers observed that competition to sign the biggest names in sports and entertainment would prevent marketers from demanding drug tests in every case. After tennis star Billie Jean King was sued for palimony by a woman, "we were one of the only companies that did not drop her," said Nike spokesman Kevin Brown. He added that "Nike isn't going to follow its athletes around with Dixie Cups." A spokesman for Wheaties cereal said, "We have a reputation and a history to uphold." Those endorsers, he explained, "aren't just a face on the Wheaties boxes; they're named a Wheaties Champion. So you could say we do a little character checking." Collins thought advertisers saw the issue of potentially problem endorsers as something they would rather avoid than deal with: "the issue is not new, but the ability to dodge it is shrinking." To that point, 1987, no morality clause had ever been used in court to hold an agent or an endorser liable for damage done to the sales or image of a product because of the star's behavior.[21]

Bruce Willis and Cybill Shepherd did ads for Seagram's Golden Wine Cooler and the Beef Industry Council, respectively. Both were suddenly dropped. Shepherd sealed her fate after the *Family Circle* magazine quoted her as saying she did not eat much red meat and was concerned about fatty foods. Cattlemen were also reported to be outraged when she became pregnant before she got married. Another slip by Shepherd occurred when she was hawking L'Oreal hair color but admitted to a reporter that she did not use hair coloring. Seagram's put up with Willis's exorbitant fee (over $2 million a year) when the cooler market was thriving, but the company cooled to him in the summer of 1987 when he overplayed his image and was arrested at his Hollywood Hills home after a raucous party. A story in the tabloid press that he had a drinking problem, combined with a campaign against alcohol by his new wife Demi Moore, also did not help his standing with Seagram. Squibb broadcast its last commercial for Theragran-M multivitamins starring Billie Jean King on the day she admitted to having had a lesbian relationship.[22]

Mike Tyson, 22, defeated Michael Spinks for the world heavyweight boxing championship in the summer of 1988. But his appeal as an endorser, wrote journalist Patrick McGeehan, "dropped precipitously as newspaper and magazine stories painted the boxer as a spoiled wife-beater caught in a maze of greed and manipulation." First to back off was Pepsi, which had spent an estimated $3.5 million to be the fight's sole sponsor and to use Tyson in a television and print campaign for Diet Pepsi. It had been considering paying Tyson $8 million plus for a long-term endorsement contract but, in light of the revelations, declared it had no plans to use him beyond the present campaign. A battery marketer that had inquired about using Tyson suddenly backed off. Several other companies, including RJR Nabisco and 3M, reportedly were interested in Tyson before the fight but then were claiming they never had any intention of using him as a spokesman. In the weeks before the fight Tyson was reported to have beaten his wife, actress Robin Givens, and to have given away a luxury auto after he drove it into a parked car, amongst other revelations of bad boy behavior. Prior to all those reports on his behavior, industry observers had rated his endorsement potential as very high. Art Kaminsky, whose New York-based Athletes & Artists represented several top athletes, maintained that if Tyson continued on as undefeated heavyweight champion and kept his nose clean, "he could be one of the biggest athletes in the history of endorsements." His conservative estimate was that Tyson could make from $5 million to $7 million in product endorsements. Some of that could have come from abroad. In Japan, Tyson then appeared in television spots for Suntory beer.[23]

When Canadian sprinter Ben Johnson had his world-record victory in the 1988 Olympic 100-meter dash nullified after he tested positive for steroids, it set off more alarm bells among advertisers. Johnson had signed up for an estimated $5 million in commercial contracts. Some advertisers were said to be shying away from a reliance on star endorsers, opting instead for the sponsorship of tournaments and other events; other advertisers were scrutinizing athletes more closely. Some accomplished that by rewriting the language in contracts, testing athletes for drugs, or bringing in private investigators. Welch Foods, Inc., "grilled" 5'3" Tyrone "Mugsy" Bogues, the NBA's shortest player, "for hours" before signing him for an ad campaign showing Welch's determination to take on the big boys in the soft drink business. Pepsi spokesman Tod J. Mackenzie said, with respect to dropping Tyson, that "he would not be an appropriate spokesman, given the recent allegations." One company that presented itself as always standing behind the athletes involved in controversies was Nike, which then spent about $19 million a year on endorsements and promotions. Without athletes "what we stand for disappears," said Nike official Elizabeth C. Dolan. "We use our judgment," said Dolan. "We generally don't dump athletes for something like that," referring to pitcher Dwight Gooden.[24]

At the start of the 1990s, reporter Bob Geiger noted some of the celebrities then involved in well-covered controversies: Pete Rose for alleged gambling; Steve Garvey for his soap opera of marriage, divorce and reported illegitimate children; and, of course, still Ben Johnson. Nova Lanktree, director of Burns Sports Celebrity Service, commented that to be an endorser, "For all practical purposes, you must be pretty perfect." A morals clause from her company, between an unidentified advertiser and celebrity endorser, read: "We shall have the right to terminate this agreement upon immediate written notice in the event our client is of the belief that artist's actual or alleged conduct occurring or reported subsequent to execution of this agreement and client's and the public's perception thereof create the result that a public association of artist with our client may be injurious to or embarrassing to our client or inconsistent with the best interests, reputation or marketing position of the product." According to that clause, the decision of the client, or advertiser, "shall be conclusive." In other words, commented Geiger, advertisers using such clauses could terminate a contract on the basis of perception alone, not necessarily fact. Agents for athletes endorsing products typically requested far more liberal provisions for their clients, allowing contract termination only if the athlete was convicted of a felony. That flurry of sports figures making headlines for unsporting behavior was, said Lanktree, "a bombardment of our value system. It's hard to deal with an Olympic hero [Ben Johnson] using steroids." For example, the California Egg Board dropped Oakland Athletics baseball star Jose Canseco from its roster of endorsers after police found a gun in his car. Geiger felt San Francisco 49er quarterback Joe Montana represented the "pretty perfect" sports star. Others he placed in that category were Earvin "Magic" Johnson, Michael Jordan, Orel Hershiser, Bo Jackson, and Wayne Gretzky. In a riskier category were the athlete endorsers used by the Gillette company in its "Animals" campaign for Right Guard Sport Stick deodorant. Used in that campaign were Los Angeles Dodger star Kirk Gibson, the NBA's Charles Barkley, boxer "Marvelous" Marvin Hagler, and outspoken football player Brian Bosworth. Gary Cohen, associate product manager for Gillette's Right Guard, said, regarding the riskier endorsers in that campaign: "We were concerned with, 'do they have a history of drugs or gambling?' It comes down to a judgment call. You can't fault [advertisers] for using celebrities."[25]

Still, some advertisers sought out those athletes with a higher potential to become bad boys; some thought they worked better. Reporter Peter Newcomb mentioned 20-year-old (in 1990) tennis star Andre Agassi and all his temper tantrums. "America loves a guy who can make the big bucks and then thumb his nose at the world," said sports psychologist William Beausay. "Society has changed over the last 30 years. We went from a society where people had respect for one another to one where the primary concern is for oneself. The athlete of today reflects that change." With his trademark bad manners, remarked Newcomb, Agassi had become a celebrity. Belgium's Donnay company paid Agassi over $1 million per year to promote its tennis rackets, while Nike had just resigned him to a contract for an estimated $2 million annually to endorse its sneakers and apparel. In Newcomb's opinion, modesty in athletes was out, with arrogance — forearm bashes, chest smashes, end-zone dances, and so on — being dominant. John McEnroe was said in this account to have brought being obnoxious to a fine art by regularly throwing tantrums and screaming at line judges on the tennis court. "This cost him thousands of dollars in fines and won him thousands of lines of nasty ink in the nation's sports pages," observed Newcomb. "Did it hurt McEnroe's off-court business? Hardly." McEnroe then still took in $3 million a year in endorsements, although he was in the twilight of his career. "Advertisers must play the obnoxiousness game with great care…. Finding a long-term company spokesman is a different matter," argued Newcomb. "Gimmicks are okay, serious controversy is not." Cited as examples of athletes who had gone too far were Mike Tyson and Jose Canseco. The latter had a history of failing to show up for scheduled photo shoots. On top of that, Canseco had been stopped several times in the preceding year for speeding and other vehicular violations. "But what really scared sponsors was Canseco's arrest in April, 1989 for carrying an unregistered handgun." Drawing only $500,000 in endorsement income for 1990, the baseball slugger was considered to no longer be in the testimonial big time.[26]

First-degree murder charges were laid in June 1994 against 46-year-old O.J. Simpson for the June 12 stabbing death of his ex-wife, Nicole, and restaurant waiter Ronald Goldman, and after a much-watched 75-minute freeway pursuit of Simpson by the police, aired live around the country. He had pled guilty in 1989 to charges of beating Mrs. Simpson (the pair had married in 1985 and divorced in 1992). It was another blow for the celebrity endorsement business. While he had not done ads for Hertz for years, that company nonetheless distanced itself to the point of issuing a terse "no comment" to all questions; it did not even do the usual courtesy of wishing him well, and so forth. The only ad he was then appearing in was a 30-minute infomercial for Interactive Network. While he was on camera for a total of only 90 seconds in that commercial, the whole thing was immediately pulled from the air. Simpson had been a groundbreaker in opening up the endorsement field more fully for black celebrities; his ads for Hertz (a 19-year pairing) remained legendary as an example of effective endorsements. So successful was he as a testifier that *Advertising Age* once named him Presenter of the Year. Besides Hertz rental cars, Simpson had endorsed TreeSweet Products orange juice, Acme Boot's Dingo Boot and Hyde Athletic Industries Spot-Bilt athletic shoes. As well, he had been a national spokesman for General Motors Chevrolet division, Foster Grant sunglasses, Schick shavers, Royal Crown Cola, and Wilson Sporting Goods.[27]

Earlier in 1994, tennis player Jennifer Capriati lost her endorsement deal with tennis racket maker Prince Manufacturing when she was arrested on marijuana charges. PepsiCo, Inc., could not walk away fast enough from Michael Jackson after the pop singer was accused of molesting a young boy. On the other hand, Wilson Sporting Goods forgave golfer John Daly's trouble with alcohol abuse when they resigned him in June 1994 to a ten-year endorsement contract, the longest golf deal in the company's history. Basketball's Charles Barkley then commanded among the highest fees of any athlete for his commercials for Nike, despite his reputation for being a "bad boy" and being controversial. "The controversy and risk were appealing to us," said Bill Halladay, associate creative director at Bates USA West agency, which hired Barkley to do a spot for Hyundai's Sonata family sedan. While Barkley was often described as a "bad boy," he was perhaps more accurately categorized as obnoxious or mouthy; he was at quite a remove from real bad boys, such as Canseco and Simpson.[28]

Ian Sandman, marketing services manager for Regent Sports Corporation, commented in 1994 that baseball's Darryl Strawberry (then a member of the San Francisco Giants) used to be one of their biggest athletes: "But because of all the negativity surrounding his name, people stopped buying gloves with his signature, and we had to disassociate ourselves from him." Strawberry, a former endorser for Regent, had been waived by the Los Angeles Dodgers earlier in the 1994 season after admitting that he had a drug problem.[29]

For endorsing Fila's sneakers, basketball's Grant Hill would receive about $25 million over five years, reported Randall Lane at the end of 1996. "Despite what Dennis Rodman, Charles Barkley, Deion Sanders and a rogue's gallery of other thuggish professional athletes might have you believe," he added, "the nice guys are finishing first where it counts: the product endorsement deals that determine whether an athlete is merely well paid or gets very rich." He argued there was a backlash against the showboats of sports. Mark McCormack, president of sports marketing giant International Management Group, remarked that "these endorsements follow the sociological mood of the country. Suddenly being a nice person is not boring — it's good." U.S. companies that year paid out an estimated $1 billion to perhaps 2,000 athletes for endorsement deals and licensing rights — said to be a tenfold increase from a decade earlier. Michael Jordan looked only at multiyear deals that paid him at least $10 million. Additionally, the $1 billion sum was reinforced by around $10 billion more spent to advertise and promote those associations.[30]

Lane reported that Hertz no longer used pro athletes in their ads, while Pepsi and Kodak were mortified when Mike Tyson was accused of beating his wife and later jailed for rape. Risks from endorser bad behavior were even greater for small companies, compared to national advertisers. When Dallas Cowboys football star Michael Irvin was caught in 1996 in a motel with go-go dancers and drugs, it was only a minor blip at Nike (he was one of their endorsers), which alone spent perhaps $100 million a year on endorsement contracts. However, 13 Toyota dealerships that had paid Irvin $120,000 to do a series of commercials pulled the ads and absorbed the $400,000 spent on production costs. After Irvin refused to return his fee — or a $55,000 Land Cruiser vehicle he had been lent for the life of the deal — the dealerships sued him. Later the case was settled out of court. Green Bay Packers quarterback Brett Favre had everything going for him to be in high demand as an endorser — talent, a winning team, and good looks. But in 1995 he admitted he was addicted to painkillers. A year later Favre estimated that his admission had cost him $2 million in lost endorsement money. With regard to that loss estimate, Nova Lanktree, a Chicago-based matcher of celebrities and advertisers, said: "I think he's being conservative." After winning golf's PGA Championship in 1991, John Daly was touted as the next Jack Nicklaus. Then he had problems with alcohol and marital difficulties, and his endorsement income plummeted accordingly. As of 1996 Daly still made over $1 million a year off the links, but that paled in comparison with other golfers— Tiger Woods had just signed deals worth some $60 million over five years, before he played his first tournament as a pro.[31]

In his long piece in *Forbes*, Lane acknowledged an article from 1990 in the same magazine wherein it was declared the formula to be a successful endorser seemed to be: "Outlandish behavior draws attention; attention draws dollars." However, he explained, inevitably that formula lost its power when everybody started throwing tantrums. "Merely boorish behavior no longer stands out," he added. Lane did a Lexis/Nexis database search that revealed 18,300 hits on Dennis Rodman's name in the previous year, three times as many as for "nice guy" Arnold Palmer. Yet despite all his attention seeking behavior, Rodman could only pull down $2 million in endorsements in 1996, compared to Palmer's $15 million. Said David Falk, Michael Jordan's agent and business manager since 1984: "Guys like Rodman, Brian Bosworth, Jim McMahon — that's fad marketing. If you're going to be marketed over the long term, it can't be a circus act." Charles Barkley had emphatically declared, "I am not a role model," in a Nike ad three years earlier. Yet, observed Lane, his endorsement take had roughly halved since 1994. Sensing this change in the public mood, in which obnoxiousness was replaced by niceness as the dominant trait sought in endorsers, argued Lane, Andre Agassi had reinvented himself, reducing his tirades, and so forth. Although his tournament performance was erratic, the makeover reportedly had done wonders for his endorsement income, which had increased from $4.5 million to $13 million per year.[32]

By Lane's reckoning, of the $203 million earned in endorsements and licensing income in the prior year by the world's 40 highest paid athletes, $175 million went to athletes with "sterling" reputations. Jordan, Palmer, and Shaquille O'Neal, "super nice guys," alone took in over $70 million of that total. Pete Sampras, then the world's top tennis player, made $8 million from endorsements that year, twice his take from four years earlier, "when he was considered a good player but too nice and boring off the court." When San Francisco 49er quarterback Steve Young replaced the legendary Joe Montana, he had almost no endorsement income. Five years later his off-field income was greater than any other football player on that top 40 list — $4 million that year. Young, a descendent of Brigham Young, gave a part of his salary to the Mormon Church, and did not smoke or drink. Part of Young's secret, explained Lane, was knowing how to chitchat with the executives. Speaking at sales meetings or trade shows and occasionally supplying some star power to a corporate function were then part of almost every major endorsement deal. Young understood that by befriending and impressing the executives, "he gives himself an easy value-added." Agreeing with that sentiment was baseball star Cal Ripken Jr., who remarked, "You want to make sure you give [the sponsors] what they want, so that it translates into good business. Otherwise you have no value."[33]

Back in 1994, athletic shoe maker Fila was looking for a nice guy endorser as it ended a rocky and unsatisfactory $500,000-a-year relationship with boxer Riddick Bowe. It was reported that Fila was not too happy that Bowe started getting into fights at press conferences while wearing Fila gear. Said Howe Burch, Fila vice-president for advertising: "As a small company, we have to be very careful that we choose the right guys. We don't care if they're the best athlete in the world if he or she isn't a solid citizen." Burch decided to make an offer to one of the three top college players ready to enter the NBA, Glenn Robinson, Jason Kidd, and Grant Hill. But Robinson turned out to be "greedy," demanding a $100 million NBA contract (after a holdout he came to terms for $68 million). Then Burch started negotiations with Kidd; in the middle of those talks, however, Kidd was linked to a hit-and-run accident in California. Fila backed away. That left Hill, who became Fila's dominant star endorser. With Hill carrying the sneaker marketing load on his back, Fila became the third largest sneaker maker in the United States. Company sales rose 37 percent in 1995, and 40 percent more in 1996. A likeable personality had a long marketing life, felt Lane, long after he had left his sport. Arnold Palmer had not played golf seriously in 20 years, at that point, but he still made $15 million a year. Joe Montana and Nolan Ryan made about $4 million each.[34]

Golfer John Daly entered the 1991 PGA Championship as the longest of long shots but won and became the hottest thing in golf. Soon he got an endorsement contract with Wilson Sporting Goods to endorse their golf equipment. After an early bout of problems with alcohol, Wilson expressed its faith in Daly by resigning him to a ten-year contract in 1994. However, within a few years his public bouts with alcoholism cost him his marriage, his top ranking in golf, and after a drinking binge in 1997 his Wilson contract. He entered rehabilitation. Later that year the 31-year-old (he also won the 1995 British Open) signed an endorsement deal with Callaway Golf (manufacturers of Big Bertha clubs). That contract required the golfer to be sober around-the-clock and to take part in a daily alcohol counseling program. The longer he avoided the bottle the more money he would make. Few companies, though, were expected to follow that lead because, said an account, "The point of endorsement, after all, is to publicize the virtues of the product, not the problems of the athlete."[35]

Basketball star Kobe Bryant was described as what risk-averse marketers desired: a spectacular, Jordan-like ballplayer who did not get into trouble. He starred for the Los Angeles Lakers, McDonald's, Sprite, and until 2002, Adidas. Also, his face was on the label for Nutella, a hazelnut and chocolate spread with his endorsement—"Try Kobe's favorite." In June 2003 Bryant signed a five-year deal with Nike worth an estimated $40 million. Just two weeks later he was arrested in Colorado and later charged with the sexual assault of a 19-year-old employee of the hotel where he had stayed. Freed on bail, Bryant denied the charges but did concede he had committed adultery with the woman. Later he was indicted to stand trial in the case. Even if Bryant was ultimately found not guilty, the erosion of his image made it possible to compel the companies he endorsed to cut their ties with him. In August Nutella declared that earlier in the year it had already decided not to renew Bryant's contract (due to expire in January 2004) but that in view of developments, Kobe's image on Nutella labels and promotional material was being phased out. Nike, McDonald's, and Sprite all voiced their support for the player, in carefully worded statements. His contract with McDonald's expired later in 2004, while the Sprite pact ended in 2005. At the time of his arrest, no Bryant commercials were running. Bob Williams, president of Burns Sports and Celebrities, pointed out that "at this point, there's minimal damage to the companies, because the commercials aren't running, and for consumers, it's out of sight, out of mind." Williams estimated Bryant's endorsement income at $11 million to $13 million a year. Speculation then was that Nike probably had the right to immediately terminate its contract with the Lakers star (through a morals clause), but it was conceded that his high profile might have given him enough leverage for a narrowly defined morals clause that would have made it difficult to terminate the deal for anything short of a felony conviction. Also, Nike had a reputation for always standing behind their athletes.[36]

As more bad behavior was exhibited by endorsers and as the problem of picking if not the perfect endorser, then at least one who avoided drugs, the police blotter, and so on, became more difficult, a novel solution rapidly rose in popularity. Why not use dead people? Long after their passing, sports legends such as Jim Thorpe, Jesse Owens, and Vince Lombardi appeared in ads for products they probably never even dreamed of. Some of the pairings included Casey Stengel for NEC America's computer system, and Joe Louis, Marilyn Monroe, Albert Einstein, and Abbott and Costello for Wendy's fast food. Reportedly, though, the true "Sultan of Sales," among the dead celebrity endorsers, was Babe Ruth. That was in 1991, after he had been dead for 42 years. Ruth's image was licensed to nearly 250 companies, ranging from giants such as IBM, Sears, and Coca-Cola to smaller businesses such as a New York City condominium project, a legal-research firm, and a Philadelphia bank. Dave Burns, president of Burns Sports Celebrity Services (a firm that matched athletes and advertisers), said that Ruth was probably the most colorful and "fantastic" athlete who ever lived: a man who was "an attention-grabber like no one else, a supersalesman." Even though Ruth was a notorious drinker and womanizer, his image, added Burns, was "a great one. His legend will never fade." The United Valley Bank of Philadelphia used Ruth and teammate Lou Gehrig to promote free checking for senior citizens. Above a photo of the Yankee greats was the pitch: "If you're old enough to remember them, you can forget about paying for checking." Fees to use Babe Ruth as an endorser ranged from $500 for one-time, single market ads to $100,00 for a multimedia national campaign. "When Ruth was alive, his endorsements were limited to an occasional brand of cigar, top hats or chewing tobacco," observed journalist Glen Macnow. "As recently as 1984 Ruth's heirs were getting less than $100 a year for the use of his image. Then the heirs hired Curtis Management Group to coordinate the licensing of the Babe's name and face. Soon Curtis signed agreements authorizing Ruth T-shirts, figurines, collector china, bubble gum cards, and teddy bears. For 1991, Ruth's endorsement and licensing income was expected to be around $500,000.[37]

Macnow reported that Curtis had carved out a sizable niche as agent to the dead, with its client list doubling in each of the previous four years. As well as having more than 50 athletes on its roster, it represented the heirs of Fred Astaire, Mark Twain, Humphrey Bogart, and James Dean, among others. In 1988 the Converse athletic shoe company started using James Dean in a magazine ad campaign for its Jack Purcell brand of sneakers after someone in the firm's Boston ad agency discovered a 1955 photo of the actor wearing the clearly labeled shoes. Sales reportedly shot up over 50 percent in the following year. Explaining the appeal of using dead celebrities, Marty Blackman, president of the New York City ad agency Blackman & Raber, remarked that "the finality of death not only sets in stone, so to speak, a person's accomplishments, it also presents a finality of his character. You know that Babe Ruth isn't going to go into drug rehabilitation.... These days, that's a big plus." When the Montauk Manor resort on Long Island decided to promote itself as a center for business conferences, it ran a photo of Will Rogers in its ad—for an endorsement fee of $1,000. Laws in most states gave heirs exclusive rights over a celebrity's image. Typical was California, where the right to own, protect, and commercially exploit the dead person's name, likeness and persona lasted for 50 years after the star's demise.[38]

Ford used Nat King Cole and his song "Unforgettable" in 1981, 16 years after the singer's death. Mercedes ran a campaign for its E-class cars in 1996 that featured the following dead celebrities: Clark Gable, Gary Cooper, Marlene Dietrich, Bing Crosby, and Errol Flynn.[39]

If bad boy behavior seemed to be centered mainly on athletes, that was because it reflected the central role that athletes had in endorsements in the modern era. They had long replaced film stars as the dominant type of celebrity endorser. Actors had held that spot when everybody in America went to the movies (usually more than once a week), when acting stars were larger than life and appeared in several different movies a year. But films had long lost that dominance. Sports did not fill that void the way movies had—much of America was not sports-oriented—but it came closer than anything else. One could have no interest in sports but could not have avoided running into the names of Michael Jordan and Tiger Woods and Arnold Palmer, for example. Sports figures were also in the media limelight on a regular basis, within their own sporting venues, and thus any bad behavior was more likely to come to light, and then be passed on to the public. Additionally, Nike may have paid out as much as 10 percent of the endorsement fee total, and they signed up sports figures.

10

Statistics, Money, and Effectiveness, 1975–2003

Celebrities grab eye, but credibility is low.
—*Automotive News*, 1977.

Advertisers used to believe that stardust added glamour, excitement, prestige, and a touch of class to the product and rapidly catapulted it into the heavens.　　　　— McCollum Spielman, 1988.

[Marketers] are spending a lot of money on celebrities to get attention and recall, but it's not necessarily making them more effective in selling their product.　　　　— Mark Gleason, 1992.

Fees paid out to endorsers escalated dramatically in the modern era. John Emmerling, president of his own New York ad agency, remarked in 1976 that the highest testimonial fees went to superstars, such as Gregory Peck (who supposedly got $1 million from Travelers insurance) and Jack Benny (who got the same amount from the Wool Bureau); Henry Ford received $1 million from GAF, but over four years, while Peter Sellers got the same sum from TWA for its short-lived and unsuccessful campaign. "But these are mega-bucks for mega-stars," explained Emmerling. "The closer-to-average costs for using a well-known personality today run at least $100,000."[1]

David Burns, of Burns Sports Celebrity Service in Chicago, said in 1978 that most athletes collected $10,000 to $15,000 for a typical one-year endorsement contract. Norman Reich, vice-president of International Creative Management, said that in 1979 the big stars were paid around $200,000 for a national endorsement contract, with payments peaking at $1 million for superstars such as Peck. Back in the early 1960s, he recalled, when stars rarely agreed to television endorsements—because of a worry they would lose prestige—Edward G. Robinson got the peak price of $50,000 for General Foods' Maxwell House coffee.[2]

By 1980 the highest fees, $1 million plus, went to the likes of Jimmy Stewart (for Firestone Tire & Rubber) and James Garner (Polaroid). That sum was for commercials only. If other tasks were asked of them, such as appearances at conventions or trade shows, they were paid extra amounts. Top-paid athletes then were Jack Nicklaus and Arnold Palmer, who each commanded $20,000 for a one-day assignment. Muhammad Ali's asking price for a one-day booking was $15,000; Minnesota Viking quarterback Fran Tarkenton (recently retired) was willing to appear before a sales group for $10,000. Decathlon great Bruce Jenner, football's Don Meredith, and O.J. Simpson each then got $5,000 to $10,000 for a one-day booking, while most other known athletes commanded a fee of from $3,000 to $5,000 per day.[3]

Brokerage firm E.F. Hutton & Company agreed to a deal in April 1986 that paid Bill Cosby an estimated $3 million for about ten television commercials, print ads, and Hutton-sponsored concerts by the comic. That campaign was judged a failure.[4]

The 30 highest paid athletes in the world made a total of about $230 million in 1990. Over one-third of that income came from pitching products (see Appendix D). By this time a number of solo-performing athletes had become instantly recognizable around the globe, what with more television and satellite transmission of sports. That instant recognition, on an increasingly global basis, was what marketers wanted. Said Philip de Picciotto, managing director of Advantage International, a Washington, D.C.–based sports agent: "Tennis players and golfers are especially marketable internationally because they play around the world." Besides being more readily recognizable, individual athletes enjoyed other business advantages over team players. For one thing, golfers, tennis players and race car drivers were allowed to wear company logos when they competed; athletes in team uniforms could not. (One exception to that was shoes: in basketball, for example, players could wear whatever brand they liked, that is, the brand they endorsed).[5]

For the year August 1996 through July 1997, the athletes who received the most endorsement money were: 1. Michael Jordan, $38 million; 2. Shaquille O'Neal, $23 million; 3. Arnold Palmer, $16 million; 4. Andre Agassi, $15.8 million; 5. Jack Nicklaus, $14.5 million. Excluding O'Neal, those four totaled $84.3 million that year, while in 1990 (from Appendix D) they combined to take $26.5 million.[6]

Sam Bradley reported in 1996 that around 20 percent of all commercials used some sort of celebrity endorsement, with 10 percent of all advertising dollars going to celebrity endorsers. According to *Forbes*, in 1995 $111 million of the $229 million earned by the top ten athletes came from endorsements. Said Erin Patton, Nike marketing manager: "The endorser is one-half added value and one-half an emotional bond ... an emotional connection with the consumer." General Mills (Wheaties cereal had long been a big user of endorsement ads) marketing assistant Pam Becker remarked that "Celebrities are used when a brand is trying to establish a certain personality after it has already established itself." George Dickerman, president of Spalding Sports Worldwide, observed that "Endorsements seem to have much greater influence with younger audiences." Trade publication *Brandweek* published a list in February 1996 (see Appendix E) of celebrity endorsers and the firms they shilled for. The list was not complete.[7]

With so much money spent on endorsement fees, and with a dramatic increase in the prevalence of those ads, advertisers wondered more and more just how effective such ads were, compared to the nontestimonial variety. Ernest Rockey, president of the Gallup & Robinson (G&R) research firm, felt that advertisers who planned to use celebrity endorsers should bear in mind that it was more important how they were used rather than who was used. A celebrity testifier, he argued, could compete with the ad message and even "upstage the product." According to a study done in 1973 by G&R, 15 percent of all prime time television ad spots featured celebrities. As well, the study revealed that a celebrity gave a commercial a 12 percent premium above the normal recall level for an ad, confirming findings from previous G&R studies. However, 47 percent of those celebrity ads did not come up to the norm, indicating stars had to be used correctly to produce an effective ad, explained Rockey.[8]

Expanding on that theme was John Emmerling, president of the ad agency John Emmerling, Inc., in 1976. Believing that without exception stars were used to attract attention, he warned they would simply attract attention to themselves unless there was a well-planned idea that hooked them into the advertiser's product. During the 1950s and 1960s, with the growth of television, he recalled, a few celebrities began to show up on the tube hawking products. But most Hollywood stars looked down their noses at the idea of making commercials, so the supply of stars willing to testify was limited. Thus, an advertiser could not search for the star that was exactly right — one who had some special relevance to the product, he explained. Also, most ads then were 60 seconds in length and there were fewer of them in total, less clutter. By 1976, argued Emmerling, the situation had changed and "your 30-second commercial is fighting for its life in a cluttered jungle." For Emmerling there were two tests to be used to evaluate a proposed celebrity ad campaign. The first test was to subtract the star. By that he meant the advertiser should hold up the storyboard that featured a star and imagine that the somebody was a nobody. If there was a strong selling idea then the commercial should still work. If the ad fell flat, it meant starting over to draft a new ad. The second test was to multiply the celebrity. He meant the advertiser should ask himself if 20 other stars could do the job just as well as the one celebrity already selected. If the answer was yes, that meant the advertiser had fallen into a trap "and viewers will probably recall seeing your star, but won't be able to link your product to that recollection," said Emmerling. However, if the answer was no, it meant the advertiser had picked a celebrity with the relevant "hook" to the product and probably had a potentially powerful piece of advertising. An example of a star-with-a-hook cited was the use of acerbic comic Don Rickles as a cranky customer in a National Car Rental campaign.[9]

To try and answer the question of whether or not celebrities were the best way to advertise a small car, the publishers of the trade publication *Automotive News* sent out a questionnaire in 1977 to 1,000 households selected from *Better Homes and Gardens* subscribers. The response rate was 88 percent. According to the survey results, car ads that featured a well-known personality were best able to catch a consumer's attention, but they also had the least amount of credibility. When asked which kind of ads best caught their attention, respondents replied as follows: 41.9 percent picked use of a well-known personality discussing the car's merits; 29.4 percent said direct factual and statistical comparisons of similar competitive makes; 24.5 percent cited a road test demonstration ad that emphasized certain points about the car; 20.8 percent said testimonials from current owners; 11.9 percent gave no reply. Asked which kind of ad was the most believable, 68.7 percent cited the factual and statistical comparison type of ad; 27.6 percent said the road test demonstration; 23.9 percent said testimonials from current owners; 3.1 percent cited well-known personalities discussing the car; 10.9 percent gave no reply.[10]

Arguing against the idea of needing a hook or a degree of relevancy between celebrity and product in order to have a successful campaign was business writer Gerry Scorse. In his opinion, O.J. Simpson for Hertz, Karl Malden for American Express, and Jane Russell for Playtex 18-hour bra were all examples of relevant pairings, while Laurence Olivier for Polaroid, Catherine Deneuve for Mercury Marquis cars, and Lorne Greene for Alpo dog food were all examples of irrelevant pairings. Yet all those campaigns had been judged to be highly successful. "When stars appear viewers do not first demand proof of product relevancy. Stars fascinate. Where ordinary mortals might get no more than a yawn, stars get attention," concluded Scorse. Relevance, he firmly believed, had little to do with it.[11]

Still, that was a minority opinion. Another who agreed that stars worked best as endorsers when care was taken to match their personalities with products and ad copy was the research firm McCollum Spielman & Company. They reached that conclusion in 1980 after examining data from hundreds of celebrity commercial tests conducted over the previous 12 years; their results were put in an eight-page report mailed out to scores of their clients, and others. To get an idea on how well celebrities functioned as salespeople, they looked at data on brand awareness amid television's commercial clutter and on attitude shift. They found that only 41 percent of all celebrity commercials they tested obtained above-average scores in those categories, and only 19 percent were above average in both. Among the celebrity presenters who scored well in their research were: Joe Namath for Brut; O.J. Simpson for Hertz; Don Meredith for Lipton tea; Robert Young for Sanka; Karl Malden for American Express; and Jane Wyatt for Minute Maid juice. George Burns for a cat food and Joan Rivers for a convenience food did not register as believable, leading the study to conclude that comedians were "quite risky" endorsers. Jack Palance and William Conrad also scored poorly in food product ads. Beautiful women, as a category, sometimes succeeded, but sometimes did not. Successful beautiful women included: Cheryl Tiegs for Cover Girl and Clairol; Catherine Deneuve for Chanel; Candice Bergen for Cle; Jennifer O'Neill for Cutex; and Jaclyn Smith for Wella; failures in that category included Brigitte Bardot for a face cream and Raquel Welch for a hair coloring. As for nonentertainment personalities, ranging from ex-astronauts to corporate executives, McCollum Spielman concluded that such endorsers would have "limited appeal and effectiveness ... most such people tend to score poorly in voice, appearance and personality ratings." Attempting to shoot down the argument, spread by star packagers they said, that celebrity endorsements had shown "astounding" growth recently, McCollum Spielman observed that its own data, and that of the Gallup & Robinson research firm, indicated that while celebrity usage as testifiers had been up "steadily" in the past decade, it had "always accounted for less than 10 percent of all commercials aired in both program and station breaks."[12]

Contradicting that conclusion, just a year later in 1981, was a study by Gallup & Robinson that reported there had been more than a 70 percent increase over the past decade in the use of movie, television, entertainment and sports stars as endorsers in prime-time television commercials alone. G&R declared that celebrity commercials offered advertisers a 10 percent premium in persuasiveness. However, a report by U.S. advertising agency Ogilvy & Mather (O&M) claimed celebrity commercials actually reduced the persuasiveness factor by 21 percent. "This finding seems to be in line with some of the criticisms of the use of celebrities," said

O&M vice-president Kathryn Feakins. Chief among those criticisms was that celebrities got attention but distracted from the product message. A reason cited by reporter Jules Arbose for the growth of endorsement ads was that there was no longer the stigma attached to making television commercials that made the practice anathema to big name stars in the past. In fact, one advertising executive remarked: "There is more money being made by actors promoting products during the commercial breaks now than by the actors taking part in the television shows themselves."[13]

Advertising Age conducted a phone survey in 1983 of 1,250 consumers across the country to find out their feelings about the use of well-known personalities as advertising spokespeople. Results suggested that such usage might not have bought the product awareness advertisers expected since most celebrity endorsers made little impression on consumers, while those who did were not considered very believable. Bill Cosby was mentioned by 103 respondents as the first celebrity endorser to come to mind from the advertising they had seen; Chrysler chairman lee Iacocca placed second with 56 mentions; Victoria Principal came third with 35 mentions; Bob Hope was fourth with 24 citations; while ABC sports broadcaster and former football star Don Meredith came fifth with 16 mentions.[14]

In some cases, from that *Advertising Age* survey, consumers remembered the celebrity better than the product. Eight respondents correctly identified James Garner as a shill for Polaroid; four incorrectly remembered him in Kodak commercials. Only 59 percent of the sample could recall any advertising that used a celebrity endorser from among all the advertising they had seen, heard or read in the previous 30 days. Highest recall was for consumers aged 25 to 34, with 72 percent of respondents in that category able to name an ad that used a personality; 18 to 24 age group, 67 percent; 45 to 54, 59 percent; 55 to 64, 47 percent; aged 65 and over, 40 percent. Of those respondents with incomes between $20,000 and $39,999, 68 percent were aware of celebrity advertising; of these with incomes of less than $10,000, 47 percent could recall such ads. Only 25 percent of the sample said they thought most celebrity spokespeople actually used the products or services they represented; 64 percent were convinced the celebrities did not; 11 percent were not sure. Men were more skeptical than women, and doubts about endorsers' truthfulness rose with income. Fifty-four percent said a celebrity's simultaneous endorsing of several different products made no difference in that person's believability; 33 percent of the respondents felt an endorser's believability was hurt by representing several products.[15]

Researchers Charles Atkin and Martin Block noted in 1983 that research conducted by social psychologists over the past 30 years demonstrated that a source perceived as highly credible was more persuasive than a low credibility sender. Celebrity endorsers, they said, were considered to be highly dynamic, with attractive and engaging personal qualities. Audiences may also have trusted the advice provided by some famous people. Cited was a 1975 study showing that celebrities were featured in 15 percent of prime-time television commercials, while another study a few years later reported that proportion was up to 20 percent. Several reasons existed to explain why a famous endorser might be influential, said Atkin and Block: celebrities attracted attention to the advertisement in the cluttered stream of messages; they were seen as entertaining and as trustworthy due to an apparent lack of self-interest. That final element was said to be due to the widespread attribution that major stars did not really work for the endorsement fee, but were motivated by a genuine affection for the product. In one experiment, an advertisement for a fictitious brand of Sangria wine featured an endorsement attributed to a celebrity (actor Al Pacino), a professional expert, the company president, or a noncelebrity endorser. College students read the ads and rated the ads on believability, and intent to purchase. Across those measures, the celebrity condition produced the highest scores. None of the other three endorsers were as influential as the famous testifier.[16]

Other researchers proposed that the celebrity would be more effective for products with high psychological or social risk, involving such elements as good taste, self-image, and opinions of others. The expert endorser was seen as most appropriate for products associated with high financial performance, or physical risk, while the typical unknown consumer was considered to be the best endorsing source for low-risk products. That led Atkin and Block to think that celebrities should be effective in promoting alcohol, since it involved substantial psychological and social risk but minimal financial and performance risk. In order to test that assumption, they designed three versions of nearly identical pairs of ads that featured either a celebrity or a noncelebrity testifier. For example, one pair was for a whiskey, with one half of the pair featuring actor Telly Savalas while the other half featured an unfamiliar male endorser, dressed similar to Savalas, and so on. Results, based on ratings produced by 196 subjects (half 13 to 17 years old, half ranged in age from 18 to 77) found that advertisements featuring celebrity endorsers produced consistently more favorable impact than the noncelebrity ads. Celebrity endorsers were perceived as significantly more trustworthy and competent, and slightly more attractive. Finally, the likelihood of actually purchasing the alcohol product was only slightly greater for those exposed to the famous endorser, but the slight difference on that scale was not significant.[17]

Atkin and Block concluded the use of famous people to endorse alcohol products was highly effective with teenagers, while the impact on older people "was limited." The image of the product tended to be more favorable when a famous endorser was shown; however, that did not lead to a significant difference in behavioral intention to purchase the product.[18]

Researcher Jon Freiden looked at four types of endorsers in 1984 — celebrity, company CEO, expert, typical consumer. Gender of the spokespeople was varied, but no difference was found on that variable. A total of 226 respondents (adults and college students) were involved. Each looked at an ad and then filled out a questionnaire about it. Celebrities used were actors Paul Newman and Linda Evans. Results reportedly varied for type of endorser. For example, if the goal was to elicit awareness of the product, then, said Freiden, a celebrity probably worked the best. However, if the goal was to relay a feeling of trust, a technician or expert was likely the better choice. He also found that attitudes expressed by younger consumers differed substantially from those expressed by older consumers. Generally, students were more positive toward the ads than were the adults.[19]

For three years in the 1980s, Bob Hope, Ted Danson, Billy Dee Williams, and Don Johnson appeared in spots for the Crafted With Pride in the U.S.A. Council, but in doing research for a new campaign, Warwick Advertising found that noncelebrities tested better than did big names. Warwick senior vice-president Sean Driscoll remarked that in the campaign's initial stage, when they told consumers to look for the Made in the U.S.A. label, celebrities were very successful in driving up awareness. But when the campaign was in the second stage, telling consumers that the label meant value-added, "that message didn't ring true coming from the mouths of celebrities." When Video Storyboard Tests conducted a survey in 1987, they found that only 16 percent of the people polled felt "very positive about celebrity endorsers, while 55 percent believed that celebrities only did such ads for the money. Around the same time, a survey by the Roper Organization revealed that celebrity endorsements might have been the least convincing advertising technique of them all — disbelieved, in fact, by 70 percent of consumers. Next came hidden camera ads (disbelieved by 67 percent); then came ads that used company representatives (58 percent); and then comparative ads that named competitors (53 percent). Roper's survey found the most credible commercials were those that based their claims on consumer surveys.[20]

Ogilvy & Mather founder and legendary adman David Ogilvy had long preached that celebrity ads prompted above-average product recall but stimulated below-average sales. Research firm McCollum Spielman presented data that celebrities did better than average at breaking through ad clutter and getting associated with a brand, but in terms of persuasion those celebrity ads were "no better than any other form of commercial." That firm argued it was still easy "to be trapped into the romance of a star. Advertisers used to believe that stardust added glamour, excitement, prestige, and a touch of class to the product and rapidly catapulted it into the heavens." According to McCollum Spielman, star endorsements were still commonplace because celebrities attracted attention; there was no longer a stigma associated with doing commercials, and "talent brokers are much more effective." That stigma had ended in the 1970s, they said, when Laurence Olivier accepted $1 million to promote Polaroid.[21]

Video Storyboard Tests president Dave Vadeha said in 1989 that even the ability of celebrities to attract attention was slipping, as was their persuasiveness and their entertainment value. The frustrations of dealing with celebrities, he felt, had led a lot of advertisers to create their own stars as a way of controlling their destiny and to eliminate the worry of bad behavior. Examples he gave of created celebrities were American Isuzu Motors' Joe Isuzu and Anheuser-Busch's Spuds Mackenzie for Bud Light beer. Despite the many problems involved with celebrity pitchmen, Vadeha said a handful of marketers would always turn to them. "When an agency uses celebrities, it is clearly an apology," he said. "They're trying to say, 'I'm sorry, I don't know what to say about the product, so I'll have someone important say nothing for me.' It's an easy way out." A survey of more than 1,000 adult television viewers by Video Storyboard revealed that only 17 percent of those polled approved of celebrities in ads, down from 26 percent in 1984, the first year they had conducted the survey. Sixteen percent of the respondents said celebrities persuaded them to buy products, down from 22 percent in 1984; 24 percent said famous faces attracted their attention, compared to 33 percent in 1984. Fifty-two percent said celebrities lacked credibility, up from 39 percent in 1984, while 64 percent said celebrities did commercials only for the money, up from 50 percent. Thirty-seven percent of those polled said they did not think the endorsers actually used the products, up from 27 percent in 1984. One exception was Bill Cosby, who, said Vadeha, had been the most convincing and believable celebrity endorser in consumer polls for the previous eight years.[22]

Researcher Grant McCracken argued that typecasting played an important role in pairing actors with products, as "it is precisely this typecasting that makes celebrities so useful to the endorsement process. It is the accumulated meanings of celebrities that make them so potent a source of significance." Thus, he argued, actor Meryl Streep had limited value as a celebrity endorser because she was largely free of "accumulated meanings," and that the same was probably true for George C. Scott. Without type-casting, actors were said to be unable to bring clean and unambiguous meanings to the products they endorsed.[23]

Shekar Misra and Sharon Beatty were researchers who believed that celebrity endorsers were an unnecessary risk unless they were logically related to the product, unless there was a pairing between the personality or attributes of the spokesperson and that of the product. An example given of such a congruent pairing was John Houseman and Smith Barney (a successful campaign), while an example of an incongruent match was Houseman with McDonald's (an unsuccessful campaign). Misra and Beatty conducted an experiment with three mythical products and two celebrity endorsers (actors Clint Eastwood and Carol Burnett). Product ads were created for Unitough Jeans (congruent with the characteristics of East-wood, incongruent with Burnett); a board game called Funnybone (con-gruent with Burnett, incongruent with Eastwood); Aroma coffee (neither congruent nor incongruent with the endorsers). Results in this experi-ment revealed that recall of brand information was significantly higher when the spokesperson was congruent with the brand. That was true for recall measured immediately after exposure to the ads, as well as for recall measured after a one-week delay. In addition, brand affect was found to have been significantly more positive in the congruent condition than in the incongruent and irrelevant conditions.[24]

An experiment in 1991 by Roobina Ohanian looked at the impact of a celebrity's attractiveness, expertise and trustworthiness on a respondent's intention to purchase a product. Ohanian had respondents list celebrities and suggest products for them to sell. From those lists came four fictional ads: Linda Evans promoted a new perfume, Madonna a new line of designer jeans, John McEnroe a line of tennis rackets, and Tom Selleck a new brand of men's cologne. Then 578 subjects were each exposed to one ad and asked to fill out a questionnaire. Results revealed that subject age and gen-der had no differential effect on the evaluation of celebrities or on inten-tion to purchase. Also, the attractiveness and trustworthiness of the celebrity had no significant effect on the subjects' intentions to purchase the products endorsed by each of the four celebrities. Only the perceived expertise of the famous people was a significant factor explaining the sub-jects' intentions to purchase. That is, McEnroe was rated as having the highest expertise, and his ad received the highest intention to purchase rat-ing; Selleck was second on both counts. Ohanian speculated that attrac-tiveness was not relevant at least partly because all celebrities were attractive and that the subjects did not associate a high level of trustworthiness to celebrities because they knew the stars got high fees for endorsing. "For celebrity spokespersons to be truly effective, they should be knowledgeable, experienced, and qualified to talk about the product," Ohanian concluded. "Attempts should be made to employ celebrity spokespersons who have direct connections with their endorsed products and who are perceived to be experts by the target respondents."[25]

David Shani and Dennis Sandler conducted a study the day after football's Super Bowl XXIV, which, they said, strongly confirmed that a star endorsement by itself was not enough. Respondents were first asked to indicate which celebrities, from a given list, had been featured in endorsement ads during the telecast, and then to identify the product that was endorsed by the celebrity. Joe Montana was identified as an endorser by 70 percent of the subjects, while 18 percent correctly identified the product he endorsed (Diet Pepsi); Jay Leno, 66 percent, 53 percent (Doritos); Michael J. Fox, 64 percent, 35 percent (Pepsi); Bo Jackson, 54 percent, 42 percent (Nike); Lee Iacocca, 29 percent, 25 percent (Chrysler); Fred Savage, 27 percent, 17 percent (Pepsi).[26]

A study released in 1991 by the Total Research Corporation tried to measure the perceived quality of 54 celebrities as endorsers. A telephone survey of 2,000 respondents revealed the top five were: Bob Hope, Bill Cosby, Walter Cronkite, George Bush, and Clint Eastwood. Rated as the bottom five were: Hugh Hefner, Donald Trump, Madonna, Roseanne Barr, and Jerry Falwell. John Morton, senior vice-president of Total Research, pointed out that Kodak had the highest quality rating score of any product or celebrity, at 84; Bill Cosby had a score of 75. Once you got into the top echelon of brands, said Morton, even a highly rated star like Cosby "could be doing harm to a Kodak because he is not as perfect, doesn't have as unblemished an image." He said it appeared that brands had better images than celebrities because brands spent money creating a certain feeling in people, whereas celebrities did not have the resources to do anything comparable.[27]

Research System Corporation released a study in 1992 on the persuasiveness of television ad spots. Company senior vice-president Mark Gleason explained that what they had found from reviewing more than 5,000 commercials was that celebrities did not enhance or detract from the success of a commercial. He added, "The point is that [marketers] are spending a lot of money on celebrities to get attention and recall, but it's not necessarily making them more effective in selling their products."[28]

Jagdish Agrawal and Wagner Kamakura looked at the effect announcements of celebrity endorsement deals had on the stock market prices of the shares of the firms signing such deals, in 1995. Their sample contained 110 cases representing announcements of celebrity endorsement by 35 firms involving 87 celebrities. Results revealed a significant percentage of "positive abnormal returns" to the sponsoring firms on the day the deal was announced. "Overall, these results clearly indicate a positive impact of celebrity endorsements on expected future profits, which lends objective market level support to the use of celebrity endorsers in advertising," they concluded.[29]

Dave Vadeha was back with another Video Storyboard survey result in 1996. This time the public's approval rating of celebrities as endorsers had fallen to 17 percent — its lowest level since 1988 — after peaking at 28 percent in 1993. Only 14 percent of the respondents believed that celebrities were more convincing than other endorsers, while 63 percent believed celebrities that hawked products did it only for the money. Also, an all-time high mark for the survey had 43 percent of respondents believing that the famous spokespeople did not even use the products that they endorsed.[30]

11

Conclusion

As the 1900s began, testimonial ads were little used, as they suffered from a bad reputation after a notorious association with patent medicines and their outrageous claims. However, much of that bad reputation had faded from memory by the end of World War I. A tremendous upsurge in advertising in general in the 1920s, in tandem with the rapid rise of mass production and mass consumption that decade (the advent of the modern consumer society), drew endorsement ads back into the mainstream as they became an integral part of the advertising industry. Hollywood personalities quickly became the focus of those ads, the favored category of celebrity to use as an endorser. It was a position they would hold for many decades. Athletes were used at this time, but relatively sparingly. Actors dominated because the movies— and their personalities— engaged almost all of the general public, while sports did not. Later, radio and television would be mined for endorsers as those mediums became popular and dominant. Still, it was Hollywood actors who commanded the biggest endorsement money, at least until the mid–1970s or so. Screen stars were larger than life; television stars were smaller.

National advertisers in many cases mounted extensive and long-running campaigns using multiple celebrities over the life of the campaign, and even within a single ad. Pioneering testimonial campaigns, such as those run for Pond's face cream, Lux bar soap, and Fleischmann's Yeast, were all viewed as successful and tended to draw other marketers into the endorsement field. Cigarette manufacturers used testimonial ads probably more than any other industry group. One reason for advertisers to turn to endorsement ads was that the method was not very costly in the 1920s. That is, in many cases endorsers received very little money for their testimony — something that was definitely not true in later years. Reportedly, Lux paid no money at all to use literally hundreds of Hollywood screen stars (including the most famous) in its campaign, with the actors supposedly content with the publicity they received for themselves, their

189

studio, and their current film. Lux did keep those women supplied with
soap.

By the end of the 1920s, endorsement ads had become noticed so much
that they became the subject of a widespread media debate, both in industry trade publications and in the general media. It was a debate that centered on the ethics of testimonial ads. Much of that debate focused on
whether or not an endorsement ad could be ethical if the testimony supplied by the endorser had been solicited and paid for by the marketer.
Another point addressed was whether such ads should be used if they were
solicited at all — as opposed to spontaneously supplied by a testifier —
regardless of whether or not a payment was involved. Also debated was
whether it was ethical if someone endorsed a product that they had in fact
never used. Fakery and misrepresentation were at the forefront of the
debate. Overwhelmingly, the industry declared itself opposed to the
solicited testimonial and to the paid testimonial, regardless that the
solicited and paid-for ad might have been sincere. The fact that such una-
nimity had no effect on the prevalence of testimonial ads at that time or
in later years indicated that little was involved in the industry's publicly
declared opposition other than rhetoric.

Endorsement ads had a high enough profile in the 1920s that they
drew ridicule from well-known people of the time. Both James Thurber
and Sinclair Lewis attacked testimonial ads in scathing fashion. Clearly the
industry's public utterances against the "insincere" testimonial were part
of a position to forestall any federal government intervention or regulation of endorsement ads, something the advertising industry worried
about. In fact, the FTC did intervene at the start of the 1930s. But, for
unclear reasons, the agency elected to proceed on a case they were unlikely
to win and then prosecuted that case poorly, as if they wanted to lose. Following that defeat, the federal government stepped out of the endorsement arena and did not re-enter again, in any meaningful way, although
from time to time it performed some minor tinkering in the area. Over
time, endorsement ads had always drawn more attention than their numbers likely warranted. Using selected years, ranging from 1926 to 1998,
endorsements in magazine ads had ranged from about 2 percent to 18 percent of all full-page ads, while their proportion of television ads had been
perhaps in the 10 to 20 percent range.

With respect to endorsement ads, the 1930s were similar to the 1920s
with the notable exception that in the later period there was next to no
debate on the ethics of endorsement ads. The "insincere" testimonial — that
is, one that was solicited and paid for — had become an accepted part of
the American advertising scene. And that was in the face of much obvious

misrepresentation in some of those ads. For example, nonsmokers testified regularly for tobacco companies that they smoked a particular brand, while smokers with no brand preference swore they smoked only, say, Camels.

Having reached a certain level in the U.S. advertising industry, endorsement ads went into a long period, lasting from 1940 to 1974, roughly, in which they sort of stagnated, as they neither gained nor lost ground. Little attention was paid to them in the media. One reason was that it was a transition period in which movies went into a huge decline, due to the arrival of television. Film stars were not the commanding figures they once were while television stars had not yet emerged in the stature and numbers necessary to replace them. During this time the middleman organization (a company that arranged pairings between celebrities and advertisers or their ad agencies) arrived to stay. Such organizations had existed in the past, but they were very few in number and none of them lasted. Sports agents became more important to athletes, as they took over bargaining for their clients. Both agents and middleman firms would become integral parts of the boom in endorsement ads in the modern era. They were all aggressive in pursuing endorsement deals for their clients, be they athletes or movie stars, far more aggressive than the celebrities themselves would have been.

Within the advertising world, almost all agreed that a boom in testimonial ads started around 1975 and has continued up to the present time. Once again a great deal of attention was devoted to the subject. With respect to print ads in magazines, there was little evidence to suggest endorsement ads formed a higher proportion of total ads in the modern period, compared to the past. The situation for television was unclear. However, there were far more ads in the modern period than in the past, so if testimonial ads just held the same percentage as in the past they would have appeared to be much more prevalent. For example, a half-hour television show in the 1950s or 1960s had a program length of about 26 minutes— today it is no more than 22 minutes, a doubling of commercial time.

During the 1920s and 1930s, endorsement ads were dominated by companies that used multiple celebrities over time, such as Lux, or Chesterfield cigarettes. In the modern era the field was dominated by individual personalities who endorsed a number of companies over a period of time, such as Bill Cosby, Michael Jordan and Tiger Woods. And more and more, those celebrity endorsers have been athletes.

Again, the ethics of the ads themselves were rarely mentioned. Instead, focus was placed on what might have been called the ethics of the endorser. In the past an endorser could have found his reputation tarnished after he misguidedly endorsed somebody's miracle cure. Now the worry was that a product's image would be tarnished after its endorser was revealed as a drug abuser, or stood accused of a felony. Debated in the modern era was the issue of how to avoid the bad boy endorser and/or what to do if you were an advertiser and found your testifier had suddenly turned into a bad boy. The search for the perfect endorser was so fraught with peril that it led some marketers to turn to dead celebrities as endorsers. If a worry was that, in using as a testifier a celebrity who had been dead for, say, 20 years he might not command much public attention, comfort could be taken from the fact that he would at least produce no surprises.

Absent from virtually all of the attention to endorsement ads previous to 1975 was any discussion on their effectiveness. That is, no research had been done to show that ads that featured celebrity endorsers were more effective in selling goods than were ads that featured noncelebrity endorsers, or no endorsements at all. All along it seemed to be accepted as a given that such ads were successful. Only in the modern era was the question of efficacy discussed, if not resolved. Over time, there was little disagreement over the idea that endorsement ads attracted the reader's or viewer's attention. And while research done in recent times had always reached that conclusion, it was not the same as showing those ads actually sold more products. There was no solid scientific evidence one way or the other. Within the advertising industry some swore that endorsement ads worked and were worth the extra money involved, while others took an opposite position. Anecdotal evidence did exist. Hollywood stars had long been known to have the ability to send people stampeding off to buy a certain item of clothing, or adopt a particular hair style, and so on, based only on the star's appearance. When Fila signed Grant Hill to be its main endorser, sales of its athletic shoes increased dramatically over the following two years after the Hill ads began to run. But Fila had committed what was for it a huge amount of money to sign Hill, and to ensure it got its money's worth it bought more ad time and space. Was its sales increase due to Hill, or just more ads, or something else?

With advertising being an even more pervasive part of our lives now than in the past and with marketers battling for consumer dollars, it is likely that the endorsement ad will remain a part of the ad campaigns of national advertisers as they try every strategy they can think of to come out on top, regardless of what any evidence says or does not say about a particular form of advertising. The search for the perfect endorser is fated to continue.

Appendix A

Prevalence of Endorsement Ads: Selected Years, Selected Publications, 1926–1998

Only full-page (or longer) endorsement ads were counted. For each year listed for each publication, issues were analyzed for the period January 1 to June 30 inclusive.

	Total Ads	Total Cig. Ads	% of Ads End.	% of Cig. Ads End.	% of Cig. Ads in total Ads	% of Cig. End. to Total End.
Saturday Evening Post 1928	1941	0	4.17	—	—	—
Saturday Evening Post 1938	774	20	7.75	65	2.58	21.7
Life 1938	297	25	17.51	76	8.42	36.54
Life 1948	1178	40	6.62	42.5	3.4	21.8
Life 1958	1136	61	3.61	11.48	5.37	17.1

(Cig.-Cigarettes, End.-Endorsed)

	Total Ads	Total Endorsed Ads	% of Ads Endorsed
Good Housekeeping 1938	172	29	16.86
Good Housekeeping 1948	192	22	11.46
Good Housekeeping 1958	284	8	2.82
Good Housekeeping 1968	357	8	2.24
Good Housekeeping 1978	554	35	6.32
Good Housekeeping 1988	379	14	3.69
Good Housekeeping 1998	387	19	4.91

Appendix A

	Total Ads	Total Endorsed Ads	% of Ads Endorsed
American Magazine 1926	289	27	9.3
American Magazine 1936	111	20	18.0
American Magazine 1946	154	3	1.9
American Magazine 1956	48	8	16.7
Newsweek 1936	185	18	9.7
Newsweek 1946	562	15	2.7
Newsweek 1956	442	29	6.6
Newsweek 1966	432	18	4.2

Appendix B

Lux Soap Ads Endorsed by Hollywood Actors in *Variety*, 1932–1949

This list was compiled from the full-page back cover ads only that appeared from 1932 to 1949, inclusive.

1934
Apr 3 Norma Shearer
Aug 21 Joan Blondell
Sept 4 Ginger Rogers
Oct 2 Claudette Colbert
Oct 16 Dolores Del Rio
Oct 30 Grace Moore
Nov 13 Goldwyn Girls and Ethel
   Merman
Nov 27 Yvonne Printemps
Dec 11 Nancy Carroll
Dec 25 Irene Dunne

1935
Jan 1 Joan Crawford
Mar 13 Ann Sothern and Merle
   Oberon
Mar 27 Gloria Stuart and Glenda
   Farrell
Apr 10 Claudette Colbert and
   Joan Bennett
May 15 Claudette Colbert
May 29 Jeanette MacDonald
June 12 Jean Arthur
June 26 Ruth Chatterton
July 10 Miriam Hopkins
July 24 Grace Moore
Nov 27 Jean Arthur
Dec 11 Eleanor Powell

1936
Jan 29 Goldwyn Girls, included
   Ethel Merman and
   Sally Eilers
Feb 19 Loretta Young
Mar 11 Sylvia Sidney
Apr 8 Mae Clark, Evalyn Knapp
   and Joan Marsh
May 6 Barbara Stanwyck
May 27 Claudia Morgan, Peggy
   Conklin and Mary Philips
June 17 Margaret Lindsay
July 15 Anne Shirley
Oct 14 Gladys George
Nov 18 Mae West
Dec 23 Joan Blondell and Glenda
   Farrell

1937
Mar 24 Doris Nolan and
   Gertrude Niesen
Apr 2 Carole Lombard
June 2 Miriam Hopkins
June 30 Harriet Hilliard
July 14 Frances Farmer
Aug 18 Joan Bennett
Aug 25 Eleanor Powell
Sept 8 Madeleine Carroll
Oct 6 Loretta Young

195

Dec 1 Ann Dvorak and Tamara
Geva
Dec 15 Ann Sheridan and Marcia
Ralston

1938

Feb 2 Margot Grahame and
Franciska Gaal
Apr 20 Myrna Loy
June 8 Rosemary Lane and
Gloria Dickson
July 27 Ginger Rogers
Sept 14 Jean Arthur
Nov 9 Janet Gaynor
Dec 21 Joan Bennett and Ann
Sothern

1939

May 10 Barbara Stanwyck
July 5 Gail Page, Priscilla Lane,
Lola Lane, Rosemary Lane
(The Lane Sisters)
Sept 20 Carole Lombard, Kay
Francis, Helen Vinson
Oct 11 Loretta Young
Oct 18 Alice Faye
Oct 25 Anna Neagle
Nov 1 Arleen Whelan
Dec 6 Bette Davis, Olivia De
Havilland

1940

Feb 14 Edna Best
Apr 24 Rita Johnson, Bonita
Granville, Diana Lewis
May 1 Merle Oberon, Geraldine
Fitzgerald, Binnie
Barnes
May 8 Joan Blondell, Lana
Turner
May 22 Alice Faye
July 17 Joan Crawford
Sept 25 Linda Darnell
Oct 9 Deanna Durbin
Nov 6 Madeleine Carroll,
Paulette Goddard

1941

Mar 19 Carole Lombard
Mar 26 Deanna Durbin
Apr 16 Bette Davis
Apr 30 Alice Faye
May 14 Merle Oberon

May 28 Irene Dunne
Sept 24 Dorothy Lewis, Barbara
Jo Allen
Oct 29 Maureen O'Hara, Anna
Lee
Nov 26 Claudette Colbert

1942

Apr 1 Susan Hayward, Paulette
Goddard
Apr 29 Marlene Dietrich
May 6 Joan Bennett
June 17 Binnie Barnes
July 15 Teresa Wright
Oct 14 Rosalind Russell
Dec 16 Ida Lupino
Dec 23 Joan Leslie
Dec 30 Maria Montez

1943

Jan 20 Dorothy Lamour, Paulette
Goddard, Veronica Lake,
Betty Hutton
Feb 24 Deanna Durbin
Mar 31 Anne Shirley, Carole
Landis
Apr 21 Rosalind Russell
May 12 Claire Trevor, Evelyn
Keyes
Sept 22 Claudette Colbert,
Paulette Goddard, Veronica
Lake

1944

Mar 8 Lynn Bari
Mar 22 Loretta Young
Apr 26 Rita Hayworth
May 3 Rise Stevens
May 10 Vera Zorina
July 26 Claudette Colbert,
Shirley Temple
Aug 16 Joyce Reynolds, Ann
Harding
Sept 20 Teresa Wright
Nov 22 Virginia Bruce

1945

Jan 31 Merle Oberon
Mar 14 Veronica Lake, Marjorie
Reynolds
Apr 4 Sonja Henie
May 16 Dorothy Lamour
June 20 Diana Lynn

June 27 Virginia Mayo, Vera-
  Ellen
July 18 Evelyn Keyes
Nov 21 Betty Grable, June Haver
1946
Feb 20 Claudette Colbert
Apr 3 Rita Hayworth
May 15 Joan Fontaine
May 29 Lana Turner
July 10 Virginia Mayo
Aug 7 Alexis Smith, Jane Wyman
Sept 11 Lauren Bacall

Oct 16 Evelyn Keyes
Dec 18 Janis Paige
1947
Apr 23 Dorothy Lamour
June 11 Hedy Lamarr
June 25 Jane Wyman
July 9 Joan Crawford
Aug 13 Ilona Massey
Aug 27 Myrna Loy
Oct 8 Rita Hayworth
Nov 5 Joan Caulfield
Dec 3 Sylvia Sidney

Appendix C

Endorsement Contracts of the Dionne Quintuplets through Early 1937

This list of contracts shows company name, amount of money received by the quintuplets' family as of January 31, 1937, and (in brackets) the date the contract was signed and the date of its expiration.

Alexander Doll Company $25,828.37 — manufacture and sale of dolls and dolls' clothing (25 Feb 1936 and 31 Dec 1937). Covers 5 percent of quint product sales and was a renewal of a 6 Feb 1935 contract.

Aluminum Manufacturing $5,057.59 — manufacture and sale of aluminum dishes (17 Mar 1936 and 1 Apr 1938). Covers five percent on quint product sales.

Harry S. Bond $1,000 — manufacture of shoes, boots and rubbers (2 Nov 1936 and 15 Jan 1942). Covers royalty of two cents to eight cents per pair, with minimum guarantee of $47,500.

Brown and Bigelow $58,097.17 — manufacture and sale of calendars and remembrance cards (10 Jan 1936 and 31 Dec 1939). Covers 7.5 percent on quint product sales.

Colgate-Palmolive-Peet $8,750 — advertise use by the quints of Colgate Ribbon and Dental Cream (2 July 1936 and 2 July 1939). Flat rate contract for $27,500.

Corn Products Refining Company $6,666.66 — advertise the use of Karo, a corn syrup, by quints (1 Nov 1936 and 1 Nov 1939). Flat rate contract for $45,000.

Herz and Kory $2,500 — manufacture and sale of children's purses and bags (26 Mar 1936 and 30 Sept 1938). Covers 5 percent on quint product sales.

Lehn and Fink $5,850 — advertising of Hinds honey and Almond Cream (Jan 1937 and 15 Aug 1939). Renewal of 8 Feb 1935 contract.

Lever Brothers $2,500 — advertise the use of Lux for washing quint's clothing (28 Nov 1936 and 1 Jan 1940). Flat rate contract for $25,000.

Libby, McNeill and Libby — supply and advertise use by children of homogenized baby foods, tomato juice and pineapple juice (2 Apr 1936 and 26 Jan 1937). Flat rate contract for $8,500.

Monocraft Products $2,500 — manufacture and sale of jewelry, ornamental and novelty items (21 Apr 1936 and 1 Sept 1938). Covers 5 percent on quint product sales with a minimum guarantee of $10,000.

McCormack's Limited $10,000 — sale of biscuits, cookies and crackers (Feb 1936 and 1 Apr 1940). Covers a $37,500 minimum guarantee with a royalty of $1.50 per ton.

Palmolive Company $8,750 — advertise the use by the quints of Palmolive soap (2 July 1936 and 2 July 1939). Flat rate contract of $27,500.

Quaker Oats Company $15,500 — advertise use by the quints of Quaker Oats cereals. Payments include $2,500 received 6 Dec 1935 for a special premium picture right (May 1935 and 1 June 1939). Flat rate contract of $15,000.

Samuel Rosen $35,000 — manufacture and sale of candy products known as Lolly Pop (20 Aug 1936 and 31 Jan 1938). Contract provides for renewal with a minimum guarantee of $7,500 per year. Five percent on quint product sales.

Stern and Herff $2,994.70 — manufacture and sale of children's coat ensembles, hats and berets (6 May 1935 and 15 Dec 1937). Covers 5 percent on quint product sales.

Tiny Town Togs $10,416.71 — manufacture and sale of children's dresses (30 Apr 1935 and 31 Oct 1937). Covers 5 percent on quint product sales.

United Drug Company $2,125 — advertise the use by quints of Puretest Cod Liver Oil and First-Aid Absorbent Cotton (Apr 1935 and 26 July 1937). Flat rate contract of $2,125.

Vincent and Hughes $3,258.09 — sale of framed pictures of the quints. Covers 7.5 percent of sales.

John C. Wellwood $5,000 — manufacture and sale of ribbons (Jan 1936 and 1 Apr 1938). Covers 5 percent royalty.

NEA Service, Inc. $12,333.19 — manufacture and distribution of still pictures of quints (1 Apr 1936 and 31 Dec 1937). Flat rate contract of $63,888.73. A renewal of 10 Jan 1935 contract. $3,000 received upon renewal of contract.

Pathe News Features, Inc. $40,485.51 — manufacture of motion pictures for news features and short reel subjects (19 June 1936 and 1 Jan 1938). Covers 25 percent and 40 percent of gross revenues.

Twentieth Century-Fox Film $50,000 — to produce one motion picture of feature length to be generally released for public exhibition purposes not later than 1 Mar 1936 (8 Nov 1935). Flat rate contract of $50,000.

Twentieth Century-Fox Film $250,000 — to produce three feature-length pictures. The three to be generally released for public exhibition purposes not later than 1939 (7 May 1936). Flat rate plus royalty depending on earnings of the pictures.

Source: P.H. Erbes, "Those precocious Dionnes." *Printers' Ink* 179 (1 April 1937): 6–8, 12, 113.

Appendix D

Highest Paid Athletes from Sports and Endorsements, 1990, Estimated

Rank	Athlete	Sport	Salary/Winnings	Other	Total
			In Millions of Dollars		
1	Mike Tyson	boxing	27.6	1.6	29.2
2	Buster Douglas	boxing	25.0	1.0	26.0
3	Sugar Ray Leonard	boxing	12.0	1.0	13.0
4	Ayrton Senna	car racing	9.0	1.0	10.0
5	Alain Prost	car racing	8.0	1.0	9.0
6	Jack Nicklaus	golf	0.6	8.0	8.6
7	Greg Norman	golf	1.5	7.0	8.5
8	Michael Jordan	basketball	2.1	6.0	8.1
9	Arnold Palmer	golf	0.1	8.0	8.1
10	Evander Holyfield	boxing	8.0	0.1	8.1
11	Boris Becker	tennis	1.2	6.0	7.2
12	Nigel Mansell	car racing	6.0	1.0	7.0
13	Steffi Graf	tennis	1.1	5.0	6.1
14	Jose Canseco	baseball	5.5	0.5	6.0
15	Wayne Gretzky	hockey	3.0	3.0	6.0
16	Andre Agassi	tennis	1.0	4.5	5.5
17	Stefan Egberg	tennis	1.5	4.0	5.5
18	Ivan Lendl	tennis	1.3	4.0	5.3
19	Diego Maradona	soccer	2.0	3.0	5.0
20	Don Mattingly	baseball	4.5	0.3	4.8
21	Bo Jackson	baseball/football	2.0	2.5	4.5
22	Gabriela Sabatini	tennis	0.5	4.0	4.5
23	Magic Johnson	basketball	2.5	2.0	4.5
24	Robin Yount	baseball	4.2	0.3	4.5
25	Joe Montana	football	1.4	3.0	4.4
26	Patrick Ewing	basketball	3.6	0.6	4.2

Rank	Athlete	Sport	Salary/Winnings	Other	Total
			In Millions of Dollars		
27	Greg LeMond	cycling	1.7	2.5	4.2
28	Gerhard Berger	car racing	3.0	1.0	4.0
29	Curtis Strange	golf	0.8	3.0	3.8
30	Will Clark	baseball	3.7	0.1	3.8

Source: Peter Newcomb and Christopher Palmeri. "Throw a tantrum, sign a contract." *Forbes* 146 (20 Aug 1990): 70.

Appendix E

Celebrity Endorsers by Company, February 1996

Aamco
Jim Brolin

Ace Hardware
John Madden

Adidas
Steffi Graf
John Starks
University of
Nebraska

Adler Books
Tom Kite

Allen Sport
Jim Plunkett

Almaden Wine
George Burns

American Express
Jerry Seinfeld

Amway
Shaquille O'Neal

And 1
Larry Johnson

Anheuser-Busch
Dale Earnhardt
Hanson Brothers
Charlton Heston
Rachel Hunter
Dan Marino
Paul Newman
Lou Rawls
George Strait

Apple Computer
George Clinton
Todd Rundgren

Arnold Palmer Golf
Arnold Palmer
Steve Stricker
Tom Wargo

AT&T
Whitney Houston

Beck's Beer
James Woods

Bell Atlantic
James Earl Jones

BellSouth
Dixie Carter

Ben Hogan
Tom Kite

Buick
Digger Phelps

Burger King
Tony Dorsett
Lou Holtz
Bo Jackson
Keith Jackson
Ronnie Lott
Jim McMahon
Warren Moon
Joe Paterno

Cadillac
Arnold Palmer
Barry Sanders

Campbell Soup
Wayne Gretzky

Cannondale Bikes
Missy Giove
Tinker Juarez
Alison Sydor

Canon
Andre Agassi

Carnival Cruise Lines
Frank Gifford
Kathie Lee Gifford

Chevrolet
Greg Norman
Picabo Street

Choice Hotels
Ed McMahon

Chrysler
Greg Kinnear
Tom Kite

Cobra Golf
Ben Crenshaw
Beth Daniel
Hale Irwin
Greg Norman

Coca-Cola
Wayne Gretzky
Karch Kiraly
Emmitt Smith
Lucky Vanous

Como Sport
Susan Anton
Hale Irwin

Compaq Computers
Hakeem Olajuwon

Converse
Larry Bird
Julius Erving
Larry Johnson
Rick Pitino
Latrell Sprewell

Danskin
Nadia Comaneci

Dynastar
Jean-Luc Brassard
Deb Compagnoni
Chris Evert
Marc Giradelli
Tommy Moe
Picabo Street
Alberto Tomba

Etonic
Bill Rodgers

Ewing Athletics
Patrick Ewing

Fairway Blues
Liselotte Neumann

Fila
Jason Alexander
Mitch Butler
Naomi Campbell
Chris Elliot
Dale Ellis
Hersey Hawkins
Grant Hill
Kathy Ireland
Jamal Mashburn
Eddie Murray
Mike Powell
Ruben Sierra
Jerry Stackhouse
Kent Steffes
Alberto Tomba
Vendela

Frontier
Corey Pavin

General Mills
Deion Sanders
Steve Young

GMC Trucks
Grant Hill

Gulfstream
Jack Nicklaus

Hanes Hosiery
Fran Drescher

Hanes Underwear
Michael Jordan

Hardees
Bill Fagerbakke
Jerry Van Dyke

Hartmarx
Jack Nicklaus

Head Sportswear
Gabriela Sabatini

Infiniti
Jonathan Pryce

Intellimedia
Tom Kite

K2 Skis
Phil Mahre
Steve Mahre

Kellogg
Grant Hill
Michael Jordan

Kmart
Penny Marshall
Rosie O'Donnell

Kraft Foods
Bill Cosby

L.A. Gear
Wayne Gretzky
Brett Hull
Karl Malone
Mark Messier

La Mode
Phil Mickelson

L'eggs
Jamie Lee Curtis

Lincoln-Mercury
Jack Nicklaus

Louisville Hockey
Dave Gagner

Mike Gartner
Curtis Joseph
Mark Messier
Keith Tkachuk

Lyle & Scott
Sandy Lyle

Lynx Golf
Fred Couples

Marriott Hotels
Dick Cavett

MasterCard
Tom Watson

Maxfli Golf
Fred Couples
Jay Haas
Jack Nicklaus
Greg Norman
Tom Watson

McDonald's
Charles Barkley
Larry Bird
Drew Bledsoe
Phil Hartman
Michael Jordan
Grant Hill
Dan Marino
Barry Sanders
Emmitt Smith

MCI
Whoopi Goldberg
Janis Joplin
Grace Kelly

Mercedes-Benz
Bill Blass
Donna Karen
Ed McMahon
Isaac Mizrahi

Milk Council
Jennifer Aniston
Christie Brinkley
Natasha Kinski
Lisa Kudrow
Vanessa Williams

Miller Brewing
Larry Bird
Larry Dixon

Keith Jackson
Lee Janzen
Bobby Rahal
Pat Riley
Duffy Waldorf
Rusty Wallace

Minolta
John Sparks

Movado Watches
Pete Sampras

Munsingwear
Larry Gilbert
Blaine McCallister
Jesper Parnevik
J.C. Snead

National Car Rental
Dudley Moore

Nicklaus Golf
Jack Nicklaus

Nike
Andre Agassi
Troy Aikman
Charles Barkley
Drew Bledsoe
James Carville
George Clinton
Jim Courier
Duke University
Sergei Federov
Georgetown University
Ken Griffey Jr.
Penny Hardaway
Reggie Jackson
Michael Jordan
Jackie Joyner-Kersee
Jason Kidd
Carl Lewis
Reggie Miller
Cam Neely
Dan O'Brien
Pennsylvania State University
Mary Pierce
Scottie Pippen
Cal Ripken Jr.
David Robinson

Dennis Rodman
Pete Sampras
Barry Sanders
Deion Sanders
Junior Seau
Monica Seles
Sterling Sharpe
John Stockton
Picabo Street
Sheryl Swoopes
Syracuse University
Thurman Thomas
Steve Young
University of Iowa
University of Michigan

Nintendo
Ken Griffey Jr.

Nobody Beats the Wiz
Boomer Esiason
Joe Namath
Phil Simms

Oakley Sunglasses
Michael Jordan

Office Depot
Arnold Palmer

Outback Steakhouse
Rachel Hunter

Pennzoil
Arnold Palmer

PepsiCo
Andre Agassi
Cindy Crawford
Ken Griffey Jr.
Shaquille O'Neal
Jerry Rice
Michael Richards
Deion Sanders
Steve Young

Pizza Hut
Waylon Jennings
Jerry Jones
Rush Limbaugh
John McEnroe
Peter McNeeley
Monkees

Willie Nelson
Anthony Quinn
David Robinson
Dennis Rodman
Pete Sampras
Deion Sanders
Ringo Starr
Donald Trump
Ivana Trump

Pontiac
Ward Burton
Bobby Hamilton
Kyle Petty

Prince Sports
Michael Chang
Jimmy Connors
Andrei Medvedev

Puma
Diego Maradona

Quaker Oats
Michael Jordan
Wendy Kaufman

Rayovac
Michael Jordan

Reebok
Derek Atkins
Kim Batten
Roger Clemens
Clyde Drexler
Juan Gonzales
Steve Holman
Shawn Kemp
Greg Lloyd
Rebecca Lobo
Ken Norton Jr.
Shaquille O'Neal
Rhett Periman
Glenn Robinson
Sam Russell
Emmitt Smith
Frank Thomas

Revlon
Cindy Crawford

Roadmaster
Arnold Palmer
Suzanne Somers
Jake Steinfeld

Rolex
Arnold Palmer

Schick
Jerry Stackhouse

Sega
Deion Sanders

Spalding
Adam Johnson
Rebecca Lobo
Hakeem Olajuwon
Shaquille O'Neal
Nancy Reno
Julie Smith
Craig Stadler
Rebecca Staley
Payne Stewart
Lee Trevino

Sprint
Candice Bergen

Sprite
Grant Hill

Taco Bell
Spike Lee
Hakeem Olajuwon
Shaquille O'Neal
Jack Palance

Taylor Made Golf
Michael Bradley
Brad Bryant

Lee Janzen
Tom Lehman
Mark O'Meara
Kenny Perry

TGI Friday's
Jim Meskimen

Thomson Electronics
Pete Sampras

Titleist/Foot-Joy
David Duval
Tom Kite
Davis Love III
Curtis Strange

Tommy Armour Golf
Brian Barnes
Jeff Gallagher
John Huston
Nancy Lopez
Davis Love III

Tretorn
Bjorn Borg

Uncle Ben's Rice
Hakeem Olajuwon

**United Sports
Technologies**
John Daly

Visa
Hakeem Olajuwon
Scottie Pippen

Wendy's
B.B. King
Dave Thomas

Wilson
Barry Bonds
Joe Carter
John Daly
Shawon Dunston
Stefan Edberg
Steffi Graf
Penny Hardaway
Grant Hill
Michael Jordan
Shawn Kemp
Bernhard Langer
Greg Maddux
Todd Martin
Mark McCumber
Alonzo Mourning
Kirby Puckett
Pete Sampras
Deion Sanders
Vijay Singh

Yonex
Amy Benz
Vicki Goetze
Scott Hoch
Phil Mickelson
Monica Seles
James Worthy

Source: Sam Bradley. "Marketers are always looking for good pitches." *Brandweek* 37 (26 Feb 1996): 36–37.

Chapter Notes

Chapter 1

1. Arthur J. Cramp. "Testimonials—mainly medical." *American Mercury* 17 (August 1929): 444–445.
2. Donald David. "Use the testimonial." *Advertising Agency Magazine* 49 (October 12, 1956): 60.
3. Charles Merz. "A custom of the country." *Outlook and Independent* 151 (April 10, 1929): 583.
4. Loring W. Batten Jr. "It was a racket in 1889." *Printers' Ink* 156 (September 10, 1931): 20.
5. Bennett Cerf. "Endorsements, Inc." *Saturday Review* 39 (June 16, 1956): 7.
6. Ray Giles. "Testimonial techniques of forty years ago." *Advertising & Selling* 15 (October 1, 1930): 22–23.
7. Ibid., pp. 70–71.
8. "The Trade Commission jumbles the testimonial puzzle." *Printers' Ink* 150 (January 30, 1930): 49.
9. Cramp, "Testimonials," p. 445.
10. Ibid., p. 447.
11. Ibid., p. 449.
12. Ibid., pp. 449–450.
13. Ibid., p. 448.
14. Alva Johnston. "Testimonials C.O.D." *Outlook and Independent* 157 (March 18, 1931): 398–399.

Chapter 2

1. "Collecting on picture names." *Variety*, February 4, 1919, p. 56.
2. "Tiring of advertising tie-up screen stars and studios refuse commercial offers." *Variety*, November 14, 1928, p. 4.
3. "Smith Brothers to wage war on the-ater cough." *Printers' Ink* 145 (November 29, 1928): 10.
4. Walter Goodman. "Elsa Maxwell loves Mazola." *Nation* 182 (April 14, 1956): 295.
5. Arthur J. Cramp. "Testimonials—mainly medical." *American Mercury* 17 (August 1929): 44.
6. Ibid.
7. "Will Rogers gives testimonial copy a new twist." *Printers' Ink* 130 (February 12, 1925): 33–34.
8. "Melachrino enlists nobility in new campaign." *Printers' Ink* 134 (February 4, 1926): 60.
9. H.S. Gardner. "The paid testimonial is taking the cure." *Advertising & Selling* 12 (April 17, 1929): 18, 46.
10. Morton J. Simon. "Endorsement and testimonial copy." *Advertising Agency and Advertising & Selling* 44 (October 1951): 163–164.
11. Cramp, "Testimonials," p. 450.
12. "J. Walter Thompson Company." *Fortune* 36 (November 1947): 226.
13. Alva Johnston. "Testimonials, C.O.D." *Outlook and Independent* 157 (March 18, 1931): 398.
14. Ibid., p. 399.
15. Ibid.
16. "J. Walter Thompson Company," 226.
17. Goodman, "Elsa Maxwell love Mazola," p. 296.
18. "The inside of the testimonial racket." *Advertising & Selling* 16 (January 7, 1931): 20.
19. Ibid., p. 21.
20. Ibid.
21. Ibid., p. 56.
22. Ibid., p. 58.
23. Willis Brindley. "How to get worthwhile testimonials for your business."

Printers' Ink 125 (November 22, 1923): 25–26.

24. Ibid., pp. 26–27.

25. A.L. Townsend. "Industrial advertising that features the testimonial of indirection." *Printers' Ink* 126 (February 21, 1924): 125.

26. Ibid., p. 126, 129.

27. "Simplicity in testimonial copy." *Printers' Ink* 128 (August 28, 1924): 114.

28. A.L. Townsend. "Choice of the cull in letters from users." *Printers' Ink* 128 (September 11, 1924): 77, 84.

29. "Quaker Oats reverses a copy trend." *Printers' Ink* 136 (August 5, 1926): 10, 12.

30. "Proper use of testimonials." *Printers' Ink* 140 (July 28, 1927): 104.

31. C.B. Larrabee. "All that I am I owe to (name your own product)." *Printers' Ink* 142 (January 26, 1928): 17–18.

32. Ibid., pp. 19–20.

33. W. Livingston Larned. "A powerful way of using testimonials." *Printers' Ink* 128 (August 21, 1924): 67–68.

34. Ibid., p. 68.

35. C.B. Larrabee. "Eminent scientists say and our conclusive tests prove ____." *Printers' Ink* 142 (February 2, 1928): 65.

36. Ibid., pp. 65–66.

37. Henry Lee Staples. "The Hollister treatment of testimonials." *Advertising & Selling* 12 (March 6, 1929): 24, 92.

38. A.E. Little. "Who believes in testimonials? We all do." *Printers' Ink* 143 (April 5, 1928): 69–70, 72.

Chapter 3

1. D.M. Hubbard. "Is the bought-and-paid-for testimonial harming advertising." *Printers' Ink* 137 (December 9, 1926): 3.

2. Ibid., p. 4.

3. Ibid., pp. 4, 6.

4. Ibid., p. 6.

5. Ibid., pp. 6, 8.

6. Claude C. Hopkins. "A testimonial." *Forum and Century* 79 (March 1928): 479–480.

7. "Does advertising need a new code of practice?" *Advertising & Selling* 12 (March 6, 1929): 19–20.

8. Ibid., p. 20.

9. Ibid., pp. 54, 57–58.

10. A.W. Erickson. "The tainted testimonial." *Printers' Ink* 146 (March 7, 1929): 3.

11. Ibid., pp. 3–4.

12. Raymond Rubicam. "When is the testimonial tainted." *Printers' Ink* 146 (March 14, 1929): 17–20.

13. "The publisher's attitude toward testimonial censorship." *Advertising & Selling* 12 (March 20, 1929): 12, 32.

14. "From Peruna to piffle." *Nation* 128 (March 27, 1929): 364.

15. Roy Dickinson "What the consumer thinks of the modern testimonial." *Printers' Ink* 146 (March 28, 1929): 17–19.

16. Charles Merz. "A custom of the country." *Outlook and Independent* 151 (April 10, 1929): 583–584.

17. Ibid.

18. Ibid., p. 584.

19. "Paid testimonials denounced in Better Business survey." *Advertising & Selling* 12 (March 20, 1929): 20.

20. Edward L. Greene. "National Better Business Bureau issues report on purchased testimonials." *Advertising & Selling* 12 (April 17, 1929): 38.

21. H.S. Gardner. "The paid testimonial is taking the cure." *Advertising & Selling* 12 (April 17, 1929): 17, 46.

22. C.T. Southwick. "Blame the intermediary for the tainted testimonial." *Printers' Ink* 147 (April 18, 1929): 128.

23. Stanley Resor. "Personalities and the public." *Advertising & Selling* 12 (April 17, 1929): 27.

24. Ibid., p. 80.

25. Ibid., pp. 80–82.

26. Frederick C. Kendall. "Do paid testimonials pay?" *Magazine of Business* 55 (May 1929): 537.

27. James Thurber. "Let's have a set of rules for our testimonial industry." *Magazine of Business* 55 (May 1929): 538.

28. Sinclair Lewis. "Sinclair Lewis looks at advertising." *Advertising & Selling* 13 (May 15, 1929): 60, 66.

29. Ibid., p. 17.

30. G. Lynn Sumner. "Is the tainted testimonial increasing advertising costs?" *Advertising & Selling* 13 (May 29, 1929): 23.

31. Ibid., pp. 24, 80.

32. "A.N.A. declares against paid testimonial advertising." *Printers' Ink* 147 (June 6, 1929): 73–74.

33. "Four A's takes a stand on testimonials." *Printers' Ink* 138 (July 18, 1929): 144.

34. Earnest Elmo Calkins. "Testimonial advertising to date." *Advertising & Selling* 15 (September 17, 1930): 18.

35. Robert Tinsman. "I believe." *Advertising & Selling* 15 (December 10, 1930): 28.
36. Alva Johnston. "Testimonials, C.O.D." *Outlook and Independent* 157 (March 18, 1931): 398.

Chapter 4

1. "The Trade Commission jumbles the testimonial puzzle." *Printers' Ink* 150 (January 30, 1930): 49.
2. Ibid., pp. 49–50.
3. "Paid testimonial ban has sweeping implications." *Business Week*, February 5, 1930, p. 8.
4. "Ban misleading ads of sporting goods." *New York Times*, May 8, 1930, p. 15.
5. "German courts condemn paid testimonials." *Advertising & Selling* 18 (December 9, 1981): 22.
6. Ibid., pp. 22–23.
7. "Coming — a showdown on paid testimonials." *Printers' Ink* 157 (December 24, 1931): 10.
8. Ibid., pp. 10, 12.
9. "Testimonials." *New Republic* 69 (December 30, 1931): 173.
10. "Cutex in court." *Advertising & Selling* 18 (January 6, 1932): 23.
11. "Testimonials, the law and the Trade Commission." *Printers' Ink* 158 (January 7, 1932): 105–106.
12. Northam Warren wins paid testimonial appeal." *Printers' Ink* 159 (June 9, 1932): 36.
13. "Testimonials can be bought, but not sold." *Business Week*, June 22, 1932, p. 13.
14. "Dismisses testimonial complaints." *Printers' Ink* 163 (April 6, 1933): 63.
15. "Unprofessional advertising." *American Journal of Public Health* 21 (June 1931): 657–658.
16. Meta Pennock. "Ethics of health publicity as it involves testimonials." *Printers' Ink* 157 (December 24, 1931): 61.
17. Solon R. Barber. "Quelling the quacks." *Hygeia* 11 (May 1933): 407.
18. Ibid., pp. 408–410.
19. "New Camel campaign." *Printers' Ink* 163 (June 29, 1933): 42.
20. "1 Senator (possibly 10) advertises a cigarette." *New York Times*, February 2, 1937, p. 3.
21. "Cigarette testimonial signers— and how they get that way." *Printers' Ink* 207 (April 14, 1944): 17–18.

22. Ibid., pp. 18, 80.
23. Ibid., pp. 82–84, 86, 88.
24. "J. Walter Thompson Company." *Fortune* 36 (November 1947): 226; Ad. *Variety*, July 18, 1933, p. 40.
25. Ibid.
26. Ibid., pp. 226, 228.
27. "$1,000." *Advertising & Selling* 16 (April 1, 1931): 21.
28. John McDonough. "When auto marques wish upon a star." *Advertising Age* 67 (January 8, 1996): S16.
29. "Studio ad ban is boon for freelancers." *Variety*, October 6, 1931, p. 3.
30. "Stars' ad coin walloping Hays ban." *Variety*, January 19, 1932, p. 3.
31. "Film ad men decry star testimonials." *New York Times*, January 7, 1932, p. 16.
32. "Studio gold rush tie-up." *Variety*, May 29, 1935, p. 3.
33. "Screen players bally a brewery; Hays froths, Ed Sullivan so-whats?" *Variety*, August 14, 1940, p. 2.
34. Lawrence M. Hughes. "Should you hitch your business to a star?" *Sales Management* 44 (March 1, 1939): 22.
35. Ibid., p. 23.
36. Ibid., p. 24.
37. Ibid.
38. Mrs. Roosevelt got advertising fee." *New York Times*, September 29, 1933, p. 3.
39. Arthur F. Marquette. "Ad adventures of Quaker Oats, quints & Amelia Earhart." *Advertising Age* 48 (January 24, 1977): 49.
40. P.H. Erbes Jr. "Those precocious Dionnes." *Printers' Ink* 179 (April 1, 1937): 8.
41. James Forkan. "Quints marketing value not what it used to be, to companies or parents." *Advertising Age* 44 (February 26, 1973): 2, 164.
42. Maurine Christopher. "Mrs. Roosevelt brought dignity to ad role." *Advertising Age* 55 (April 30, 1984): 54.
43. Andrew M. Howe. "Testimonial drama." *Printers' Ink* 184 (July 28, 1938): 3–4.
44. John Caples. "How to conduct prize contests to secure testimonial letters." *Advertising & Selling* 25 (June 6, 1935): 32.
45. Ibid., pp. 32, 56.
46. Ibid., p. 56.
47. Edward H. Gardner. "Seductive testimonials." *Printers' Ink* 173 (December 12, 1935): 33, 41, 44.
48. Mark O'Dea. "In defense of testimonials." *Printers' Ink* 174 (February 27, 1936): 58.

49. "Ad class hears Mrs. Richardson." *New York Times*, March 23, 1937, p. 42.

Chapter 5

1. "All for love." *New Yorker* 24 (January 8, 1949): 20–21.
2. Ibid., p. 21.
3. George Moses. "New angle on testimonials." *Advertising Agency* 48 (January 1955): 92–93.
4. "Big name hunter." *Fortune* 52 (September 1955): 164.
5. "Autograph hunter." *American Magazine* 160 (December 1955): 46.
6. Walter Goodman. "Elsa Maxwell loves Mazola." *Nation* 182 (April 14, 1956): 295–297.
7. Bennett Cerf. "Endorsements, Inc." *Saturday Evening Post* 39 (June 16, 1956): 7.
8. "Testimonial advertising takes on a global look." *Advertising Agency Magazine* 50 (August 30, 1957): 16.
9. "Use of experts' opinions in advertising." *Advertising & Selling* 38 (March 1945): 177.
10. Morton J. Simon. "A lawyer looks at advertising testimonials." *Advertising Agency and Advertising & Selling* 43 (December 1950): 67.
11. Morton J. Simon. "Endorsement and testimonial copy." *Advertising Agency and Advertising & Selling* 44 (October 1951): 163–164.
12. Edwin F. Meier. "The case for endorsements." *Advertising & Selling* 38 (March 1945): 172.
13. "FTC hits Amstar for testimonials in its ads." *Advertising Age* 42 (July 19, 1971): 3, 48.
14. "Guidelines proposed for testimonial ads." *Broadcasting* 83 (December 4, 1972): 27–28.
15. "Advertising: a finer screen for plugs." *Business Week*, June 9, 1975, p. 28.
16. "More truth in advertising." *Time* 105 (June 2, 1975): 6.
17. Perry B. Johns. "How Caterpillar Tractor gets its testimonials." *Advertising & Selling* 37 (September 1944): 76, 140.
18. Conrad F. Stuhlman. "How to get prestige testimonials." *Printers' Ink* 224 (August 20, 1948): 31.
19. Ibid., pp. 31–33.
20. Ibid., p. 68.

21. "Personna capitalizes big name endorsements in dealer helps." *Sales Management* 55 (October 1, 1945): 79.
22. Maurine Christopher. "Mrs. Roosevelt brought dignity to ad role." *Advertising Age* 55 (April 30, 1984): 54.
23. Susan Murray. "Our man Godfrey." *Television and New Media* 2 (August 2001): 187–189.
24. Ibid., pp. 190–193.
25. John McDonough. "When auto marques wish upon a star." *Advertising Age* 67 (January 8, 1996): S16, S26.
26. Ibid., p. S26.
27. Peter Newcomb and Christopher Palmeri. "Throw a tantrum, sign a contract." *Forbes* 146 (August 20, 1990): 68.
28. "Selling stars." *Newsweek* 54 (August 24, 1959): 66.
29. "Strike one." *Time* 78 (August 18, 1961): 68.
30. Gay Talese. "Diamonds are a boy's best friend." *New York Times Magazine*, October 1, 1961, pp. 39, 59–60.
31. "The name game." *Forbes* 104 (August 15, 1969): 31–32.
32. Frank Deford. "Hot pitchmen in the selling game." *Sports Illustrated* 31 (November 17, 1969): 112, 115.
33. Ibid., pp. 116–117.
34. Ibid., p. 117.
35. Stuart W. Little. "The celebrity commercials industry." *Saturday Review* 53 (April 11, 1970): 55–56.
36. "Doubling a player's salary." *Forbes* 108 (October 15, 1971): 66.
37. "Who do you trust?" *Time* 102 (December 31, 1973): 8.
38. "Notes and comments." *New Yorker* 50 (November 1, 1974): 37.
39. "Something of value." *Nation* 190 (April 2, 1960): 286; "The name game." *Forbes* 104 (August 15, 1969): 30; Little, "The celebrity commercials industry," pp. 55, 69.
40. "Study shows stamps of approval influence women in buying." *Printers' Ink* 213 (December 7, 1945): 157.
41. "Do's and don'ts for copy writers." *Advertising & Selling* 41 (December 1948): 72.
42. Corey Ford. "Minutes of the annual meeting of the endorsers' club held at the clubhouse on February 2, 1949." *New Yorker* 24 (February 12, 1949): 47.
43. Monroe F. Dreher. "On behalf of tes-

timonials." *Printers' Ink* 242 (March 20, 1953): 47–49.

44. "Testimonial ads get nod in Starch study." *Printers' Ink* 246 (February 19, 1954): 21.

45. John Revett. "Brother recalls Reagan rise." *Advertising Age* 52 (January 12, 1981): 3, 72.

46. Dreher, "On behalf of testimonials," pp. 49–50.

Chapter 6

1. James P. Forkan. "From soap seller to star and back again proves lucrative mix for actors." *Advertising Age* 45 (September 2, 1974): 24; James P. Forkan. "Commercial actors squeezed by stars, real people." *Advertising Age* 46 (November 17, 1975): 142; "Karl Malden for American Express wins AA star presenter award." *Advertising Age* 47 (May 31, 1976): 1.

2. James. P. Forkan. "TV regulars strike gold in adland." *Advertising Age* 48 (June 20, 1977): 3, 84.

3. "Karl Malden for American Express," pp. 1, 37.

4. "How the campaign was born." *Advertising Age* 47 (May 31, 1976): 37.

5. Louis J. Haugh. "O. J. tops year's star presenters." *Advertising Age* 48 (June 20, 1977): 1, 82.

6. John Revett. "Cosby top star presenter of 1978." *Advertising Age* 49 (July 12, 1978): 1; Jennifer Pendleton. "One step to a winning sales pitch." *Advertising Age* 50, sec. 2 (July 30, 1979): S1.

7. James P. Forkan. "Dangerfield is star presenter." *Advertising Age* 54 (August 1, 1983): 3; Jeff Jensen. "Jordan still kind of ad presenter game." *Advertising Age* 65 (April 25, 1994): 59.

8. Barry Farrell. "Celebrity market." *Harper's Magazine* 251 (December 1975): 108.

9. Dick Reibold. "Look to the stars for sales pitches." *Advertising Age* 50, sec. 2 (March 26, 1979): S20–S21.

10. "Few unreachable for testimonials." *Television/Radio Age* 33 (January 20, 1986): 49.

11. Andrew Tanzer. "The celebrity is the message." *Forbes* 138 (July 14, 1986): 88–89.

12. "Madonna in Japan." *Fortune* 114 (September 15, 1986): 9.

13. Stephen Rae. "How celebrities make killings on commercials." *Cosmopolitan* 222 (January 1997): 166.

14. Russell Baker. "Where are you now, Joe DiMaggio." *New York Times*, June 29, 1975, p. 6.

15. Roger Rosenblatt. "Our spring vacation." *New Republic* 174 (April 10, 1976): 32–33.

16. Farrell, "Celebrity market," pp. 108–109.

17. James P. Forkan. "Talent-hunter Lloyd Kolmer declares celebrity endorsers are overpriced." *Advertising Age* 47 (November 29, 1976): 62.

18. Maxine Marx. "Monday memo." *Broadcasting* 92 (January 24, 1977): 10.

19. "Do you know Barney's?" *National Review* 29 (August 19, 1977): 959.

20. James V. O'Gara. "Personality cult an ad glut, Van Slyke says." *Advertising Age* 48 (November 7, 1977): 54.

21. "The big new celebrity boom." *Business Week*, May 22, 1978, p. 77.

22. Ainsworth Howard. "More than just a passing fancy." *Advertising Age* 50, sec. 2 (July 30, 1979): S2, S4.

23. Arthur J. Bragg. "Celebrities in selling more than just tinsel." *Sales and Marketing Management* 124 (February 4, 1980): 30, 33.

24. Ibid., pp. 31–32.

25. Ibid., pp. 34–36.

26. Harry Stein. "Have name, will huckster." *Saturday Evening Post* 252 (November 1980): 26.

27. Stephen Gale. "Commercial success." *Black Enterprise* 12 (December 1981): 53–54.

28. Richard B. Miller "Celebrity spokesmen in banking — here's Ed!" *Bankers Magazine* 165 (July/August 1982): 54.

29. Richard B. Miller. "Celebrity salespeople — do they work for financial institutions?" *Bankers Monthly Magazine* 103 (May 1986): 12–13.

30. Sid Bernstein. "Celebrities lose glamour." *Advertising Age* 55 (September 10, 1984): 18.

31. Stratford P. Sherman. "When you wish upon a star." *Fortune* 112 (August 19, 1985): 66.

32. Ibid., pp. 66, 68–69.

33. Ibid., pp. 72–73.

34. Laura Clark. "Celebrity pitchmen's ranks grow." *Automotive News*, November 2, 1987, p. 18.

35. Steven W. Colford. "Athlete endorsers

fouled by slayings." *Advertising Age* 61 (March 19, 1990): 64.

36. Stephen Glass. "Ad and subtract." *New Republic* 215 (December 16, 1996): 20.

37. Stephen Rae, "How Celebrities," pp. 164, 166.

38. Ibid., p. 167.

Chapter 7

1. Nils Howard. "Playing the endorsement game." *Dun's Review* 110 (August 1977): 43, 45.

2. Ibid., p. 45

3. Ibid., p. 46.

4. Ibid.

5. Melissa Ludtke. "Big scores in the ad game." *Sports Illustrated* 47 (November 7, 1977): 50.

6. Dick Reibold. "Look to the stars for sales pitches." *Advertising Age* 50, sec. 2 (March 26, 1979): S20–S21.

7. Cynthia E. Hardie. "Valvoline zooms with racers." *Advertising Age* 50, sec. 2 (July 30, 1979): S12–S13.

8. Robert Raissman. "First come touchdowns, then endorsements." *Advertising Age* 53, sec. 2 (April 19, 1982): M2.

9. Vic Ziegel. "This fighter for hire." *New York* 15 (June 14, 1982): 69–70.

10. "Tennis stars—the super salespeople." *Glamour* 80 (July 1982): 115.

11. Ibid., p. 213.

12. Marilyn A. Harris. "The smash women are making in tennis." *Business Week*, April 8, 1985, p. 92.

13. Frank Rasky. "He shoots! He scores! He sells!" *Canadian Business* 56 (August 1983): 28.

14. Ibid., pp. 31–32.

15. "Companies are getting tennis pros in their court." *Business Week*, June 18, 1984, p. 51.

16. "Million dollar sneaker deals." *Black Enterprise* 14 (July 1984): 40.

17. Maria E. Recio. "Michael Jordan scores big—on and off the court." *Business Week*, December 3, 1984, pp. 78, 82.

18. David Greising. "The NBA may feel a void but Jordan Inc. will play on." *Business Week*, October 18, 1993, p. 38.

19. Julie Liesse and Jeff Jensen. "Whole new game without Jordan." *Advertising Age* 64 (October 11, 1993): 48.

20. Jeff Jensen. "Jordan still king of ad presenter game." *Advertising Age* 65 (April 25, 1994): 59.

21. Marc Peyser. "No heirs to Air Jordan." *Newsweek* 133 (January 25, 1999): 54–55.

22. Laura Clark. "Automakers try for hole in one." *Automotive News*, August 15, 1998, p. 54.

23. Scott Donaton. "Competitive edge." *Advertising Age* 60 (June 26, 1989): 26.

24. David Shani and Dennis Sandler. "Celebrity alone isn't a sure hit." *Marketing News* 25 (August 5, 1991): 8.

25. Ian Hamilton. "Talent, character, and style: the Nike athlete." *Harvard Business Review* 70 (July/August 1992): 95.

26. Jeanne Whalen and Jeff Jensen. "Is Shaquille the Air apparent to endorser crown." *Advertising Age* 64 (October 11, 1993): 49.

27. Randall Lane. "Prepackaged celebrity." *Forbes* 152 (December 20, 1993): 86–87.

28. Ibid., pp. 87–88, 90.

29. Ross Diamond. "Drink up and play the game." *New Statesman* 131 (July 1, 2002): 24–25.

30. Stuart Elliott. "Big game's messages got lost among the stars." *New York Times*, February 1, 1994, pp. D1, D7.

31. Kim Cleland. "Field of dreams or schemes?" *Advertising Age* 65 (April 25, 1994): 3, 59.

32. "Robotic, yes—but dapper." *Business Week*, July 4, 1994, p. 6.

33. "Survey ranks top athlete endorsers." *Sporting Goods Business* 27 (July 1994): 44.

34. Chris Roush. "Big George and the over-the-hill gang." *Business Week*, November 21, 1994, p. 70.

35. "Gauging the popularity of athlete endorsers." *Marketing Magazine* 100 (December 4, 1995): 20–21.

36. Dave Vadeha. "Campaign clout." *Advertising Age* 67 (February 12, 1996): 33.

37. Mike Stachura. "Tiger money: justifying his millions." *Golf Digest* 47 (November 1996): 60–61.

38. "A league of their own." *Sports Illustrated* 91 (July 5, 1999): 31.

39. Michael Bamberger. "Mining Woods for gold." *Sports Illustrated* 93 (September 25, 2000): 27.

40. Stefan Fatsis. "Muscling out supplement income." *Wall Street Journal*, November 30, 2001, p. W14.

41. "Endorsers." *U.S. News & World Report* 134 (June 2, 2003): 8.

42. Jack McCallum. "You gotta carry that weight." *Sports Illustrated* 99 (October 27, 2003): 68–74.

43. Ginanne Brownell. "Brand it like Beckham." *Newsweek* 141 (June 30, 2003): 88+.

Chapter 8

1. Susan Cheever Crowley. "Rum friends." *Newsweek* 91 (May 22, 1978): 69.

2. "Let the stellar seller beware." *Time* 111 (May 22, 1978): 66.

3. James P. Forkan. "You can reach for the stars, talent agents say." *Advertising Age* 50 (April 23, 1979): 53.

4. Marie Krakow. "Cause celebre and the celebrities." *Advertising Age* 50, sec. 2 (July 30, 1979): S16.

5. "Athletes' status in ads reviewed by BATF." *Beverage Industry* 71 (October 16, 1981): 1, 10.

6. "Alcohol ban: the view from BATF." *Broadcasting* 108 (February 25, 1985): 72.

7. Steven W. Colford. "Do celebrities, alcohol mix?" *Advertising Age* 56 (February 25, 1985): 1, 82.

8. "Is what's-his-name a celebrity?" *Advertising Age* 56 (February 25, 1985): 18.

9. Steven W. Colford. "BATF dries up athlete ad ban." *Advertising Age* 57 (May 12, 1986): 2, 105.

10. "Drug company stops celebrity ads." *FDA Consumer* 25 (December 1991): 4.

11. "Dr. celebrity." *Consumer Reports* 64 (May 1999): 8–9.

12. Melody Petersen. "Heartfelt advice, hefty fees." *New York Times*, August 11, 2002, sec. 3, p. 1.

13. Ibid., p. 14.

14. Gail DeGeorge. "The SEC flags Joe Montana." *Business Week*, February 24, 1992, p. 36.

15. Glenn Collins. "A.M.A. pulls back from endorsements of health products." *New York Times*, August 21, 1997, pp. A1, D6.

16. Christine Gorman. "Doctor's dilemma." *Time* 150 (August 25, 1997): 64.

17. Phillip J. Longman. "Endorsements for sale." *U.S. News & World Report* 123 (September 1, 1997): 11.

18. Marian Burros. "Endorsements raise money and questions." *New York Times*, October 22, 1997, p. F3.

19. Ibid.

20. "Grrrreat … for whom?" *Consumer Reports* 63 (June 1998): 10.

21. John Lippman. "Now playing: movie testimonials starring studio workers, actors." *Wall Street Journal*, June 18, 2001, p. B8.

22. "Hollywood's ad ethics gap." *Advertising Age* 72 (June 25, 2001): 16.

23. Ira Teinowitz. "Court overrules FTC in diet ad case." *Advertising Age* 73 (November 18, 2002): 6.

24. Ibid.

Chapter 9

1. Nils Howard. "Playing the endorsement game." *Dun's Review* 110 (August 1977): 45.

2. "Spitz/Schick tie called worst sports promo ever." *Advertising Age* 46 (October 27, 1975): 2, 76.

3. John Emmerling. "Want a celebrity in your ad? O.K., but watch your step." *Advertising Age* 47 (November 1, 1976): 64.

4. Lynn Langway. "Selling by starlight." *Newsweek* 89 (January 10, 1977): 61.

5. Bourne Morris. "Will a personality sell a product better? Pros & cons." *Advertising Age* 50 (February 5, 1979): 44.

6. Ainsworth Howard. "More than just a passing fancy." *Advertising Age* 50, sec. 2 (July 30, 1979): S4.

7. Kate Eaton. "Between winners, there's the bomb." *Advertising Age* 50, sec. 2 (July 30, 1979): S10.

8. Arthur J. Bragg. "Celebrities in selling more than just tinsel." *Sales and Marketing Management* 124 (February 4, 1980): 34.

9. Sid Bernstein. "Celebrities lose glamour." *Advertising Age* 55 (September 10, 1984): 18.

10. "Oops!" *Madison Ave* 26 (September 1984): 22.

11. William Gloede. "Gaffebusters check on celebs." *Advertising Age* 55 (October 8, 1984): 1, 101.

12. Stratford P. Sherman. "When you wish upon a star." *Fortune* 112 (August 19, 1985): 72–73.

13. Grant McCracken. "Who is the celebrity endorser? Cultural foundations of the endorsement process." *Journal of Consumer Research* 16 (December 1989): 311.

14. Christy Marshall. "It seemed like a good idea at the time." *Forbes* 140 (December 28, 1987): 98.

15. Emily DeNitto. "Why we're divorcing Burt Reynolds." *Advertising Age* 64 (August 23, 1993): 4.

16. "The big new celebrity boom." *Business Week*, May 22, 1978, p. 77.

17. Stephen Gale. "Commercial success." *Black Enterprise* 12 (December 1981): 56.

18. "Star quality." *Economist* 302 (January 24, 1987): 64.

19. Larry G. Collins. "Drug tests for endorsers?" *Advertising Age* 58 (April 6, 1987): 1, 84.

20. Larry G. Collins. "Drugs affect ad contracts." *Advertising Age* 58 (April 13, 1987): 3.

21. Ibid., p. 102.

22. Bernice Kanner. "Are the stars out tonight?" *New York* 21 (February 8, 1988): 22, 24, 26.

23. Patrick McGeehan. "Endorsement KO?" *Advertising Age* 59 (July 4, 1988): 3.

24. Ron Stodghill III. "Athletes, drugs and very nervous advertisers." *Business Week*, October 17, 1988, p. 36.

25. Bob Geiger. "The good guys finish first." *Advertising Age* 61 (March 5, 1990): S1, S4.

26. Peter Newcomb and Christopher Palmieri. "Throw a tantrum, sign a contract." *Forbes* 146 (August 20, 1990): 71, 73.

27. Christy Fisher. "The nightmare." *Advertising Age* 65 (June 20, 1994): 1, 8.

28. Larry Armstrong. "Still starstruck." *Business Week*, July 4, 1994, p. 38.

29. "Marketers cautious in athlete selection." *Sporting Goods Business* 27 (August 1994): 30.

30. Randall Lane. "Nice guys finish first." *Forbes* 158 (December 16, 1996): 237.

31. Ibid., pp. 238–239.

32. Ibid., pp. 239–240.

33. Ibid., pp. 240–241.

34. Ibid., pp. 241–242.

35. Timothy M. Ito. "Pass the club. Hold the drink." *U.S. News & World Report* 122 (June 9, 1997): 18.

36. Richard Sandomir. "With Bryant in court, marketers might flee." *New York Times*, August 6, 2003, p. D1.

37. Glen Macnow. "Undying support." *Nation's Business* 79 (February 1991): 26.

38. Ibid., pp. 26, 28.

39. John McDonough. "When auto marques wish upon a star." *Advertising Age* 67 (January 8, 1996): S26.

Chapter 10

1. John Emmerling. "Want a celebrity in your ad? O.K., but watch your step." *Advertising Age* 47 (November 1, 1976): 63.

2. "The big new celebrity boom." *Business Week*, May 22, 1978, p. 80; James P. Forkan. "You can reach for the stars, talent agents say." *Advertising Age* 50 (April 23, 1979): 52.

3. Arthur J. Bragg. "Celebrities in selling more than just tinsel." *Sales and Marketing Management* 124 (February 4, 1980): 36.

4. Brian Moran. "Cosby's image pays dividends." *Advertising Age* 57 (May 12, 1986): 105.

5. Peter Newcomb and Christopher Palmieri. "Throw a tantrum, sign a contract." *Forbes* 146 (August 20, 1990): 68.

6. "Jordan again leads athlete-endorsers." *New York Times*, August 30, 1996, p. D5.

7. Sam Bradley. "Marketers are always looking for good pitches." *Brandweek* 37 (February 26, 1996): 36.

8. James P. Forkan. "Commercial actors squeezed by stars, real people." *Advertising Age* 47 (November 17, 1975): 142.

9. John Emmerling. "Want a celebrity in your ad?" pp. 63–64.

10. Joseph J. Bohn. "Celebrities grab eye, but credibility is low." *Automotive News*, December 12, 1977, p. 30.

11. Gerry Scorse. "Nonrelevant stars hurt creative pride." *Advertising Age* 50, sec. 2 (July 30, 1979): S11.

12. James P. Forkan. "Product matchup key to effective star presenters." *Advertising Age* 51 (October 6, 1980): 42.

13. James R. Arbose. "Harnessing the appeal of celebrities and cartoon characters to boost sales." *International Management* 36 (March 1981): 24–25.

14. Scott Hume. "Stars are lacking luster as ad presenters." *Advertising Age* 54 (November 7, 1983): 3.

15. Ibid., p. 92.

16. Charles Atkin and Martin Block. "Effectiveness of celebrity endorsers." *Journal of Advertising Research* 23 (February/March 1983): 57.

17. Ibid., pp. 58–60.

18. Ibid., pp. 60–61.

19. Jon B. Freiden. "Advertising spokesperson effects: an examination of endorser type and gender on two audiences." *Journal*

of Advertising Research 24 (October/November 1984): 35–36, 40.

20. Bernice Kanner. "Are the stars out tonight?" *New York* 21 (February 8, 1988): 22.

21. Ibid., pp. 22, 24.

22. Scott Donaton. "Celebs' star sinking in ads." *Advertising Age* 60 (August 28, 1989): 48.

23. Grant McCracken. "Who is the celebrity endorser? Cultural foundations of the endorsement process." *Journal of Consumer Research* 16 (December 1989): 311, 316.

24. Shekhar Misra and Sharon E. Beatty. "Celebrity spokesperson and brand congruence." *Journal of Business Research* 21 (September 1990): 160–161, 165, 170.

25. Roobina Ohanian. "The impact of celebrity spokespersons' perceived image on consumers' intention to purchase." *Journal of Advertising Research* 31 (February/March 1991): 47–52.

26. David Shani and Dennis Sandler. "Celebrity alone isn't a sure hit." *Marketing News* 25 (August 5, 1991): 8.

27. Steven W. Colford. "How to find the right spokesman." *Advertising Age* 62 (October 28, 1991): 17.

28. Scott Hume. "Best ads don't rely on celebrities." *Advertising Age* 63 (May 25, 1992): 20.

29. Jagdish Agrawal and Wagner A. Kamakura. "The economic worth of celebrity endorsers: an event study analysis." *Journal of Marketing* 59 (July 1995): 56–57, 60.

30. Dave Vadeha. "Campaign clout." *Advertising Age* 67 (September 2, 1996): 18.

Bibliography

Ad. *Variety*, July 18, 1933, pp. 40–41.

"Ad class hears Mrs. Richardson." *New York Times*, March 23, 1937, p. 42.

"Advertising: a finer screen for plugs." *Business Week*, June 9, 1975, p. 28.

Agrawal, Jagdish, and Wagner A. Kamakura. "The economic worth of celebrity endorsers: an event study analysis." *Journal of Marketing* 59 (July 1995): 56–62.

"Alcohol ban: the view from BATF." *Broadcasting* 108 (February 25, 1985): 72+.

"All for love." *New Yorker* 24 (January 8, 1949): 20–21.

"A.N.A. declares against paid testimonial advertising." *Printers' Ink* 147 (June 6, 1929): 73–74+.

Arbose, Jules R. "Harnessing the appeal of celebrities and cartoon characters to boost sales." *International Management* 36 (March 1981): 24–25+.

Armstrong, Larry. "Still starstruck." *Business Week*, July 4, 1994, p. 38.

"Athletes' status in ads reviewed by BATF." *Beverage Industry* 71 (October 16, 1981): 1, 10.

Atkin, Charles, and Martin Block. "Effectiveness of celebrity endorsers." *Journal of Advertising Research* 23 (February/March 1983): 57–61.

"Autograph hunter." *American Magazine* 160 (December 1955): 46.

Baker, Russell. "Where are you now, Joe DiMaggio?" *New York Times Magazine*, June 29, 1975, p. 6.

Bamberger, Michael. "Mining Woods for gold." *Sports Illustrated* 93 (September 25, 2000): 27.

"Ban misleading ads of sporting goods." *New York Times*, May 8, 1930, p. 15.

Barber, Solon R. "Quelling the quacks." *Hygeia* 11 (May 1933): 407–410.

Batten, Loring W., Jr. "It was a racket in 1889." *Printers' Ink* 156 (September 10, 1931): 20.

Bernstein, Sid. "Celebrities lose glamour." *Advertising Age* 55 (September 10, 1984): 18.

Big name hunter." *Fortune* 52 (September 1955): 164.

"The big new celebrity boom." *Business Week*, May 22, 1978, pp. 77, 80.

Bohn, Joseph J. "Celebrities grab eye, but credibility is low." *Automotive News*, December 12, 1977, p. 30.

Bradley, Sam. "Marketers are always looking for good pitches." *Brandweek* 37 (February 26, 1996): 36–37.

Bragg, Arthur J. "Celebrities in selling more than just tinsel." *Sales and Marketing Management* 124 (February 4, 1980): 30–36.

Brindley, Willis. "How to get worthwhile testimonials for your business." *Printers' Ink* 125 (November 22, 1923): 25–27.

Brownell, Ginanne. "Brand it like Beckham." *Newsweek* 141 (June 30, 2003): 88+.

Burros, Marian. "Endorsements raise money and questions." *New York Times*, October 22, 1997, p. F3.

Calkins, Earnest Elmo. "Testimonial advertising to date." *Advertising & Selling* 15 (September 17, 1930): 18.

Caples, John. "How to conduct prize

contests to secure testimonial letters." *Advertising & Selling* 25 (June 6, 1935): 32, 56.

Cerf, Bennett. "Endorsements, Inc." *Saturday Review* 39 (June 16, 1956): 7–8.

Christopher, Maurine. "Mrs. Roosevelt brought dignity to ad role." *Advertising Age* 55 (April 30, 1984): 54.

"Cigarette testimonial signers—and how they get that way." *Printers' Ink* 207 (April 14, 1944): 17–18+.

Clark, Laura. "Automakers try for hole in one." *Automotive News*, August 15, 1988, p. 54.

_____. "Celebrity pitchmen's ranks grow." *Automotive News*, November 2, 1987, p. 18.

Cleland, Kim. "Field of dreams or schemes?" *Advertising Age* 65 (April 25, 1994): 3, 59.

Colford, Steven W. "Athlete endorsers fouled by slayings." *Advertising Age* 61 (March 19, 1990): 64.

_____. "BATF dries up athlete ad ban." *Advertising Age* 57 (May 12, 1986): 2, 105.

_____. "Do celebrities, alcohol mix?" *Advertising Age* 56 (February 25, 1985): 1, 82.

_____. "How to find the right spokesman." *Advertising Age* 62 (October 28, 1991): 17.

"Collecting on picture names." *Variety*, February 4, 1919, p. 56.

Collins, Glenn. "A.M.A. pulls back from endorsements of health products." *New York Times*, August 21, 1997, pp. A1, D6.

Collins, Larry G. "Drug tests for endorsers?" *Advertising Age* 58 (April 6, 1987): 1, 84.

_____. "Drugs affect ad contracts." *Advertising Age* 58 (April 13, 1987): 3, 102.

"Coming—a showdown on paid testimonials." *Printers' Ink* 157 (December 24, 1931): 10, 12.

"Companies are getting tennis pros in their court." *Business Week*, June 18, 1984, p. 51.

Cowley, Susan Cheever. "Rum friends." *Newsweek* 91 (May 22, 1978): 69.

Cramp, Arthur J. "Testimonials—mainly medical." *American Mercury* 17 (August 1929): 444–451.

"Cutex in court." *Advertising & Selling* 18 (January 6, 1932): 23–24.

David, Donald. "Use the testimonial." *Advertising Agency Magazine* 49 (October 12, 1956): 60.

Deford, Frank. "Hot pitchmen in the selling game." *Sports Illustrated* 31 (November 17, 1969): 110–112+.

DeGeorge, Gail. "The SEC flags Joe Montana." *Business Week*, February 24, 1992, p. 36.

DeNitto, Emily. "Why we're divorcing Burt Reynolds." *Advertising Age* 64 (August 23, 1993): 4.

Diamond, Ross. "Drink up and play the game." *New Statesman* 131 (July 1, 2002): 24–25.

Dickinson, Roy. "What the consumer thinks of the modern testimonial." *Printers' Ink* 146 (March 28, 1929): 17–20.

"Dismisses testimonial complaints." *Printers' Ink* 163 (April 6, 1933): 63.

"Do you know Barney's?" *National Review* 29 (August 19, 1977): 959.

"Does advertising need a new code of practice?" *Advertising & Selling* 12 (March 6, 1929): 19–20+.

Donaton, Scott. "Celebs' star sinking in ads." *Advertising Age* 60 (August 28, 1989): 48.

_____. "Competitive edge." *Advertising Age* 60 (June 26, 1989): 26.

"Do's and don'ts for copy writers." *Advertising & Selling* 41 (December 1948): 72.

"Doubling a player's salary." *Forbes* 108 (October 15, 1971): 66–67.

"Dr. celebrity." *Consumer Reports* 64 (May 1999): 8–9.

Dreher, Monroe F. "On behalf of testimonials." *Printers' Ink* 242 (March 20, 1953): 47–50.

"Drug company stops celebrity ads." *FDA Consumer* 25 (December 1991): 4.

Eaton, Kate. "Between winners, there's the bomb." *Advertising Age* 50, sec. 2 (July 30, 1979): S10.

Elliott, Stuart. "Big game's messages got lost among the stars." *New York Times*, February 1, 1994, pp. D1, D7.

Emmerling, John. "Want a celebrity in your ad? O.K., but watch your step." *Advertising Age* 47 (November 1, 1976): 63–64.

"Endorsers." *U.S. News & World Report* 134 (June 2, 2003): 8.

Erbes, P.H., Jr. "Those precocious Dionnes." *Printers' Ink* 179 (April 1, 1937): 6–8, 12, 113.

Erickson, A.W. "The tainted testimonial." *Printers' Ink* 146 (March 7, 1929): 3–4.

Farrell, Barry. "Celebrity market." *Harper's Magazine* 251 (December 1975): 108–110.

Fatsis, Stefan. "Muscling out supplemental income." *Wall Street Journal*, November 30, 2001, p. W14.

"Few unreachable for testimonials." *Television/Radio Age* 33 (January 20, 1986): 49.

"Film ad men decry star testimonials." *New York Times*, January 7, 1932, p. 16.

Fisher, Christy. "The nightmare." *Advertising Age* 65 (June 20, 1994): 1, 8.

Ford, Corey. "Minutes of the annual meeting of the Endorsers' Club held at the clubhouse on February 2, 1949." *New Yorker* 24 (February 12, 1949): 44+.

Forkan, James P. "Commercial actors squeezed by stars, real people." *Advertising Age* 46 (November 17, 1975): 142–143.

_____. "Dangerfield is Star Presenter." *Advertising Age* 54 (August 1, 1983): 3, 32.

_____. "From soap seller to star and back again proves lucrative mix for actors." *Advertising Age* 45 (September 2, 1974): 24.

_____. "Product matchup key to effective star presenters." *Advertising Age* 51 (October 6, 1980): 42.

_____. "Quints marketing value not what it used to be, to companies or parents." *Advertising Age* 44 (February 26, 1973): 2, 164.

_____. "Talent-hunter Lloyd Kolmer declares celebrity endorsers are overpriced." *Advertising Age* 47 (November 29, 1976): 62.

_____. "TV regulars strike gold in adland." *Advertising Age* 48 (June 20, 1977): 3, 84.

_____. "You can reach for the stars, talent agents say." *Advertising Age* 50 (April 23, 1979): 52–53.

"Four A's takes a stand on testimonials." *Printers' Ink* 148 (July 18, 1929): 144.

Freiden, Jon B. "Advertising spokesperson effects: an examination of endorser type and gender on two audiences." *Journal of Advertising Research* 24 (October/November 1984): 33–36+.

"From Peruna to piffle." *Nation* 128 (March 27, 1929): 364.

"FTC hits Amstar for testimonials in its ads." *Advertising Age* 42 (July 19, 1971): 3, 48.

Gale, Stephen. "Commercial success." *Black Enterprise* 12 (December 1981): 51–54+.

Gardner, Edward H. "Seductive testimonials." *Printers' Ink* 173 (December 12, 1935): 33+.

Gardner, H.S. "The paid testimonial is taking the cure." *Advertising & Selling* 12 (April 17, 1929): 17–18, 46.

"Gauging the popularity of athlete endorsers." *Marketing Magazine* 100 (December 4, 1995): 20–21.

Geiger, Bob. "The good guys finish first." *Advertising Age* 61 (March 5, 1990): S1, S4.

"German courts to condemn paid testimonials." *Advertising & Selling* 18 (December 9, 1931): 22–23+.

Giles, Ray. "Testimonial technique of forty years ago." *Advertising & Selling* 15 (October 1, 1930): 22–23+.

Glass, Stephen. "Ad and subtract." *New Republic* 215 (December 16, 1996): 18, 20.

Gloede, William. "Gaffebusters check on celebs." *Advertising Age* 55 (October 8, 1984): 1, 101.

Goodman, Walter. "Elsa Maxwell loves Mazola." *Nation* 182 (April 14, 1956): 295–297.

Gorman, Christine. "Doctor's dilemma." *Time* 150 (August 25, 1997): 64.

Greene, Edward L. "National Better Business Bureau issues report on purchased testimonials." *Advertising & Selling* 12 (April 17, 1929): 38+.

Greising, David. "The NBA may feel a void but Jordan Inc. will play on." *Business Week*, October 18, 1993, p. 38.

"Grrrreat ... for whom?" *Consumer Reports* 63 (June 1998): 10.

"Guidelines proposed for testimonial ads." *Broadcasting* 83 (December 4, 1972): 27–28.

Hamilton, Ian. "Talent, character, and style: the Nike athlete." *Harvard Business Review* 70 (July/August 1992): 95.

Hardie, Cynthia E. "Valvoline zooms with racers." *Advertising Age* 50, sec. 2 (July 30, 1979): S12–S13.

Harris, Marilyn A. "The smash women are making in tennis." *Business Week*, April 8, 1985, p. 92.

Haugh, Louis J. "O. J. tops year's star presenters." *Advertising Age* 48 (June 20, 1977): 1, 82.

"Hollywood's ad ethics gap." *Advertising Age* 72 (June 25, 2001): 16.

Hopkins, Claude C. "A testimonial." *Forum and Century* 79 (March 1928): 479–480.

"How the campaign was born." *Advertising Age* 47 (May 31, 1976): 37.

Howard, Ainsworth. "More than just a passing fancy." *Advertising Age* 50, sec. 2 (July 30, 1979): S2, S4.

Howard, Nils. "Playing the endorsement game." *Dun's Review* 110 (August 1977): 43–46.

Howe, Andrew M. "Testimonial drama." *Printers' Ink* 184 (July 28, 1938): 3–4.

Hubbard, D.M. "Is the bought-and-paid-for testimonial harming advertisers." *Printers' Ink* 137 (December 9, 1926): 3–4+.

Hughes, Lawrence M. "Should you hitch your business to a star?" *Sales Management* 44 (March 1, 1939): 22–24.

Hume, Scott. "Best ads don't rely on celebrities." *Advertising Age* 63 (May 25, 1992): 20.

———. "Stars are lacking luster as ad presenters." *Advertising Age* 54 (November 7, 1983): 3, 92.

"The inside of the testimonial racket."

Advertising & Selling 16 (January 7, 1931): 20–21+.

"Is what's-his-name a celebrity?" *Advertising Age* 56 (February 25, 1985): 18.

Ito, Timothy M. "Pass the club. Hold the drink." *U.S. News & World Report* 122 (June 9, 1997): 18.

"J. Walter Thompson Company." *Fortune* 36 (November 1947): 226, 228.

Jensen, Jeff. "Jordan still king of ad presenter game." *Advertising Age* 65 (April 25, 1994): 3, 59.

Johns, Perry B. "How Caterpillar Tractor gets its testimonials." *Advertising & Selling* 37 (September 1944): 76+.

Johnston, Alva. "Testimonials, C.O.D." *Outlook and Independent* 157 (March 18, 1931): 398–399.

"Jordan again leads athlete-endorsers." *New York Times*, August 30, 1996, p. D5.

Kanner, Bernice. "Are the stars out tonight?" *New York* 21 (February 8, 1988): 22+.

"Karl Malden for American Express wins AA star presenter award." *Advertising Age* 47 (May 31, 1976): 1, 37.

Kendall, Frederick C. "Do paid testimonials pay?" *Magazine of Business* 55 (May 1929): 537–538.

Krakow, Marie. "Cause celebre and the celebrities." *Advertising Age* 50, sec. 2 (July 30, 1979): S1, S16.

Lane, Randall. "Nice guys finish first." *Forbes* 158 (December 16, 1996): 236–242.

———. "Prepackaged celebrity." *Forbes* 152 (December 20, 1993): 86–88+.

Langway, Lynn. "Selling by starlight." *Newsweek* 89 (January 10, 1977): 61–62.

Larned, W. Livingston. "A powerful way of using testimonials." *Printers' Ink* 128 (August 21, 1924): 67–68.

Larrabee, C.B. "All that I am I owe to (name your own product)." *Printers' Ink* 142 (January 26, 1928): 17–20, 25.

———. "Eminent scientists say and our own conclusions prove ____." *Printers' Ink* 142 (February 2, 1928): 65–66+.

"A league of their own." *Sports Illustrated* 91 (July 5, 1999): 31.

"Let the stellar seller beware." *Time* 111 (May 22, 1978): 66.

Lewis, Sinclair. "Sinclair Lewis looks at advertising." *Advertising & Selling* 13 (May 15, 1929): 17–18+.

Liesse, Julie, and Jeff Jensen "Whole new game without Jordan." *Advertising Age* 64 (October 11, 1993): 1, 48.

Lippman, John. "Now playing: movie testimonials starring studio workers, actors." *Wall Street Journal*, June 18, 2001, p. B8.

Little, A.E. "Who believes testimonials? We all do." *Printers' Ink* 143 (April 5, 1928): 69–70+.

Little, Stuart W. "The celebrity commercials industry." *Saturday Review* 53 (April 11, 1970): 55–56+.

Longman, Phillip J. "Endorsements for sale." *U.S. News & World Report* 123 (September 1, 1997): 11.

Ludtke, Melissa. "Big scorers in the ad game." *Sports Illustrated* 47 (November 7, 1977): 50.

Macnow, Glen. "Undying support." *Nation's Business* 79 (February 1991): 26, 28.

"Madonna in Japan." *Fortune* 114 (September 15, 1986): 9.

"Marketers cautious in athlete selection." *Sporting Goods Business* 27 (August 1994): 30.

Marquette, Arthur F. "Ad adventures of Quaker Oats, quints & Amelia Earhart." *Advertising Age* 48 (January 24, 1977): 49.

Marshall, Christy. "It seemed like a good idea at the time." *Forbes* 140 (December 28, 1987): 98–99.

Marx, Maxine. "Monday memo." *Broadcasting* 92 (January 24, 1977): 10.

McCallum, Jack. "You gotta carry that weight." *Sports Illustrated* 99 (October 27, 2003): 68–74.

McCracken, Grant. "Who is the celebrity endorser? Cultural foundations for the endorsement process." *Journal of Consumer Research* 16 (December 1989): 310–321.

McDonough, John. "When auto marques wish upon a star." *Advertising Age* 67 (January 8, 1996): S16, S26.

McGeehan, Patrick. "Endorsement KO?" *Advertising Age* 59 (July 4, 1988): 3.

Meier, Edwin F. "The case for endorsements." *Advertising & Selling* 38 (March 1945): 172.

"Melachrino enlists nobility in new campaign." *Printers' Ink* 134 (February 4, 1926): 60.

Merz, Charles. "A custom of the country." *Outlook and Independent* 151 (April 10, 1929): 583–584.

Miller, Richard B. "Celebrity salespeople — do they work for financial institutions?" *Bankers Monthly Magazine* 103 (May 1986): 12–13.

_____. "Celebrity spokesmen in banking — here's Ed!" *Bankers Magazine* 165 (July/August 1982): 53–56.

"Million dollar sneaker deals." *Black Enterprise* 14 (July 1984): 40.

Misra, Shekhar, and Sharon E. Beatty. "Celebrity spokesperson and brand congruence." *Journal of Business Research* 21 (September 1990): 159–173.

Moran, Brian. "Cowboy's image pays dividends." *Advertising Age* 57 (May 12, 1986): 2, 105.

"More truth in advertising." *Time* 105 (June 2, 1975): 6.

Morris, Bourne. "Will a personality sell a product better? Pros and cons." *Advertising Age* 50 (February 5, 1979): 43–44.

Moses, George. "New angle on testimonials." *Advertising Age* 48 (January 1955): 92–93.

"Mrs. Roosevelt got advertising fee." *New York Times*, September 29, 1933, p. 3.

Murray, Susan. "Our man Godfrey." *Television & New Media* 2 (August 2001): 187–204.

"The name game." *Forbes* 104 (August 15, 1969): 30–32.

"New Camel campaign." *Printers' Ink* 163 (June 29, 1933): 42.

Newcomb, Peter, and Christopher Palmeri. "Throw a tantrum, sign a contract." *Forbes* 146 (August 20, 1990): 68–73.

"Northam Warren wins paid testimonial appeal." *Printers' Ink* 159 (June 9, 1932): 36.

"Notes and comments." *New Yorker* 50 (November 1, 1974): 37.

O'Dea, Mark. "In defense of testimonials." *Printers' Ink* 174 (February 27, 1936): 58.

O'Gara, James V. "Personality cult an ad glut, Van Slyke says." *Advertising Age* 48 (November 7, 1977): 54.

Ohanian, Roobina. "The impact of celebrity spokespersons' perceived image on consumers' intention to purchase." *Journal of Advertising Research* 31 (February/March 1991): 46–54.

"1 Senator (possibly 10) advertises a cigarette." *New York Times*, February 2, 1937, p. 3.

"$1,000." *Advertising & Selling* 16 (April 1, 1931): 21.

"Oops!" *Madison Ave* 26 (September 1984): 22.

"Paid testimonial ban has sweeping implications." *Business Week*, February 5, 1930, p. 8.

"Paid testimonials denounced in Better Business Bureau survey." *Advertising & Selling* 12 (March 20, 1929): 20, 92.

Pendleton, Jennifer. "One step to a winning sales pitch." *Advertising Age* 50, sec. 2 (July 30, 1979): S1, S16.

Pennock, Meta. "Ethics of health publicity as it involves testimonials." *Printers' Ink* 157 (December 24, 1931): 61–62.

"Personna capitalizes by big name endorsements in dealer helps." *Sales Management* 55 (October 1, 1945): 79.

Petersen, Melody. "Heartfelt advice, hefty fees." *New York Times*, August 11, 2002, sec. 3, pp. 1, 14.

Peyser, Marc. "No heirs to Air Jordan." *Newsweek* 133 (January 25, 1999): 54–55.

"Proper use of testimonials." *Printers' Ink* 140 (July 28, 1927): 104.

"The publisher's attitude toward testimonial censorship." *Advertising & Selling* 12 (March 20, 1929): 32, 73.

"Quaker Oats reverses a copy trend." *Printers' Ink* 136 (August 5, 1926): 10, 12.

Rae, Stephen. "How celebrities make killings on commercials." *Cosmopolitan* 222 (January 1997): 164–167.

Raissman, Robert. "First come touchdowns, then endorsements." *Advertising Age* 53, sec. 2 (April 19, 1982): M2–M3+.

Rasky, Frank. "He shoots! He scores! He sells!" *Canadian Business* 56 (August 1983): 28–32.

Recio, Maria E. "Michael Jordan scores big — on and off the court." *Business Week*, December 3, 1984, pp. 78, 82.

Reibold, Dick. "Look to the stars for sales pitches." *Advertising Age* 50, sec. 2 (March 26, 1979): S20–S21.

Resor, Stanley. "Personalities and the public." *Advertising & Selling* 12 (April 17, 1929): 27, 80–82.

Revett, John. "Brother recalls Reagan rise." *Advertising Age* 52 (January 12, 1981): 3, 72.

_____. "Cosby top star presenter of 1978." *Advertising Age* 49 (July 17, 1978): 1, 48.

"Robotic, yes — but dapper." *Business Week*, July 4, 1994, p. 6.

Rosenblatt, Roger. "Our spring vacation." *New Republic* 174 (April 10, 1976): 32–33.

Roush, Chris. "Big George and the over-the-hill gang." *Business Week*, November 21, 1994, p. 70.

Rubicam, Raymond. "When is the testimonial tainted?" *Printers' Ink* 146 (March 14, 1929): 17–20.

Sandomir, Richard. "With Bryant in court, marketers might flee." *New York Times*, August 6, 2003, p. D1.

Scorse, Gerry. "Nonrelevant stars hurt creative pride." *Advertising Age* 50, sec. 2 (July 30, 1979): S11.

"Screen players bally a brewery; Hays froths, Ed Sullivan so-whats?" *Variety*, August 14, 1940, p. 2.

"Selling stars." *Newsweek* 54 (August 24, 1957): 66.

Shani, David, and Dennis Sandler. "Celebrity alone isn't a sure hit." *Marketing News* 25 (August 5, 1991): 8.

Sherman, Stratford P. "When you wish upon a star." *Fortune* 112 (August 19, 1985): 66–69+.

Simon, Morton J. "Endorsement and testimonial copy." *Advertising Agency and*

Advertising & Selling 44 (October 1951): 163–164.

_____. "A lawyer looks at advertising testimonials." *Advertising Agency and Advertising & Selling* 43 (December 1950): 67, 94.

"Simplicity in testimonial copy." *Printers' Ink* 128 (August 28, 1924): 114.

"Smith Brothers to wage war on theater cough." *Printers' Ink* 145 (November 29, 1928): 10, 12.

"Something of value." *Nation* 190 (April 2, 1960): 286.

Southwick, C.T. "Blame the intermediary for the tainted testimonial." *Printers' Ink* 147 (April 18, 1929): 128.

"Spitz/Schick tie called worst sports promo ever." *Advertising Age* 46 (October 27, 1975): 2, 76.

Stachura, Mike. "Tiger money: justifying his millions." *Golf Digest* 47 (November 1996): 60–61.

Staples, Henry Lee. "The Hollister treatment for testimonialcocci." *Advertising & Selling* 12 (March 6, 1929): 24, 92.

"Star quality." *Economist* 302 (January 24, 1987): 64.

"Stars' ad coin walloping Hays ban." *Variety*, January 19, 1932, p. 3.

Stein, Harry. "Have name, will huckster." *Saturday Evening Post* 252 (November 1980): 26.

Stodghill, Ron, III. "Athletes, drugs and very nervous advertisers." *Business Week*, October 17, 1988, p. 36.

"Strike one." *Time* 78 (August 18, 1961): 68.

"Studio ad ban is boon for freelancers." *Variety*, October 6, 1931, p. 3.

"Studio gold rush tie-up." *Variety*, May 29, 1935, p. 3.

"Study shows stamps of approval influence women in buying." *Printers' Ink* 213 (December 7, 1945): 157.

Stuhlman, Conrad F. "How to get prestige testimonials." *Printers' Ink* 224 (August 20, 1948): 31–33+.

Sumner, G. Lynn. "Is the tainted testimonial increasing advertising cost?" *Advertising & Selling* 13 (May 29, 1929): 23–24, 80.

"Survey ranks top athlete endorsers." *Sporting Goods Business* 27 (July 1994): 44.

Talese, Gay. "Diamonds are a boy's best friend." *New York Times Magazine*, October 1, 1961, p. 39+.

Tanzer, Andrew. "The celebrity is the message." *Forbes* 138 (July 14, 1986): 88–89.

Teinowitz, Ira. "Court overrules FTC in diet ad case." *Advertising Age* 73 (November 18, 2002): 6.

"Tennis stars—the super salespeople." *Glamour* 80 (July 1982): 115, 213.

"Testimonial ads get nod in Starch study." *Printers' Ink* 246 (February 19, 1954): 21.

"Testimonial advertising takes on a global look." *Advertising Agency Magazine* 50 (August 30, 1957): 16–17.

"Testimonials." *New Republic* 69 (December 30, 1931): 173.

"Testimonials can be bought, but not sold." *Business Week*, June 22, 1932, p. 13.

"Testimonials, the law and the Trade Commission." *Printers' Ink* 158 (January 7, 1932): 105–106.

Thurber, James. "Let's have a set of rules for our testimonial industry." *Magazine of Business* 55 (May 1929): 538.

Tinsman, Robert. "I believe." *Advertising & Selling* 15 (December 10, 1930): 28, 66.

"Tiring of advertising tie-up screen stars and studios refuse commercial offers." *Variety*, November 14, 1928, p. 4.

Townsend, A.L. "Choice of the cull in letters from users." *Printers' Ink* 128 (September 11, 1924): 77–78+.

_____. "Industrial advertising that features the testimonial by indirection." *Printers' Ink* 126 (February 21, 1924): 125–126+.

"The Trade Commission jumbles the testimonial puzzle." *Printers' Ink* 150 (January 30, 1930): 49–50+.

"Unprofessional advertising." *American Journal of Public Health* 21 (June 1931): 657–658.

"Use of experts' opinions in advertising." *Advertising & Selling* 38 (March 1945): 277.

Vadeha, Dave. "Campaign clout." *Advertising Age* 67 (February 12, 1996): 33.
_____. "Campaign clout." *Advertising Age* 67 (September 2, 1996): 18.
Whalen, Jeanne, and Jeff Jensen. "Is Shaquille the Air apparent to endorser crown." *Advertising Age* 64 (October 11, 1993): 49.

"Who do you trust?" *Time* 102 (December 31, 1973): 8.
"Will Rogers gives testimonial copy a new twist." *Printers' Ink* 130 (February 12, 1925): 33–34.
Ziegel, Vic. "This fighter for hire." *New York* 15 (June 14, 1982): 69–70.

Index

225